D1686107

LEEDS BECKETT UNIVERSITY
LIBRARY
DISC...

Leeds Metropolitan University

17 0455940 2

MPEG-7 Audio and Beyond

LEEDS BECKETT UNIVERSITY

DISCARDED

LEEDS METROPOLITAN
UNIVERSITY
LIBRARY

1704SS9408
1E-B
HU-70988
10/5/06   2.3.06
006.5 KIM

MPEG-7 Audio and Beyond

Audio Content Indexing and Retrieval

Hyoung-Gook Kim
Samsung Advanced Institute of Technology, Korea

Nicolas Moreau
Technical University of Berlin, Germany

Thomas Sikora
Communication Systems Group, Technical University of Berlin, Germany

John Wiley & Sons, Ltd

Copyright © 2005 John Wiley & Sons Ltd, The Atrium, Southern Gate, Chichester,
West Sussex PO19 8SQ, England

Telephone (+44) 1243 779777

Email (for orders and customer service enquiries): cs-books@wiley.co.uk
Visit our Home Page on www.wiley.com

All Rights Reserved. No part of this publication may be reproduced, stored in a retrieval system or
transmitted in any form or by any means, electronic, mechanical, photocopying, recording,
scanning or otherwise, except under the terms of the Copyright, Designs and Patents Act 1988 or
under the terms of a licence issued by the Copyright Licensing Agency Ltd, 90 Tottenham Court
Road, London W1T 4LP, UK, without the permission in writing of the Publisher. Requests to the
Publisher should be addressed to the Permissions Department, John Wiley & Sons Ltd, The
Atrium, Southern Gate, Chichester, West Sussex PO19 8SQ, England, or emailed to
permreq@wiley.co.uk, or faxed to (+44) 1243 770620.

This publication is designed to provide accurate and authoritative information in regard to the
subject matter covered. It is sold on the understanding that the Publisher is not engaged in
rendering professional services. If professional advice or other expert assistance is required, the
services of a competent professional should be sought.

Other Wiley Editorial Offices

John Wiley & Sons Inc., 111 River Street, Hoboken, NJ 07030, USA

Jossey-Bass, 989 Market Street, San Francisco, CA 94103-1741, USA

Wiley-VCH Verlag GmbH, Boschstr. 12, D-69469 Weinheim, Germany

John Wiley & Sons Australia Ltd, 42 McDougall Street, Milton, Queensland 4064, Australia

John Wiley & Sons (Asia) Pte Ltd, 2 Clementi Loop #02-01, Jin Xing Distripark, Singapore 129809

John Wiley & Sons Canada Ltd, 22 Worcester Road, Etobicoke, Ontario, Canada M9W 1L1

Wiley also publishes its books in a variety of electronic formats. Some content that appears in print
may not be available in electronic books.

Library of Congress Cataloging in Publication Data

Kim, Hyoung-Gook.
  Introduction to MPEG-7 audio / Hyoung-Gook Kim, Nicolas Moreau, Thomas Sikora.
    p. cm.
  Includes bibliographical references and index.
  ISBN-13 978-0-470-09334-4 (cloth: alk. paper)
  ISBN-10 0-470-09334-X (cloth: alk. paper)
  1. MPEG (Video coding standard) 2. Multimedia systems. 3. Sound—Recording and
  reproducing—Digital techniques—Standards. I. Moreau, Nicolas. II. Sikora, Thomas.
  III. Title.

  TK6680.5.K56 2005
  006.6'96—dc22

                                                                    2005011807

British Library Cataloguing in Publication Data

A catalogue record for this book is available from the British Library

ISBN-13 978-0-470-09334-4 (HB)
ISBN-10 0-470-09334-X (HB)

Typeset in 10/12pt Times by Integra Software Services Pvt. Ltd, Pondicherry, India
Printed and bound in Great Britain by TJ International Ltd, Padstow, Cornwall
This book is printed on acid-free paper responsibly manufactured from sustainable forestry
in which at least two trees are planted for each one used for paper production.

Contents

Acronyms

ADSR	Attack, Decay, Sustain, Release
AFF	Audio Fundamental Frequency
AH	Audio Harmonicity
AP	Audio Power
ASA	Auditory Scene Analysis
ASB	Audio Spectrum Basis
ASC	Audio Spectrum Centroid
ASE	Audio Spectrum Envelope
ASF	Audio Spectrum Flatness
ASP	Audio Spectrum Projection
ASR	Automatic Speech Recognition
ASS	Audio Spectrum Spread
AWF	Audio Waveform
BIC	Bayesian Information Criterion
BP	Back Propagation
BPM	Beats Per Minute
CASA	Computational Auditory Scene Analysis
CBID	Content-Based Audio Identification
CM	Coordinate Matching
CMN	Cepstrum Mean Normalization
CRC	Cyclic Redundancy Checking
DCT	Discrete Cosine Transform
DDL	Description Definition Language
DFT	Discrete Fourier Transform
DP	Dynamic Programming
DS	Description Scheme
DSD	Divergence Shape Distance
DTD	Document Type Definition
EBP	Error Back Propagation
ED	Edit Distance
EM	Expectation and Maximization
EMIM	Expected Mutual Information Measure

EPM	Exponential Pseudo Norm
FFT	Fast Fourier Transform
GLR	Generalized Likelihood Ratio
GMM	Gaussian Mixture Model
GSM	Global System for Mobile Communications
HCNN	Hidden Control Neural Network
HMM	Hidden Markov Model
HR	Harmonic Ratio
HSC	Harmonic Spectral Centroid
HSD	Harmonic Spectral Deviation
HSS	Harmonic Spectral Spread
HSV	Harmonic Spectral Variation
ICA	Independent Component Analysis
IDF	Inverse Document Frequency
INED	Inverse Normalized Edit Distance
IR	Information Retrieval
ISO	International Organization for Standardization
KL	Karhunen–Loève
KL	Kullback–Leibler
KS	Knowledge Source
LAT	Log Attack Time
LBG	Linde–Buzo–Gray
LD	Levenshtein Distance
LHSC	Local Harmonic Spectral Centroid
LHSD	Local Harmonic Spectral Deviation
LHSS	Local Harmonic Spectral Spread
LHSV	Local Harmonic Spectral Variation
LLD	Low-Level Descriptor
LM	Language Model
LMPS	Logarithmic Maximum Power Spectrum
LP	Linear Predictive
LPC	Linear Predictive Coefficient
LPCC	Linear Prediction Cepstrum Coefficient
LSA	Log Spectral Amplitude
LSP	Linear Spectral Pair
LVCSR	Large-Vocabulary Continuous Speech Recognition
mAP	Mean Average Precision
MCLT	Modulated Complex Lapped Transform
MD5	Message Digest 5
MFCC	Mel-Frequency Cepstrum Coefficient
MFFE	Multiple Fundamental Frequency Estimation
MIDI	Music Instrument Digital Interface
MIR	Music Information Retrieval
MLP	Multi-Layer Perceptron

M.M.	Metronom Mälzel
MMS	Multimedia Mining System
MPEG	Moving Picture Experts Group
MPS	Maximum Power Spectrum
MSD	Maximum Squared Distance
NASE	Normalized Audio Spectrum Envelope
NMF	Non-Negative Matrix Factorization
NN	Neural Network
OOV	Out-Of-Vocabulary
OPCA	Oriented Principal Component Analysis
PCA	Principal Component Analysis
PCM	Phone Confusion Matrix
PCM	Pulse Code Modulated
PLP	Perceptual Linear Prediction
PRC	Precision
PSM	Probabilistic String Matching
QBE	Query-By-Example
QBH	Query-By-Humming
RASTA	Relative Spectral Technique
RBF	Radial Basis Function
RCL	Recall
RMS	Root Mean Square
RSV	Retrieval Status Value
SA	Spectral Autocorrelation
SC	Spectral Centroid
SCP	Speaker Change Point
SDR	Spoken Document Retrieval
SF	Spectral Flux
SFM	Spectral Flatness Measure
SNF	Spectral Noise Floor
SOM	Self-Organizing Map
STA	Spectro-Temporal Autocorrelation
STFT	Short-Time Fourier Transform
SVD	Singular Value Decomposition
SVM	Support Vector Machine
TA	Temporal Autocorrelation
TPBM	Time Pitch Beat Matching
TC	Temporal Centroid
TDNN	Time-Delay Neural Network
ULH	Upper Limit of Harmonicity
UM	Ukkonen Measure
UML	Unified Modeling Language
VCV	Vowel–Consonant–Vowel
VQ	Vector Quantization

VSM	Vector Space Model
XML	Extensible Markup Language
ZCR	Zero Crossing Rate

The 17 MPEG-7 Low-Level Descriptors:

AFF	Audio Fundamental Frequency
AH	Audio Harmonicity
AP	Audio Power
ASB	Audio Spectrum Basis
ASC	Audio Spectrum Centroid
ASE	Audio Spectrum Envelope
ASF	Audio Spectrum Flatness
ASP	Audio Spectrum Projection
ASS	Audio Spectrum Spread
AWF	Audio Waveform
HSC	Harmonic Spectral Centroid
HSD	Harmonic Spectral Deviation
HSS	Harmonic Spectral Spread
HSV	Harmonic Spectral Variation
LAT	Log Attack Time
SC	Spectral Centroid
TC	Temporal Centroid

Symbols

Chapter 2

n	time index
$s(n)$	digital audio signal
F_s	sampling frequency
l	frame index
L	total number of frames
$w(n)$	windowing function
L_w	length of a frame
N_w	length of a frame in number of time samples
$HopSize$	time interval between two successive frames
N_{hop}	number of time samples between two successive frames
k	frequency bin index
$f(k)$	frequency corresponding to the index k
$S_l(k)$	spectrum extracted from the lth frame
$P_l(k)$	power spectrum extracted from the lth frame
N_{FT}	size of the fast Fourier transform
ΔF	frequency interval between two successive FFT bins
r	spectral resolution
b	frequency band index
B	number of frequency bands
loF_b	lower frequency limit of band b
hiF_b	higher frequency limit of band b
$\Gamma_l(m)$	normalized autocorrelation function of the lth frame
m	autocorrelation lag
T_0	fundamental period
f_0	fundamental frequency
h	index of harmonic component
N_H	number of harmonic components
f_h	frequency of the hth harmonic
A_h	amplitude of the hth harmonic
V_E	reduced SVD basis
W	ICA transformation matrix

Chapter 3

X	feature matrix $(L \times F)$
L	total number of frames
l	frame index
F	number of columns in X (frequency axis)
f	frequency band index
E	size of the reduced space
U	row basis matrix $(L \times L)$
D	diagonal singular value matrix $(L \times F)$
V	matrix of transposed column basis functions $(F \times F)$
V_E	reduced SVD matrix $(F \times E)$
$\hat{X}$	normalized feature matrix
μ_f	mean of column f
μ_l	mean of row l
Γ_l	standard deviation of row l
χ_l	energy of the NASE
V	matrix of orthogonal eigenvectors
D	diagonal eigenvalue matrix
C	covariance matrix
C_P	reduced eigenvalues of D
C_E	reduced PCA matrix $(F \times E)$
P	number of components
S	source signal matrix $(P \times F)$
W	ICA mixing matrix $(L \times P)$
N	matrix of noise signals $(L \times F)$
$\check{X}$	whitened feature matrix
H	NMF basis signal matrix $(P \times F)$
G	mixing matrix $(L \times P)$
H_E	matrix H with $P = E(E \times F)$
x	coefficient vector
d	dimension of the coefficient space
λ	parameter set of a GMM
M	number of mixture components
$b_m(x)$	Gaussian density (component m)
μ_m	mean vector of component m
Σ_m	covariance matrix of component m
c_m	weight of component m
N_S	number of hidden Markov model states
S_i	hidden Markov model state number i
b_i	observation function of state S_i
a_{ij}	probability of transition between states S_i and S_j
π_i	probability that S_i is the initial state
θ	parameters of a hidden Markov model

w, b	parameters of a hyperplane
$d(w, b)$	distance between the hyperplane and the closest sample
α_i	Lagrange multiplier
$L(w, b, \alpha)$	Lagrange function
$K(\cdot, \cdot)$	kernel mapping
R_l	RMS-norm gain of the lth frame
X_l	NASE vector of the lth frame
Y	audio spectrum projection

Chapter 4

X	acoustic observation
w	word (or symbol)
W	sequence of words (or symbols)
λ_w	hidden Markov model of symbol w
S_i	hidden Markov model state number i
b_i	observation function of state S_i
a_{ij}	probability of transition between states S_i and S_j
D	description of a document
Q	description of a query
d	vector representation of document D
q	vector representation of query Q
t	indexing term
$q(t)$	weight of term t in q
$d(t)$	weight of term t in d
T	indexing term space
N_T	number of terms in T
$s(t_i, t_j)$	measure of similarity between terms t_i and t_j

Chapter 5

n	note index
$f(n)$	pitch of note n
F_s	sampling frequency
F_0	fundamental frequency
$scale(n)$	scale value for pitch n in a scale
$i(n)$	interval value for note n
$d(n)$	differential onset for note n
$o(n)$	time of onset of note n
C	melody contour
M	number of interval values in C
$m(i)$	interval value in C

$G(i)$	n-gram of interval values in C
Q	query representation
D	music document
Q_N	set of n-grams in Q
D_N	set of n-grams in D
c_d	cost of an insertion or deletion
c_m	cost of a mismatch
c_e	value of an exact match
U, V	MPEG-7 beat vectors
$u(i)$	ith coefficient of vector U
$v(j)$	jth coefficient of vector V
R	distance measure
S	similarity score
$\langle t, p, b \rangle$	time t, pitch p, beat b triplet
$\langle t_m, p_m, b_m \rangle$	melody segment m
$\langle t_q, p_q, b_q \rangle$	query segment q
n	measure number
S_n	similarity score of measure n
s_m	subsets of melody pitch p_m
s_q	subsets of query pitch p_q
i, j	contour value counters

Chapter 6

L_S	length of the digital signal in number of samples
N_{CH}	number of channels
$s_i(n)$	digital signal in the ith channel
$\Gamma_{si,sj}$	cross-correlation between channels i and j
P_i	mean power of the ith channel

Chapter 7

X_i	sub-sequence of feature vectors
μ_{X_i}	mean value of X_i
Σ_{X_i}	covariance matrix of X_i
N_{X_i}	number of feature vectors in X_i
R	generalized likelihood ratio
D	penalty

1
Introduction

Today, digital audio applications are part of our everyday lives. Popular examples include audio CDs, MP3 audio players, radio broadcasts, TV or video DVDs, video games, digital cameras with sound track, digital camcorders, telephones, telephone answering machines and telephone enquiries using speech or word recognition.

Various new and advanced audiovisual applications and services become possible based on audio content analysis and description. Search engines or specific filters can use the extracted description to help users navigate or browse through large collections of data. Digital analysis may discriminate whether an audio file contains speech, music or other audio entities, how many speakers are contained in a speech segment, what gender they are and even which persons are speaking. Spoken content may be identified and converted to text. Music may be classified into categories, such as jazz, rock, classics, etc. Often it is possible to identify a piece of music even when performed by different artists – or an identical audio track also when distorted by coding artefacts. Finally, it may be possible to identify particular sounds, such as explosions, gunshots, etc.

We use the term audio to indicate all kinds of audio signals, such as speech, music as well as more general sound signals and their combinations. Our primary goal is to understand how meaningful information can be extracted from digital audio waveforms in order to compare and classify the data efficiently. When such information is extracted it can also often be stored as content description in a compact way. These compact *descriptors* are of great use not only in audio storage and retrieval applications, but also for efficient content-based classification, recognition, browsing or filtering of data. A data descriptor is often called a *feature vector* or *fingerprint* and the process for extracting such feature vectors or fingerprints from audio is called *audio feature extraction* or *audio fingerprinting*.

Usually a variety of more or less complex descriptions can be extracted to fingerprint one piece of audio data. The efficiency of a particular fingerprint

MPEG-7 Audio and Beyond: Audio Content Indexing and Retrieval   H.-G. Kim, N. Moreau and T. Sikora
© 2005 John Wiley & Sons, Ltd

used for comparison and classification depends greatly on the application, the extraction process and the richness of the description itself. This book will provide an overview of various strategies and algorithms for automatic extraction and description. We will provide various examples to illustrate how trade-offs between size and performance of the descriptions can be achieved.

1.1 AUDIO CONTENT DESCRIPTION

Audio content analysis and description has been a very active research and development topic since the early 1970s. During the early 1990s – with the advent of digital audio and video – research on audio and video retrieval became equally important. A very popular means of audio, image or video retrieval is to annotate the media with text, and use text-based database management systems to perform the retrieval. However, text-based annotation has significant drawbacks when confronted with large volumes of media data. Annotation can then become significantly labour intensive. Furthermore, since audiovisual data is rich in content, text may not be rich enough in many applications to describe the data. To overcome these difficulties, in the early 1990s content-based retrieval emerged as a promising means of describing and retrieving audiovisual media. Content-based retrieval systems describe media data by their audio or visual content rather than text. That is, based on audio analysis, it is possible to describe sound or music by its spectral energy distribution, harmonic ratio or fundamental frequency. This allows a comparison with other sound events based on these features and in some cases even a classification of sound into general sound categories. Analysis of speech tracks may result in the recognition of spoken content.

In the late 1990s – with the large-scale introduction of digital audio, images and video to the market – the necessity for interworking between retrieval systems of different vendors arose. For this purpose the ISO Motion Picture Experts Group initiated the MPEG-7 "Multimedia Content Description Interface" work item in 1997. The target of this activity was to develop an international MPEG-7 standard that would define standardized descriptions and description systems. The primary purpose is to allow users or agents to search, identify, filter and browse audiovisual content. MPEG-7 became an international standard in September 2001. Besides support for metadata and text descriptions of the audiovisual content, much focus in the development of MPEG-7 was on the definition of efficient content-based description and retrieval specifications.

This book will discuss techniques for analysis, description and classification of digital audio waveforms. Since MPEG-7 plays a major role in this domain, we will provide a detailed overview of MPEG-7-compliant techniques and algorithms as a starting point. Many state-of-the-art analysis and description algorithms beyond MPEG-7 are introduced and compared with MPEG-7 in terms of computational complexity and retrieval capabilities.

1.2   MPEG-7 AUDIO CONTENT DESCRIPTION – AN OVERVIEW

The MPEG-7 standard provides a rich set of standardized tools to describe multimedia content. Both human users and automatic systems that process audiovisual information are within the scope of MPEG-7. In general MPEG-7 provides such tools for audio as well as images and video data.[1] In this book we will focus on the audio part of MPEG-7 only.

MPEG-7 offers a large set of audio tools to create descriptions. MPEG-7 descriptions, however, do not depend on the ways the described content is coded or stored. It is possible to create an MPEG-7 description of analogue audio in the same way as of digitized content.

The main elements of the MPEG-7 standard related to audio are:

- Descriptors (D) that define the syntax and the semantics of audio feature vectors and their elements. Descriptors bind a feature to a set of values.
- Description schemes (DSs) that specify the structure and semantics of the relationships between the components of descriptors (and sometimes between description schemes).
- A description definition language (DDL) to define the syntax of existing or new MPEG-7 description tools. This allows the extension and modification of description schemes and descriptors and the definition of new ones.
- Binary-coded representation of descriptors or description schemes. This enables efficient storage, transmission, multiplexing of descriptors and description schemes, synchronization of descriptors with content, etc.

The MPEG-7 content descriptions may include:

- Information describing the creation and production processes of the content (director, author, title, etc.).
- Information related to the usage of the content (copyright pointers, usage history, broadcast schedule).
- Information on the storage features of the content (storage format, encoding).
- Structural information on temporal components of the content.
- Information about low-level features in the content (spectral energy distribution, sound timbres, melody description, etc.).

---

[1] An overview of the general goals and scope of MPEG-7 can be found in: Manjunath M., Salembier P. and Sikora T. (2001) *MPEG-7 Multimedia Content Description Interface*, John Wiley & Sons, Ltd.

- Conceptual information on the reality captured by the content (objects and events, interactions among objects).
- Information about how to browse the content in an efficient way.
- Information about collections of objects.
- Information about the interaction of the user with the content (user preferences, usage history).

Figure 1.1 illustrates a possible MPEG-7 application scenario. Audio features are extracted on-line or off-line, manually or automatically, and stored as MPEG-7 descriptions next to the media in a database. Such descriptions may be low-level audio descriptors, high-level descriptors, text, or even speech that serves as spoken annotation.

Consider an audio broadcast or audio-on-demand scenario. A user, or an agent, may only want to listen to specific audio content, such as news. A specific filter will process the MPEG-7 descriptions of various audio channels and only provide the user with content that matches his or her preference. Notice that the processing is performed on the already extracted MPEG-7 descriptions, not on the audio content itself. In many cases processing the descriptions instead of the media is far less computationally complex, usually in an order of magnitude.

Alternatively a user may be interested in retrieving a particular piece of audio. A request is submitted to a search engine, which again queries the MPEG-7 descriptions stored in the database. In a browsing application the user is interested in retrieving similar audio content.

Efficiency and accuracy of filtering, browsing and querying depend greatly on the richness of the descriptions. In the application scenario above, it is of great help if the MPEG-7 descriptors contain information about the category of

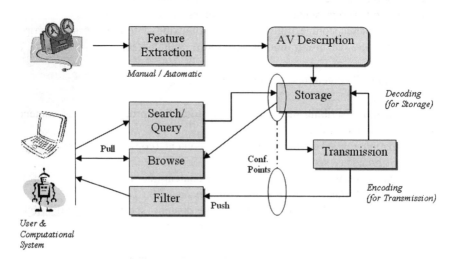

Figure 1.1   MPEG-7 application scenario

the audio files (i.e. whether the broadcast files are news, music, etc.). Even if this is not the case, it is often possible to categorize the audio files based on the low-level MPEG-7 descriptors stored in the database.

1.2.1 MPEG-7 Low-Level Descriptors

The MPEG-7 low-level audio descriptors are of general importance in describing audio. There are 17 temporal and spectral descriptors that may be used in a variety of applications. These descriptors can be extracted from audio automatically and depict the variation of properties of audio over time or frequency. Based on these descriptors it is often feasible to analyse the similarity between different audio files. Thus it is possible to identify identical, similar or dissimilar audio content. This also provides the basis for classification of audio content.

Basic Descriptors
Figure 1.2 depicts instantiations of the two MPEG-7 audio basic descriptors for illustration purposes, namely the audio waveform descriptor and the audio power descriptor. These are time domain descriptions of the audio content. The temporal variation of the descriptors' values provides much insight into the characteristics of the original music signal.

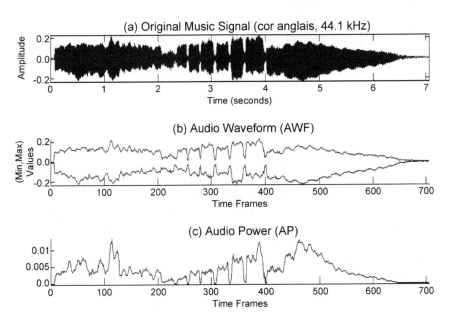

Figure 1.2 MPEG-7 basic descriptors extracted from a music signal (cor anglais, 44.1 kHz)

Basic Spectral Descriptors
The four basic spectral audio descriptors are all derived from a single time–frequency analysis of an audio signal. They describe the audio spectrum in terms of its envelope, centroid, spread and flatness.

Signal Parameter Descriptors
The two signal parameter descriptors apply only to periodic or quasi-periodic signals. They describe the fundamental frequency of an audio signal as well as the harmonicity of a signal.

Timbral Temporal Descriptors
Timbral temporal descriptors can be used to describe temporal characteristics of segments of sounds. They are especially useful for the description of musical timbre (characteristic tone quality independent of pitch and loudness).

Timbral Spectral Descriptors
Timbral spectral descriptors are spectral features in a linear frequency space, especially applicable to the perception of musical timbre.

Spectral Basis Descriptors
The two spectral basis descriptors represent low-dimensional projections of a high-dimensional spectral space to aid compactness and recognition. These descriptors are used primarily with the sound classification and indexing description tools, but may be of use with other types of applications as well.

1.2.2 MPEG-7 Description Schemes

MPEG-7 DSs specify the types of descriptors that can be used in a given description, and the relationships between these descriptors or between other DSs. The MPEG-7 DSs are written in XML. They are defined using the MPEG-7 description definition language (DDL), which is based on the XML Schema Language, and are instantiated as documents or streams. The resulting descriptions can be expressed in a textual form (i.e. human-readable XML for editing, searching, filtering) or in a compressed binary form (i.e. for storage or transmission).

Five sets of audio description tools that roughly correspond to application areas are integrated in the standard: audio signature, musical instrument timbre, melody description, general sound recognition and indexing, and spoken content. They are good examples of how the MPEG-7 audio framework may be integrated to support other applications.

Musical Instrument Timbre Tool
The aim of the timbre description tool is to specify the perceptual features of instruments with a reduced set of descriptors. The descriptors relate to notions such as "attack", "brightness" or "richness" of a sound. Figures 1.3 and 1.4 illustrate the XML instantiations of these descriptors using the MPEG-7 audio description scheme for a harmonic and a percussive instrument type. Notice that the description of the instruments also includes temporal and spectral features of the sound, such as spectral and temporal centroids. The particular values fingerprint the instruments and can be used to distinguish them from other instruments of their class.

Audio Signature Description Scheme
Low-level audio descriptors in general can serve many conceivable applications. The spectral flatness descriptor in particular achieves very robust matching of

```
<AudioDescriptionScheme  xsi:type="PercussiveInstrumentTimbreType">
  <LogAttackTime>
    <Scalar>-1.683017</Scalar>
  </LogAttackTime>
  <SpectralCentroid>
    <Scalar>1217.341518</Scalar>
  </SpectralCentroid>
  <TemporalCentroid>
    <Scalar>0.081574</Scalar>
  </TemporalCentroid>
</AudioDescriptionScheme>
```

Figure 1.3   MPEG-7 audio description for a percussion instrument

```
<AudioDescriptionScheme  xsi:type="HarmonicInstrumentTimbreType">
  <LogAttackTime>
    <Scalar>-0.150702</Scalar>
  </LogAttackTime>
  <HarmonicSpectralCentroid>
    <Scalar>1586.892383</Scalar>
  </HarmonicSpectralCentroid>
  <HarmonicSpectralDeviation>
    <Scalar>-0.027864</Scalar>
  </HarmonicSpectralDeviation>
  <HarmonicSpectralSpread>
    <Scalar>0.550866</Scalar>
  </HarmonicSpectralSpread>
  <HarmonicSpectralVariation>
    <Scalar>0.001877</Scalar>
  </HarmonicSpectralVariation>
</AudioDescriptionScheme>
```

Figure 1.4   MPEG-7 audio description for a violin instrument

audio signals, well tuned to be used as a unique content identifier for robust automatic identification of audio signals. The descriptor is statistically summarized in the audio signature description scheme. An important application is audio fingerprinting for identification of audio based on a database of known works. This is relevant for locating metadata for legacy audio content without metadata annotation.

Melody Description Tools
The melody description tools include a rich representation for monophonic melodic information to facilitate efficient, robust and expressive melodic similarity matching. The melody description scheme includes a melody contour description scheme for extremely terse, efficient, melody contour representation, and a melody sequence description scheme for a more verbose, complete, expressive melody representation. Both tools support matching between melodies, and can support optional information about the melody that may further aid content-based search, including query-by-humming.

General Sound Recognition and Indexing Description Tools
The general sound recognition and indexing description tools are a collection of tools for indexing and categorizing general sounds, with immediate application to sound effects. The tools enable automatic sound identification and indexing, and the specification of a classification scheme of sound classes and tools for specifying hierarchies of sound recognizers. Such recognizers may be used automatically to index and segment sound tracks. Thus, the description tools address recognition and representation all the way from low-level signal-based analyses, through mid-level statistical models, to highly semantic labels for sound classes.

Spoken Content Description Tools
Audio streams of multimedia documents often contain spoken parts that enclose a lot of semantic information. This information, called *spoken content*, consists of the actual words spoken in the speech segments of an audio stream. As speech represents the primary means of human communication, a significant amount of the usable information enclosed in audiovisual documents may reside in the spoken content. A transcription of the spoken content to text can provide a powerful description of media. Transcription by means of automatic speech recognition (ASR) systems has the potential to change dramatically the way we create, store and manage knowledge in the future. Progress in the ASR field promises new applications able to treat speech as easily and efficiently as we currently treat text.

The audio part of MPEG-7 contains a *SpokenContent* high-level tool targeted for spoken data management applications. The MPEG-7 *SpokenContent* tool provides a standardized representation of an ASR output, i.e. of the semantic information (the *spoken content*) extracted by an ASR system from a spoken signal. It consists of a compact representation of multiple word and/or sub-word hypotheses produced by an ASR engine. How the *SpokenContent* description should be extracted and used is not part of the standard.

The MPEG-7 *SpokenContent* tool defines a standardized description of either a word or a phone type of lattice delivered by a recognizer. Figure 1.5 illustrates what an MPEG-7 *SpokenContent* description of the speech excerpt "film on Berlin" could look like. A lattice can thus be a word-only graph, a phone-only graph or combine word and phone hypotheses in the same graph as depicted in the example of Figure 1.5.

1.2.3 MPEG-7 Description Definition Language (DDL)

The DDL defines the syntactic rules to express and combine DSs and descriptors. It allows users to create their own DSs and descriptors. The DDL is not a modelling language such as the Unified Modeling Language (UML) but a schema language. It is able to express spatial, temporal, structural and conceptual relationships between the elements of a DS, and between DSs. It provides a rich model for links and references between one or more descriptions and the data that it describes. In addition, it is platform and application independent and human and machine readable.

The purpose of a schema is to define a class of XML documents. This is achieved by specifying particular constructs that constrain the structure and content of the documents. Possible constraints include: elements and their content, attributes and their values, cardinalities and data types.

1.2.4 BiM (Binary Format for MPEG-7)

BiM defines a generic framework to facilitate the carriage and processing of MPEG-7 descriptions in a compressed binary format. It enables the compression,

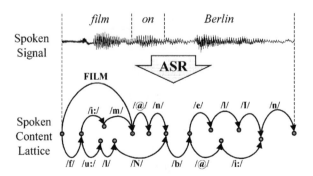

Figure 1.5 MPEG-7 *SpokenContent* description of an input spoken signal "film on Berlin"

multiplexing and streaming of XML documents. BiM coders and decoders can handle any XML language. For this purpose the schema definition (DTD or XML Schema) of the XML document is processed and used to generate a binary format. This binary format has two main properties. First, due to the schema knowledge, structural redundancy (element name, attribute names, etc.) is removed from the document. Therefore the document structure is highly compressed (98% on average). Second, elements and attribute values are encoded using dedicated source coders.

1.3 ORGANIZATION OF THE BOOK

This book focuses primarily on the digital audio signal processing aspects for content analysis, description and retrieval. Our prime goal is to describe how meaningful information can be extracted from digital audio waveforms, and how audio data can be efficiently described, compared and classified. Figure 1.6 provides an overview of the book's chapters.

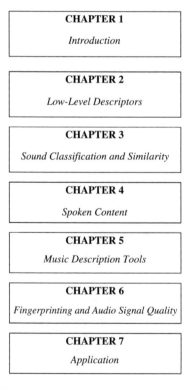

Figure 1.6 Chapter outline of the book

The purpose of Chapter 2 is to provide the reader with a detailed overview of *low-level audio descriptors*. To a large extent this chapter provides the foundations and definitions for most of the remaining chapters of the book. Since MPEG-7 provides an established framework with a large set of descriptors, the standard is used as an example to illustrate the concept. The mathematical definitions of all MPEG-7 low-level audio descriptors are outlined in detail. Other established low-level descriptors beyond MPEG-7 are introduced. To help the reader visualize the kind of information that these descriptors convey, some experimental results are given to illustrate the definitions.

In Chapter 3 the reader is introduced to the concepts of *sound similarity* and *sound classification*. Various classifiers and their properties are discussed. Low-level descriptors introduced in the previous chapter are employed for illustration. The MPEG-7 standard is again used as a starting point to explain the practical implementation of sound classification systems. The performance of MPEG-7 systems is compared with the well-established MFCC feature extraction method. The chapter provides in great detail simulation results of various systems for sound classification.

Chapter 4 focuses on MPEG-7 *SpokenContent* description. It is possible to follow most of the chapter without reading the other parts of the book. The primary goal is to provide the reader with a detailed overview of ASR and its use for MPEG-7 *SpokenContent* description. The structure of the MPEG-7 *SpokenContent* description itself is presented in detail and discussed in the context of the *spoken document retrieval* (SDR) application. The contribution of the MPEG-7 *SpokenContent* tool to the standardization and development of future SDR applications is emphasized. Many application examples and experimental results are provided to illustrate the concept.

Music description tools for specifying the properties of musical signals are discussed in Chapter 5. We focus explicitly on MPEG-7 tools. Concepts for instrument *timbre* description to specify perceptual features of musical sounds are discussed using reduced sets of descriptors. *Melodies* can be described using MPEG-7 description schemes for melodic similarity matching. We will discuss query-by-humming applications to provide the reader with examples of how melody can be extracted from a user's input and matched against melodies contained in a database.

An overview of audio fingerprinting and audio signal quality description is provided in Chapter 6. In general, the MPEG-7 low-level descriptors can be seen as providing a fingerprint for describing audio content. Audio fingerprinting has to a certain extent been described in Chapters 2 and 3. We will focus in Chapter 6 on fingerprinting tools specifically developed for the identification of a piece of audio and for describing its quality.

Chapter 7 finally provides an outline of example applications using the concepts developed in the previous chapters. Various applications and experimental results are provided to help the reader visualize the capabilities of concepts for content analysis and description.

LEEDS METROPOLITAN UNIVERSITY LIBRARY

2

Low-Level Descriptors

2.1 INTRODUCTION

The MPEG-7 low-level descriptors (LLDs) form the *foundation layer* of the standard (Manjunath *et al.*, 2002). It consists of a collection of simple, low-complexity audio features that can be used to characterize any type of sound. The LLDs offer flexibility to the standard, allowing new applications to be built in addition to the ones that can be designed based on the MPEG-7 high-level tools.

The foundation layer comprises a series of 18 generic LLDs consisting of a normative part (the syntax and semantics of the descriptor) and an optional, non-normative part which recommends possible extraction and/or similarity matching methods. The temporal and spectral LLDs can be classified into the following groups:

- Basic descriptors: audio waveform (AWF), audio power (AP).
- Basic spectral descriptors: audio spectrum envelope (ASE), audio spectrum centroid (ASC), audio spectrum spread (ASS), audio spectrum flatness (ASF).
- Basic signal parameters: audio harmonicity (AH), audio fundamental frequency (AFF).
- Temporal timbral descriptors: log attack time (LAT) and temporal centroid (TC).
- Spectral timbral descriptors: harmonic spectral centroid (HSC), harmonic spectral deviation (HSD), harmonic spectral spread (HSS), harmonic spectral variation (HSV) and spectral centroid (SC).
- Spectral basis representations: audio spectrum basis (ASB) and audio spectrum projection (ASP).

An additional silence descriptor completes the MPEG-7 foundation layer.

MPEG-7 Audio and Beyond: Audio Content Indexing and Retrieval   H.-G. Kim, N. Moreau and T. Sikora
© 2005 John Wiley & Sons, Ltd

This chapter gives the mathematical definitions of all low-level audio descriptors according to the MPEG-7 audio standard. To help the reader visualize the kind of information that these descriptors convey, some experimental results are given to illustrate the definitions.[1]

2.2 BASIC PARAMETERS AND NOTATIONS

There are two ways of describing low-level audio features in the MPEG-7 standard:

- An LLD feature can be extracted from sound segments of variable lengths to mark regions with distinct acoustic properties. In this case, the summary descriptor extracted from a segment is stored as an MPEG-7 *AudioSegment* description. An audio segment represents a temporal interval of audio material, which may range from arbitrarily short intervals to the entire audio portion of a media document.
- An LLD feature can be extracted at regular intervals from sound frames. In this case, the resulting sampled values are stored as an MPEG-7 *ScalableSeries* description.

This section provides the basic parameters and notations that will be used to describe the extraction of the frame-based descriptors. The scalable series descriptions used to store the resulting series of LLDs will be described in Section 2.3.

2.2.1 Time Domain

In the time domain, the following notations will be used for the input audio signal:

- n is the index of time samples.
- $s(n)$ is the input digital audio signal.
- F_s is the sampling rate of $s(n)$.

And for the time frames:

- l is the index of time frames.
- *hopSize* is the time interval between two successive time frames.

---

[1] See also the LLD extraction demonstrator from the Technische Universität Berlin (*MPEG-7 Audio Analyzer*), available on-line at: http://mpeg7lld.nue.tu-berlin.de/.

- N_{hop} denotes the integer number of time samples corresponding to *hopSize*.
- L_w is the length of a time frame (with $L_w \geq hopSize$).
- N_w denotes the integer number of time samples corresponding to L_w.
- L is the total number of time frames in $s(n)$.

These notations are portrayed in Figure 2.1.

The choice of *hopSize* and L_w depends on the kind of descriptor to extract. However, the standard constrains *hopSize* to be an integer multiple or divider of 10 ms (its default value), in order to make descriptors that were extracted at different *hopSize* intervals compatible with each others.

2.2.2 Frequency Domain

The extraction of some MPEG-7 LLDs is based on the estimation of short-term power spectra within overlapping time frames. In the frequency domain, the following notations will be used:

- k is the frequency bin index.
- $S_l(k)$ is the spectrum extracted from the lth frame of $s(n)$.
- $P_l(k)$ is the power spectrum extracted from the lth frame of $s(n)$.

Several techniques for spectrum estimation are described in the literature (Gold and Morgan, 1999). MPEG-7 does not standardize the technique itself, even though a number of implementation features are recommended (e.g. an L_w of 30 ms for a default *hopSize* of 10 ms). The following just describes the most classical method, based on squared magnitudes of discrete Fourier transform (DFT) coefficients. After multiplying the frames with a windowing function

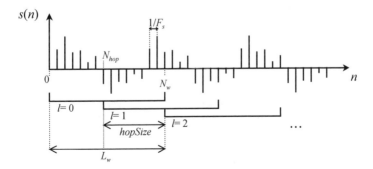

Figure 2.1 Notations for frame-based descriptors

$w(n)$ (e.g. a Hamming window), the DFT is applied as:

$$S_l(k) = \sum_{n=0}^{N_{FT}-1} s(n + lN_{hop})w(n)\exp\left(-j\frac{2\pi nk}{N_{FT}}\right) (0 \le l \le L-1; 0 \le k \le N_{FT}-1), \quad (2.1)$$

where N_{FT} is the size of the DFT ($N_{FT} \ge N_w$). In general, a fast Fourier transform (FFT) algorithm is used and N_{FT} is the power of 2 just larger than N_w (the enlarged frame is then padded with zeros).

According to Parseval's theorem, the average power of the signal in the lth analysis window can be written in two ways, as:

$$\overline{P}_l = \frac{1}{E_w}\sum_{n=0}^{N_w-1} \left|s(n + lN_{hop})w(n)\right|^2 = \frac{1}{N_{FT}E_w}\sum_{k=0}^{N_{FT}-1} |S_l(k)|^2, \quad (2.2)$$

where the window normalization factor E_w is defined as the energy of $w(n)$:

$$E_w = \sum_{n=0}^{N_w-1} |w(n)|^2. \quad (2.3)$$

The power spectrum $P_l(k)$ of the lth frame is defined as the squared magnitude of the DFT spectrum $S_l(k)$. Since the signal spectrum is symmetric around the Nyquist frequency $F_s/2$, it is possible to consider the first half of the power spectrum only ($0 \le k \le N_{FT}/2$) without losing any information. In order to ensure that the sum of all power coefficients equates to the average power defined in Equation (2.2), each coefficient can be normalized in the following way:

$$P_l(k) = \frac{1}{N_{FT}E_w}|S_l(k)|^2 \quad \text{for } k = 0 \text{ and } k = \frac{N_{FT}}{2}$$

$$P_l(k) = 2\frac{1}{N_{FT}E_w}|S_l(k)|^2 \quad \text{for } 0 < k < \frac{N_{FT}}{2}. \quad (2.4)$$

Figure 2.2 depicts the spectrogram of a piece of music (a solo excerpt of cor anglais recorded at 44.1 kHz). Power spectra are extracted through the FFT ($N_{FT} = 2048$) every 10 ms from 30 ms frames. They are represented vertically at the corresponding frame indexes. The frequency range of interest is between 0 and 22.05 kHz, which is the Nyquist frequency in this example. A lighter shade indicates a higher power value.

In the FFT spectrum, the discrete frequencies corresponding to bin indexes k are:

$$f(k) = k\Delta F \quad (0 \le k \le N_{FT}/2), \quad (2.5)$$

where $\Delta F = F_s/N_{FT}$ is the frequency interval between two successive FFT bins. Inverting the preceding equation, we can map any frequency in the range $[0, F_s/2]$ to a discrete bin in $\{0, 1, \ldots, N_{FT}/2\}$:

$$k = round(f/\Delta F) \quad (0 \le f \le F_s/2), \quad (2.6)$$

where $round(x)$ means rounding the real value x to the nearest integer.

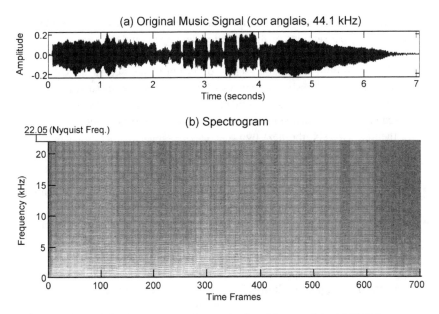

Figure 2.2   Spectrogram of a music signal (cor anglais, 44.1 kHz)

2.3   SCALABLE SERIES

An MPEG-7 *ScalableSeries* description is a standardized way of representing a series of LLD features (scalars or vectors) extracted from sound frames at regular time intervals. Such a series can be described at full resolution or after a *scaling* operation. In the latter case, the series of original samples is decomposed into consecutive sub-sequences of samples. Each sub-sequence is then summarized by a single *scaled sample*.

An illustration of the scaling process and the resulting scalable series description is shown in Figure 2.3 (ISO/IEC, 2001), where i is the index of the scaled

Original series	●●●●●●●●●●●●●●●●●●●●●●●●●●●●●●●
Scaled series	○	○	○	○		○		○○○	○	○	○	○	○
Index i	1	2	3	4		5		6 7 8	9	10	11	12	13
ratio	2			6				1	2				
numOfElements	3			2				2	6				
totalNumOfSamples	31												

Figure 2.3   Structure of a scalable series description

series. In this example, the 31 samples of the original series (filled circles) are summarized by 13 samples of the scaled series (open circles).

The *scale ratio* of a given scaled sample is the number of original samples it stands for. Within a scalable series description, the scaled series is itself decomposed into successive sequences of scaled samples. In such a sequence, all scaled samples share the same scale ratio. In Figure 2.3, for example, the first three scaled samples each summarize two original samples (scale ratio is equal to 2), the next two six, the next two one, etc.

The attributes of a *ScalableSeries* are the following:

- *Scaling*: is a flag that specifies how the original samples are scaled. If absent, the original samples are described without scaling.
- *totalNumOfSamples*: indicates the total number of samples of the original series before any scaling operation.
- *ratio*: is an integer value that indicates the scale ratio of a scaled sample, i.e. the number of original samples represented by that scaled sample. This parameter is common to all the elements in a sequence of scaled samples. The value to be used when *Scaling* is absent is 1.
- *numOfElements*: is an integer value indicating the number of consecutive elements in a sequence of scaled samples that share the same scale ratio. If *Scaling* is absent, it is equal to the value of *totalNumOfSamples*.

The last sample of the series may summarize fewer than *ratio* samples. In the example of Figure 2.3, the last scaled sample has a ratio of 2, but actually summarizes only one original sample. This situation is detected by comparing the sum of *ratio* times *numOfElements* products to *totalNumOfSamples*.

Two distinct types of scalable series are defined for representing series of scalars and series of vectors in the MPEG-7 LLD framework. Both types inherit from the scalable series description. The following sections present them in detail.

2.3.1 Series of Scalars

The MPEG-7 standard contains a *SeriesOfScalar* descriptor to represent a series of scalar values, at full resolution or scaled. This can be used with any temporal series of scalar LLDs. The attributes of a *SeriesOfScalar* description are:

- *Raw*: may contain the original series of scalars when no scaling operation is applied. It is only used if the *Scaling* flag is absent to store the entire series at full resolution.

- *Weight*: is an optional series of weights. If this attribute is present, each weight corresponds to a sample in the original series. These parameters can be used to control scaling.
- *Min, Max* and *Mean*: are three real-valued vectors in which each dimension characterizes a sample in the scaled series. For a given scaled sample, a *Min, Max* and *Mean* coefficient is extracted from the corresponding group of samples in the original series. The coefficient in *Min* is the minimum original sample value, the coefficient in *Max* is the maximum original sample value and the coefficient in *Mean* is the mean sample value. The original samples are averaged by arithmetic mean, taking the sample weights into account if the *Weight* attribute is present (see formulae below). These attributes are absent if the *Raw* element is present.
- *Variance*: is a real-valued vector. Each element corresponds to a scaled sample. It is the variance computed within the corresponding group of original samples. This computation may take the sample weights into account if the *Weight* attribute is present (see formulae below). This attribute is absent if the *Raw* element is present.
- *Random*: is a vector resulting from the selection of one sample at random within each group of original samples used for scaling. This attribute is absent if the *Raw* element is present.
- *First*: is a vector resulting from the selection of the first sample in each group of original samples used for scaling. This attribute is absent if the *Raw* element is present.
- *Last*: is a vector resulting from the selection of the last sample in each group of original samples used for scaling. This attribute is absent if the *Raw* element is present.

These different attributes allow us to summarize any series of scalar features. Such a description allows *scalability*, in the sense that a scaled series can be derived indifferently from an original series (*scaling* operation) or from a previously scaled *SeriesOfScalar* (*rescaling* operation).

Initially, a series of scalar LLD features is stored in the *Raw* vector. Each element $Raw(l)$ $(0 \leq l \leq L - 1)$ contains the value of the scalar feature extracted from the *l*th frame of the signal. Optionally, the *Weight* series may contain the weights $W(l)$ associated to each $Raw(l)$ feature.

When a scaling operation is performed, a new *SeriesOfScalar* is generated by grouping the original samples (see Figure 2.3) and calculating the above-mentioned attributes. The *Raw* attribute is absent in the scaled series descriptor. Let us assume that the *i*th scaled sample stands for the samples $Raw(l)$ contained between $l = lLo(i)$ and $l = lHi(i)$ with:

$$lHi(i) = lLo(i) + ratio - 1 \qquad (2.7)$$

where *ratio* is the scale ratio of the *i*th scaled sample (i.e. the number of original samples it stands for). The corresponding *Min* and *Max* values are then defined as:

$$Min(i) = \min_{l=lLo(i)}^{lHi(i)} Raw(l) \text{ and } Max(i) = \max_{l=lLo(i)}^{lHi(i)} Raw(l). \qquad (2.8)$$

The *Mean* value is given by:

$$Mean(i) = \frac{1}{ratio} \sum_{l=lLo(i)}^{lHi(i)} Raw(l) \qquad (2.9)$$

if no sample weights $W(l)$ are specified in *Weight*. If weights are present, the *Mean* value is computed as:

$$Mean(i) = \sum_{l=lLo(i)}^{lHi(i)} W(l)Raw(l) \Big/ \sum_{l=lLo(i)}^{lHi(i)} W(l). \qquad (2.10)$$

In the same way, there are two computational methods for the *Variance* depending on whether the original sample weights are absent:

$$Variance(i) = \frac{1}{ratio} \sum_{l=lLo(i)}^{lHi(i)} [Raw(l) - Mean(i)]^2, \qquad (2.11)$$

or present:

$$Variance(i) = \sum_{l=lLo(i)}^{lHi(i)} W(l)[Raw(l) - Mean(i)]^2 \Big/ \sum_{l=lLo(i)}^{lHi(i)} W(l). \qquad (2.12)$$

Finally, the weights $W(i)$ of the new scaled samples are computed, if necessary, as:

$$W(i) = \frac{1}{ratio} \sum_{l=lLo(i)}^{lHi(i)} W(l). \qquad (2.13)$$

2.3.2 Series of Vectors

Some LLDs do not consist of single scalar values, but of multi-dimensional vectors. To store these LLDs as scalable series, the MPEG-7 standard contains a *SeriesOfVector* descriptor to represent temporal series of feature vectors. As before, a series can be stored at the full original resolution or scaled. The attributes of a *SeriesOfVector* description are:

- *vectorSize*: is the number of elements of each vector in the series.
- *Raw*: may contain the original series of vectors when no scaling operation is applied. It is only used if the *Scaling* flag is absent to store the entire series at full resolution.

- *Weight*: is an optional series of weights. If this attribute is present, each weight corresponds to a vector in the original series. These parameters can be used to control scaling in the same way as for the *SeriesOfScalar* description.
- *Min, Max* and *Mean*: are three real-valued matrices. The number of rows is equal to the sum of *numOfElements* over the scaled series (i.e. the number of scaled vectors). The number of columns is equal to *vectorSize*. Each row characterizes a scaled vector. For a given scaled vector, a *Min, Max* and *Mean* row vector is extracted from the corresponding group of vectors in the original series. The row vector in *Min* contains the minimum coefficients observed among the original vectors, the row vector in *Max* contains the maximum coefficients observed among the original vectors and the row vector in *Mean* is the mean of the original vectors. Each vector coefficient is averaged in the same way as the *Mean* scalars in the previous section. These attributes are absent if the *Raw* element is present.
- *Variance*: is a series of variance vectors whose size is set to *vectorSize*. Each vector corresponds to a scaled vector. Its coefficients are equal to the variance computed within the corresponding group of original vectors. This computation may take the sample weights into account if the *Weight* attribute is present. This attribute is absent if the *Raw* element is present.
- *Covariance*: is a series of covariance matrices. It is represented as a three-dimensional matrix: the number of rows is equal to the sum of *numOfElements* parameters over the scaled series; the number of columns and number of pages are both equal to *vectorSize*. Each row is a covariance matrix describing a given scaled vector. It is estimated from the corresponding group of original vectors (see formula below). This attribute is absent if the *Raw* element is present.
- *VarianceSummed*: is a series of summed variance coefficients. Each coefficient corresponds to a scaled vector. For a given scaled vector, it is obtained by summing the elements of the corresponding *Variance* vector (see formula below). This attribute is absent if the *Raw* element is present.
- *MaxSqDist*: is a series of maximum squared distance (MSD) coefficients. For each scaled vector, an MSD coefficient is estimated (see formula below), representing an upper bound of the distance between the corresponding group of original vectors and their mean. This attribute is absent if the *Raw* element is present.
- *Random*: is a series of vectors resulting from the selection of one vector at random within each group of original vectors used for scaling. This attribute is absent if the *Raw* element is present.
- *First*: is a series of vectors resulting from the selection of the first vector in each group of original vectors used for scaling. This attribute is absent if the *Raw* element is present.
- *Last*: is a series of vectors resulting from the selection of the last vector in each group of original samples used for scaling. This attribute is absent if the *Raw* element is present.

As in the case of *SeriesOfScalar*, these attributes aim at summarizing a series of vectors through scaling and/or rescaling operations.

Initially, a series of vector LLD features is stored in the *Raw* attribute. Each element $Raw(l)$ $(0 \le l \le L - 1)$ contains the vector extracted from the *l*th frame of the signal. Optionally, the *Weight* series may contain the weights $W(l)$ associated to each vector.

When a scaling operation is performed, a new *SeriesOfVector* is generated. The *Min, Max, Mean* and *Weight* attributes of the scaled series are defined in the same way as for the *SeriesOfScalar* scaling operation described in Section 2.3.1 (the same formulae are applied with vectors instead of scalars). The elements of the *Covariance* matrix of the *i*th scaled sample are defined as:

$$Cov(i, b, b') = \frac{1}{ratio} \sum_{l=lLo(i)}^{lHi(i)} [Raw(l, b) - Mean(i, b)][Raw(l, b') - Mean(i, b')],$$

(2.14)

with $(0 \le b \le B - 1)$ and $(0 \le b' \le B - 1)$, where B is the size of vector $Raw(l)$, and b and b' are indexes of vector dimensions. $Raw(l, b)$ and $Mean(i, b)$ are the *b*th coefficients of vectors $Raw(l)$ and $Mean(i)$. The *VarianceSummed* attribute of the *i*th scaled sample is defined as:

$$VarianceSummed(i) = \frac{1}{ratio} \sum_{b=0}^{B-1} \sum_{l=lLo(i)}^{lHi(i)} [Raw(l, b) - Mean(i, b)]^2. \quad (2.15)$$

If weights are specified for original vectors $Raw(l)$, the computation of *Covariance* and *VarianceSummed* takes them into account in the same way as in Equation (2.12).

The *MaxSqDist* attribute of the *i*th scaled sample is defined as:

$$MaxSqDist(i) = \max_{l=lLo(i)}^{lHi(i)} \| Raw(l) - Mean(i) \|^2. \quad (2.16)$$

2.3.3 Binary Series

The standard defines a binary form of the aforementioned *SeriesOfScalar* and *SeriesOfVector* descriptors: namely, the *SeriesOfScalarBinary* and *SeriesOfVectorBinary* descriptors. These descriptors are used to instantiate series of scalars or vectors with a uniform power-of-2 *ratio*. The goal is to ease the comparison of series with different scaling ratios, as the decimation required for the comparison between two binary series is also a power of 2.

2.4 BASIC DESCRIPTORS

The goal of the following two descriptors is to provide a simple and economical description of the temporal properties of an audio signal.

2.4.1 Audio Waveform

A simple way to get a compact description of the shape of an audio signal $s(n)$ is to consider its minimum and maximum samples within successive non-overlapping frames (i.e. $L_w = hopSize$). For each frame, two values are stored:

- *minRange*: the lower limit of audio amplitude in the frame.
- *maxRange*: the upper limit of audio amplitude in the frame.

The audio waveform (AWF) descriptor consists of the resulting temporal series of these (*minRange, maxRange*) pairs. The temporal resolution of the AWF is given by the *hopSize* parameter. If desired, the raw signal can be stored in an AWF descriptor by setting *hopSize* to the sampling period $1/F_s$ of $s(n)$.

The AWF provides an estimate of the signal envelope in the time domain. It also allows economical and straightforward storage, display or comparison techniques of waveforms. The display of the AWF description of a signal consists in drawing for each frame a vertical line from *minRange* to *maxRange*. The time axis is then labelled according to the *hopSize* information.

Figure 2.4 gives graphical representations of the series of basic LLDs extracted from the music excerpt used in Figure 2.2. We can see that the MPEG-7 AWF provides a good approximation of the shape of the original waveform.

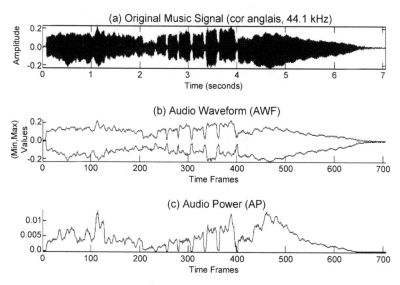

Figure 2.4 MPEG-7 basic descriptors extracted from a music signal (cor anglais, 44.1 kHz)

2.4.2 Audio Power

The audio power (AP) LLD describes the temporally smoothed instantaneous power of the audio signal. The AP coefficients are the average square of waveform values $s(n)$ within successive non-overlapping frames ($L_w = hopSize$). The AP coefficient of the lth frame of the signal is thus:

$$AP(l) = \frac{1}{N_{hop}} \sum_{n=0}^{N_{hop}-1} |s(n + lN_{hop})|^2 \quad (0 \le l \le L - 1), \qquad (2.17)$$

where L is the total number of time frames. The AP allows us to measure the evolution of the amplitude of the signal as a function of time. In conjunction with other basic spectral descriptors (described below), it provides a quick representation of the spectrogram of a signal.

An example of the AP description of a music signal is given in Figure 2.4. The AP is measured in successive signal frames and given as a function of time (expressed in terms of frame index l). This provides a very simple representation of the signal content: the power peaks correspond to the parts where the original signal has a higher amplitude.

2.5 BASIC SPECTRAL DESCRIPTORS

The four basic spectral LLDs provide time series of logarithmic frequency descriptions of the short-term audio power spectrum. The use of logarithmic frequency scales is supposed to approximate the response of the human ear.

All these descriptors are based on the estimation of short-term power spectra within overlapping time frames. This section describes the descriptors, based on the notations and definitions introduced in Section 2.2. For reasons of clarity, the frame index l will be discarded in the following formulae.

2.5.1 Audio Spectrum Envelope

The audio spectrum envelope (ASE) is a log-frequency power spectrum that can be used to generate a reduced spectrogram of the original audio signal. It is obtained by summing the energy of the original power spectrum within a series of frequency bands.

The bands are logarithmically distributed (base 2 logarithms) between two frequency edges *loEdge* (lower edge) and *hiEdge* (higher edge). The spectral resolution r of the frequency bands within the [*loEdge*,*hiEdge*] interval can be chosen from eight possible values, ranging from 1/16 of an octave to 8 octaves:

$$r = 2^j \text{ octaves } (-4 \le j \le +3). \qquad (2.18)$$

Both *loEdge* and *hiEdge* must be related to 1 kHz in the following way:

$$Edge = 2^{rn} \times 1\,\text{kHz}, \tag{2.19}$$

where r is the resolution in octaves and n is an integer value.

The default value of *hiEdge* is 16 kHz, which corresponds to the upper limit of hearing. The default value of *loEdge* is 62.5 Hz so that the default [*loEdge*, *hiEdge*] range corresponds to an 8-octave interval, logarithmically centred at a frequency of 1 kHz.

Within the default [*loEdge*, *hiEdge*] range, the number of logarithmic bands that corresponds to r is $B_{in} = 8/r$. The low (loF_b) and high (hiF_b) frequency edges of each band are given by:

$$\begin{aligned} loF_b &= loEdge \times 2^{(b-1)r} \\ hiF_b &= loEdge \times 2^{br} \end{aligned} \quad (1 \le b \le B_{in}). \tag{2.20}$$

The sum of power coefficients in band b [loF_b, hiF_b] gives the ASE coefficient for this frequency range. The coefficient for the band b is:

$$ASE(b) = \sum_{k=loK_b}^{hiK_b} P(k) \quad (1 \le b \le B_{in}), \tag{2.21}$$

where $P(k)$ are the power spectrum coefficients defined in Equation (2.4), and loK_b (resp. hiK_b) is the integer frequency bin corresponding to the lower edge of the band loF_b (the higher edge of the band hiF_b) obtained from Equation (2.6).

However, the repartition of the power spectrum coefficients $P(k)$ among the different frequency bands can be a problem, particularly for the narrower low-frequency bands when the resolution r is high. It is reasonable to assume that a power spectrum coefficient whose distance to a band edge is less than half the FFT resolution (i.e. less than $\Delta F/2$) contributes to the ASE coefficients of both neighbouring bands. How such a coefficient should be shared by the two bands is not specified by the standard. A possible method is depicted in Figure 2.5.

The B_{in} *within-band* band power coefficients are completed by two additional values: the powers of the spectrum between 0 Hz and *loEdge* and between *hiEdge* and the Nyquist frequency $F_s/2$ (provided that *hiEdge* < Nyquist frequency). These two values represent the *out-of-band* energy.

In the following, $B = B_{in} + 2$ will describe the total number of coefficients $ASE(b)$ ($0 \le b \le B-1$) forming the ASE descriptor extracted from one frame. With *loEdge* and *hiEdge* default values, the dimension of an ASE can be chosen between $B = 3$ ($B_{in} = 1$) with the minimal resolution of 8 octaves and $B = 130$ ($B_{in} = 128$) with the maximal resolution of 1/16 octave.

The extraction of an ASE vector from a power spectrum is depicted in Figure 2.6 with, as an example, the *loEdge* and *hiEdge* default values and a

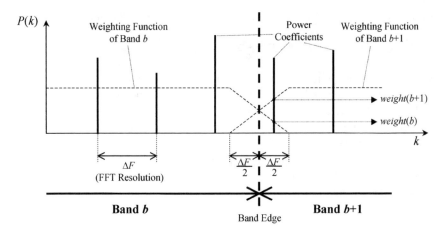

Figure 2.5 Method for weighting the contribution of a power coefficient shared by two bands

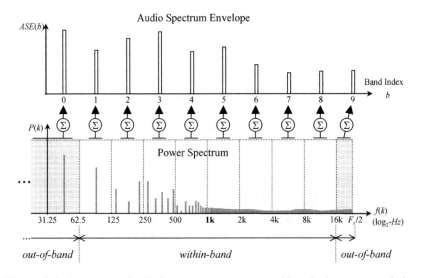

Figure 2.6 Extraction of ASE from a power spectrum with a single-octave resolution

1-octave resolution. The ASE vectors comprise 10 coefficients: 8 *within-band* coefficients plus 2 *out-of-band* coefficients.

The summation of all ASE coefficients equals the power in the analysis window, according to Parseval's theorem. More generally, this descriptor has useful scaling properties: the power spectrum over an interval is equal to the sum of power spectra over subintervals.

Figure 2.7 gives graphical representations of the basic LLDs extracted from the same music excerpt as in Figure 2.4. The ASE description is depicted in (b). Each

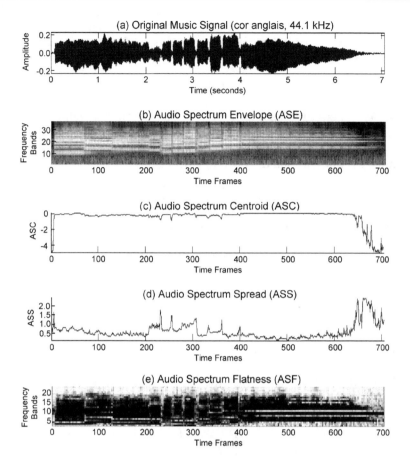

Figure 2.7 MPEG-7 basic spectral descriptors extracted from a music signal (cor anglais, 44.1 kHz)

ASE vector is extracted from 34 frequency bands and consists of 32 within-band coefficients between $loEdge = 250$ Hz and $hiEdge = 16$ kHz (i.e. a 1/4-octave resolution) and two out-of-band coefficients. ASE vectors are extracted every 10 ms from 30 ms frames and represented vertically at the corresponding frame indexes. A lighter shade indicates a higher band power value. The ASE provides a compact representation of the spectrogram of the input signal.

2.5.2 Audio Spectrum Centroid

The audio spectrum centroid (ASC) gives the centre of gravity of a log-frequency power spectrum. All power coefficients below 62.5 Hz are summed and represented by a single coefficient, in order to prevent a non-zero DC component and/or very low-frequency components from having a disproportionate weight. On the discrete frequency bin scale, this corresponds to every power coefficient falling below the index:

$$K_{low} = floor(62.5/\Delta F), \tag{2.22}$$

where $floor(x)$ gives the largest integer less than or equal to x, and $\Delta F = F_s/N_{FT}$ is the frequency interval between two FFT bins.

This results in a new power spectrum $P'(k')$ whose relation to the original spectrum $P(k)$ of Equation (2.4) is given by:

$$P'(k') = \begin{cases} \sum_{k=0}^{K_{low}} P(k) & \text{for } k' = 0 \\ P(k' + K_{low}) & \text{for } 1 \le k' \le \frac{N_{FT}}{2} - K_{low}. \end{cases} \tag{2.23}$$

The frequencies $f'(k')$ corresponding to the new bins k' are given by:

$$f'(k') = \begin{cases} 31.25 & \text{for } k' = 0 \\ f(k' + K_{low}) & \text{for } 1 \le k' \le \frac{N_{FT}}{2} - K_{low}, \end{cases} \tag{2.24}$$

where $f(k)$ is defined as in Equation (2.5). The nominal frequency of the low-frequency coefficient is chosen at the middle of the low-frequency band: $f'(0) = 31.25\,Hz$.

Finally, for a given frame, the ASC is defined from the modified power coefficients $P'(k')$ and their corresponding frequencies $f'(k')$ as:

$$ASC = \frac{\sum_{k'=0}^{(N_{FT}/2)-K_{low}} \log_2 \left(\frac{f'(k')}{1000} \right) P'(k')}{\sum_{k'=0}^{(N_{FT}/2)-K_{low}} P'(k')} \tag{2.25}$$

Each frequency $f'(k')$ of the modified power spectrum is weighted by the corresponding power coefficient $P'(k')$.

Several other definitions of the spectrum centroid can be found in the literature (Wang et al., 2000), using different spectrum coefficients (amplitude, log-power, etc.) or frequency scales (logarithmic or linear). The MPEG-7 definition, based on an octave frequency scale centred at 1 kHz, is designed to be coherent with the ASE descriptor defined in Section 2.5.1.

The ASC measure gives information on the shape of the power spectrum. It indicates whether a power spectrum is dominated by low or high frequencies and can be regarded as an approximation of the perceptual *sharpness* of the signal. The log-frequency scaling approximates the perception of frequencies in the human hearing system.

Figure 2.7 depicts the temporal series of ASC values. In this example, the spectrum is dominated by lower frequencies. The ASC values remain around 0, which means, according to Equation (2.25), that the corresponding frequency centroids remain around 1 kHz.

2.5.3 Audio Spectrum Spread

The audio spectrum spread (ASS) is another simple measure of the spectral shape. The *spectral spread*, also called *instantaneous bandwidth*, can be defined in several different ways (Li, 2000). In MPEG-7, it is defined as the second central moment of the log-frequency spectrum. For a given signal frame, the ASS feature is extracted by taking the root-mean-square (RMS) deviation of the spectrum from its centroid ASC:

$$
ASS = \sqrt{\frac{\sum_{k'=0}^{(N_{FT}/2)-K_{low}} \left[\log_2 \left(\frac{f'(k')}{1000} \right) - ASC \right]^2 P'(k')}{\sum_{k'=0}^{(N_{FT}/2)-K_{low}} P'(k')}}, \tag{2.26}
$$

where the modified power spectrum coefficients $P'(k')$ and the corresponding frequencies $f'(k')$ are calculated in the same way as for the ASC descriptor (see Equations (2.23) and (2.24)).

The ASS gives indications about how the spectrum is distributed around its centroid. A low ASS value means that the spectrum may be concentrated around the centroid, whereas a high value reflects a distribution of power across a wider range of frequencies. It is designed to help differentiate *noise-like* and *tonal* sounds.

Figure 2.7 depicts the temporal series of ASS values. Except at the onsets of notes and for the noise-like end silence, the spread remains rather low (an ASS of 0.5 corresponding to a 500 Hz spread), as expected with a solo instrument excerpt.

2.5.4 Audio Spectrum Flatness

The audio spectrum flatness (ASF) reflects the flatness properties of the power spectrum. More precisely, for a given signal frame, it consists of a series of values, each one expressing the deviation of the signal's power spectrum from a flat shape inside a predefined frequency band. As such, it is a measure of how similar an audio signal is to white noise, or, vice versa, how correlated a signal is.

The first step of the ASF extraction is the calculation of the power spectrum of each signal frame as specified in Equation (2.4). In this case, the power coefficients $P(k)$ are obtained from non-overlapping frames (i.e. the *hopSize* parameter is set to L_w, the length of the analysis windows, which is recommended to be 30 ms in this case).

Within a [*loEdge, hiEdge*] range, the spectrum is then divided into 1/4-octave-spaced log-frequency bands. These parameters must be distinguished from the *loEdge* and *hiEdge* edges used in the definition of the ASE descriptor in Section 2.5.1. Here, the values of *loEdge* and *hiEdge* must be chosen so that the intervals separating them from 1 kHz are integer multipliers of a 1/4 octave. We thus have:

$$loEdge = 2^{\frac{1}{4}n} \times 1\,\text{kHz}$$

$$hiEdge = 2^{\frac{1}{4}B} \times loEdge,$$

(2.27)

where n and B are integer parameters with the following meanings:

- The value of n determines the lower band edge. The minimum value for *loEdge* is recommended to be 250 Hz (i.e. $n = -8$).
- B is the desired number of frequency bands. After *loEdge* has been set, the value of B determines the higher band edge. The value of *hiEdge* should not exceed a frequency limit beyond which no flatness features can be properly extracted. The most obvious limitation to *hiEdge* is the Nyquist frequency. Another limitation could be the bandwidth of the original signal. The choice of parameter B must be made accordingly within these limitations.

The resulting frequency bands are proportional to those used in the definition of the ASE, thus ensuring compatibility among the different basic spectral descriptors.

However, defining frequency bands with no overlap could make the calculation of ASF features too sensitive to slight variations in sampling frequency. Therefore, the nominal edge frequencies of Equation (2.27) are modified so that the B frequency bands slightly overlap each other. Each band is thus made 10% larger in the following manner:

$$loF_b = 0.95 \times loEdge \times 2^{\frac{1}{4}(b-1)}$$
$$hiF_b = 1.05 \times loEdge \times 2^{\frac{1}{4}b} \qquad (1 \le b \le B),$$

(2.28)

with loF_b and hiF_b being the lower and upper limits of band b. We denote as loK_b and hiK_b the corresponding bins in the power spectrum, obtained from Equation (2.6).

Furthermore, in order to reduce computational costs and to adjust the frequency resolution of the spectrum to the log-frequency bands, the MPEG-7 standard specifies a method for grouping the power spectrum coefficients $P(k)$ in bands above the edge frequency of 1 kHz. The grouping is defined as follows:

- For all bands between 1 kHz and 2 kHz (i.e. four bands if *hiEdge* is greater than 2 kHz), power spectrum coefficients $P(k)$ are grouped by pairs. Two successive coefficients $P(k)$ and $P(k+1)$ are replaced by a single average coefficient $[P(k) + P(k+1)]/2$.

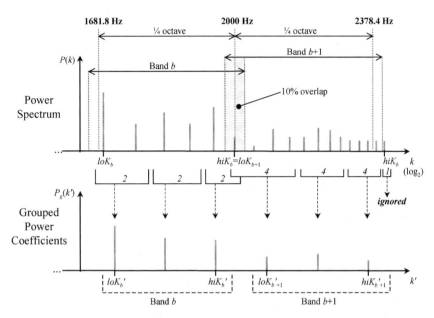

Figure 2.8 Power coefficient grouping within two consecutive bands around 2 kHz

- This grouping procedure is generalized to the following intervals of 1 octave as follows. Within all bands between 2^n kHz and 2^{n+1} kHz (where n is an integer and $n \geq 1$), each group of 2^{n+1} successive power coefficients is replaced by a single coefficient equal to their arithmetic mean. Figure 2.8 illustrates the coefficient grouping procedure within two consecutive bands b (between $f = 2^{3/4}$ kHz ≈ 1681.8 Hz and $f = 2$ kHz) and $b+1$ (between $f = 2$ kHz and $f = 2^{5/4}$ kHz ≈ 2378.4 Hz). As specified in Equation (2.28), these nominal edge frequencies are actually modified to introduce a 10% overlap represented on the schema.

- At the end of each band, the last group of coefficients may not contain the required number of values. If at least 50% of the required coefficients are available (i.e. 2^n coefficients for bands between 2^n kHz and 2^{n+1} kHz), the group is completed by using the appropriate number of coefficients at the beginning of the next band. Otherwise, no average coefficient is yielded; the power coefficients contained in the last group are simply ignored. In the example of Figure 2.8, the last group of band $b+1$ only contain one coefficient, which is ignored in the calculation of the three grouped power coefficients finally associated to $b+1$.

This grouping procedure results in a new set of power coefficients $P_g(k')$. We call loK'_b and hiK'_b the new band edge indexes of frequency bands b in the modified power spectrum (see Figure 2.8).

For each band b, a spectral flatness coefficient is then estimated as the ratio between the geometric mean and the arithmetic mean of the spectral power coefficients within this band:

$$ASF(b) = \frac{\sqrt[hiK'_b - loK'_b + 1]{\prod_{k'=loK'_b}^{hiK'_b} P_g(k')}}{\frac{1}{hiK'_b - loK'_b + 1} \sum_{k'=loK'_b}^{hiK'_b} P_g(k')} \qquad (1 \leq b \leq B). \qquad (2.29)$$

For all bands under the edge of 1 kHz, the power coefficients are averaged in the normal way. In that case, for each band b, we have $P_g(k') = P(k')$ between $k' = loK'_b = loK_b$ and $k' = hiK'_b = hiK_b$. For all bands above 1 kHz, for which a power coefficient grouping was required, only the reduced number of grouped coefficients is taken into account in the calculation of the geometric and arithmetic means.

A flat spectrum shape corresponds to a noise or an impulse signal. Hence, high ASF coefficients are expected to reflect noisiness. On the contrary, low values may indicate a harmonic structure of the spectrum. From a psycho-acoustical point of view, a large deviation from a flat shape (i.e. a low spectral flatness measure) generally characterizes the *tonal* sounds.

Figure 2.7 shows the temporal series of ASF vectors. Each ASF vector is extracted from 24 frequency bands within a 6-octave frequency interval, between $loEdge = 250\,\text{Hz}$ and $hiEdge = 16\,\text{kHz}$ (chosen to be smaller than the 22.05 kHz Nyquist frequency). A lighter shade indicates a higher spectral flatness value, meaning that the tonal component is less present in the corresponding bands.

The spectral flatness coefficients may be used as a feature vector for robust matching between pairs of audio signals. It is also possible to reduce the spectral flatness features to a single scalar by computing the mean value across the frequency band coefficients $ASF(b)$ for each frame. The resulting feature measures the overall flatness of a frame and can be used by an audio classifier (Burred and Lerch 2003, 2004).

2.6 BASIC SIGNAL PARAMETERS

The above-mentioned basic spectral LLDs give a smoothed representation of power spectra. They cannot reflect the detailed harmonic structure of periodic sounds because of a lack of frequency resolution. The following descriptors provide some complementary information, by describing the degree of harmonicity of audio signals.

2.6.1 Audio Harmonicity

The audio harmonicity (AH) descriptor provides two measures of the harmonic properties of a spectrum:

- the *harmonic ratio*: the ratio of harmonic power to total power.
- the *upper limit of harmonicity*: the frequency beyond which the spectrum cannot be considered harmonic.

They both rely on a standardized fundamental frequency estimation method, based on the local normalized autocorrelation function of the signal. This approach, widely used for local pitch estimation, is independent of the extraction of the audio fundamental frequency descriptor presented below.

2.6.1.1 Harmonic Ratio

The harmonic ratio (HR) is a measure of the proportion of harmonic components in the power spectrum. An HR coefficient is computed for each N_w sample frame of the original signal $s(n)$, with a hop of N_{hop} samples between successive frames. The extraction of an HR frame feature is standardized as follows.

For a given frame index l, the normalized autocorrelation function of the signal is first estimated as:

$$\Gamma_l(m) = \frac{\sum_{n=0}^{N_w-1} s_l(n)s_l(n-m)}{\sqrt{\sum_{n=0}^{N_w-1} s_l(n)^2 \sum_{n=0}^{N_w-1} s_l(n-m)^2}} \quad (1 \le m \le M; 0 \le l \le L-1), \quad (2.30)$$

where $s_l(n)$ is defined as $s(lN_{hop}+n)$, m is the lag index of the autocorrelation and L is the total number of frames in $s(n)$. In the definition of Equation (2.30), autocorrelation values are computed at lags ranging from $m = 1$ to $m = M$. The maximum lag M corresponds to the maximum fundamental period T_0 (or equivalently the minimum fundamental frequency) that can be estimated:

$$M = T_0^{max} F_s = \frac{F_s}{f_0^{min}}. \quad (2.31)$$

The default expected maximum period T_0^{max} is 40 ms, which corresponds to a minimum fundamental frequency of 25 Hz.

If the signal is purely periodic, the maximum values of $\Gamma_l(m)$ will be at lags m corresponding to multiples of T_0. At lags near $m = 0$ a high peak will appear, which will very likely reach values near to 1 for almost any type of audio signal, independently of its degree of periodicity. To obtain the HR, the autocorrelation is searched for the maximum, after having ignored the zero-lag peak:

$$HR = \max_{M_0 \leq m \leq M} \{\Gamma_l(m)\}, \qquad (2.32)$$

where M_0 denotes a lag immediately to the right of the zero-lag peak. One straightforward possibility is to define M_0 as the lag corresponding to the first zero crossing of the autocorrelation.

It should be noted that, in the MPEG-7 standard, the above equation is written as:

$$HR = \max_{l \leq m \leq N_{hop}} \{\Gamma_l(m)\}. \qquad (2.33)$$

It can be seen that, on the one side, the zero-lag peak is not ignored, which would result in HR values virtually always close to 1. On the other side, the rightmost limit corresponds only to a frame length, and not to the maximum lag M corresponding to the maximum fundamental period expected.

The lag that maximizes $\Gamma_l(m)$ corresponds to the estimated local fundamental period. The HR values will be close to 0 for white noise and to 1 for purely periodic signals.

Figure 2.9 gives the temporal series of HR values extracted from three different types of sounds: flute, laughter and noise. It is clear that the modified definition described in Equation (2.32) differentiates more clearly the three types of sounds.

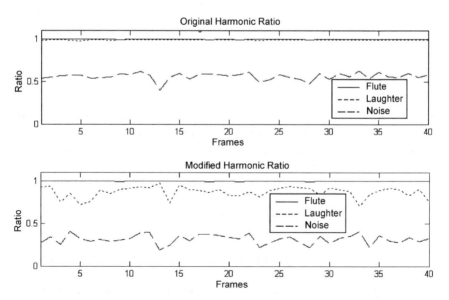

Figure 2.9 MPEG-7 HR extracted from three different types of sounds (44.1 kHz) with: top, the original HR of Equation (2.33); and bottom, the modified HR of Equation (2.32)

With both methods, flute has an HR uniformly equal to 1, as expected for a purely harmonic signal, whereas the lack of harmonicity of noise is better described with the modified HR, whose value stays below 0.5 across the whole audio segment. The results obtained with the laughter sound are also clearly different. With the original HR definition, laughter cannot be distinguished from music, whereas the modified HR definition clearly separates the two curves. This indicates, as expected, less harmonicity in laughter than in flute.

2.6.1.2 Upper Limit of Harmonicity

The upper limit of harmonicity (ULH) is an estimation of the frequency beyond which the spectrum no longer has any harmonic structure. It is based on the output/input power ratio of a time domain comb filter (Moorer, 1974) tuned to the fundamental period of the signal estimated in the previous section. The algorithm is performed as follows:

1. The comb-filtered signal is calculated as:

$$\tilde{s}_l(n) = s_l(n) - G_l s_l(n - \hat{m}) \quad (0 \leq n \leq N_w - 1), \quad (2.34)$$

where $\hat{m}$ is the lag maximizing the autocorrelation function $\Gamma_l(m)$ in Equation (2.32), which corresponds to the estimated fundamental period of frame l. The G_l factor is the optimal gain of the comb filter:

$$G_l = \frac{\sum_{j=0}^{N_w-1} s_l(j)s_l(j - \hat{m})}{\sum_{j=0}^{N_w-1} s_l(j - \hat{m})^2}. \quad (2.35)$$

2. The power spectra of the original and comb-filtered signals ($P'(k)$ and $P'_c(k)$, respectively) are computed for each frame l as described in Equation (2.23).
3. For each of the spectra $P'(k)$ and $P'_c(k)$, all the power samples falling beyond a given frequency bin k_{lim} are summed. The ratio of the two sums is then taken as follows:

$$R(k_{lim}) = \frac{\sum_{k=k_{lim}}^{(N_{FT}/2)-K_{low}} P'_c(k)}{\sum_{k=k_{lim}}^{(N_{FT}/2)-K_{low}} P'(k)}. \quad (2.36)$$

The maximum frequency bin of the spectra $k_{max} = N_{FT}/2 - K_{low}$ has been explained in Equation (2.23).
4. The ratios $R(k_{lim})$ are computed sequentially, decrementing k_{lim} from $k_{lim} = k_{max}$ down to the first frequency bin k_{ulh} for which $R(k_{lim})$ is smaller than a threshold of 0.5.

5. The corresponding frequency f_{ulh} is given by $f(k_{ulh} + K_{low})$ as defined in Equation (2.5), except if $k_{ulh} = 0$. In the later case, f_{ulh} is set to 31.25 Hz, conforming to the definition of the ASC in Equation (2.25).

6. Finally, a ULH feature is computed for each signal frame as:

$$ULH = \log_2\left(\frac{f_{ulh}}{1000}\right). \tag{2.37}$$

The conversion of the frequency limit f_{ulh} into an octave scale centred on 1 kHz makes the ULH coherent with the definitions of the ASC and ASS descriptors in Equations (2.25) and (2.26).

The two AH features HR and ULH are designed to provide a compact description of the harmonic properties of sounds. They can be used for distinguishing between *harmonic sounds* (i.e. sounds whose spectra have a harmonic structure, like musical sounds and voiced speech segments) and *non-harmonic sounds* (i.e. sounds with non-harmonic spectra, like noisy sounds and unvoiced speech segments).

2.6.2 Audio Fundamental Frequency

The audio fundamental frequency (AFF) descriptor provides estimations of the fundamental frequency f_0 in segments where the signal is assumed to be periodic. It is particularly useful to get an approximation of the pitch of any music or speech signals.

Numerous f_0 estimation algorithms are available in the literature. The standard does not specify any normative extraction method. In the following we provide an overview of several widely used pitch estimation techniques.

One of the most common approaches is the temporal autocorrelation (TA) method already described in the AH section, in Equations (2.30) and (2.32). However, even though the TA method produces exact pitch values in most cases, it may result in *doubled pitch errors* when the signal is highly periodic with short pitch periods. This means, that for a given true pitch period of T_0, the maximum value of TA may be reached at integer multiples of T_0, such as $2T_0$, $3T_0$, etc.

One way to avoid this is to use the spectral autocorrelation (SA) method, which is a transposition of the TA approach in the spectral domain. But in spite of its effectiveness in avoiding pitch doubling, the SA method may cause *pitch halving*, i.e. detect a pitch period which is an integer division of the actual T_0, such as $T_0/2$, $T_0/3$, etc.

To avoid these shortcomings, the spectro-temporal autocorrelation (STA) method (Cho *et al.*, 1998) was proposed. Combining the TA and SA approaches,

the STA pitch estimation is robust against gross pitch errors such as pitch doubling or halving. Given a pitch candidate τ, the STA is defined by:

$$\Gamma_{STA}(\tau) = \beta\Gamma_{TA}(\tau) + (1 - \beta).\Gamma_{SA}(\tau), \tag{2.38}$$

where Γ_{TA} and Γ_{SA} are the autocorrelation functions of the signal in the temporal
and spectral domains respectively, and β is a weighting factor between 0 and 1.
The fundamental period T_0 is then estimated as:

$$T_0 = \underset{\tau}{\mathrm{argmax}}[\Gamma_{STA}(\tau)], \tag{2.39}$$

and the local fundamental frequency is finally given by:

$$f_0 = \frac{1}{T_0}. \tag{2.40}$$

Although the estimation method is not normalized, the MPEG-7 standard requires
additional parameters to be provided that, along with the estimated value of f_0,
form the AFF descriptor. These parameters are:

- *loLimit*: the lower limit of the frequency range in which f_0 has been searched.
- *hiLimit*: the upper limit of the frequency range in which f_0 has been searched.
- A measure of confidence on the presence of periodicity in the analysed part
  of the signal, contained between 0 and 1. These measures are stored in the
  Weight field of a *SeriesOfScalar* (see Section 2.3.1) that stores a temporal
  series of AFF descriptors.

The confidence measure allows us to annotate different portions of a signal
according to their respective degree of periodicity. It ranges from 0, meaning
a non-periodic interval, to 1, reflecting a perfect periodicity. Although it is not
mentioned in the standard, the MPEG-7 HR descriptor (Section 2.6.1.1) could be
used as a confidence measure, since it fulfils these requirements. This measure
can be used by scaling or sound matching algorithms as a weight for handling
portions of a signal that are not clearly periodic.

Together with the AH features, the AFF provides some information on the
fine harmonic structure of a periodic sound. These features may complement a
log-frequency spectrum like the ASE descriptor (Section 2.5.1) whose frequency
resolution is too coarse to provide a detailed representation of the harmonic
peaks.

The AFF is mainly used as an estimate of the pitch of musical sounds and
voiced speech. The pitch curve of a speech signal reflects the voice intonation
and is an important prosodic feature.

Figure 2.10 depicts graphical representations of two basic signal LLDs
extracted from the same piece of music as in Figure 2.4. This musical solo
excerpt presents a clear harmonic structure with HR ≈ 1, except at the onsets of

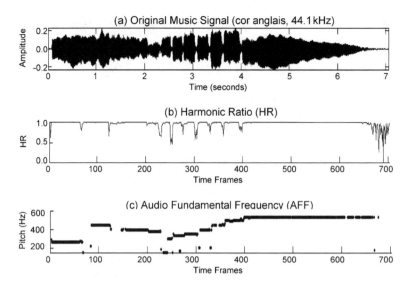

Figure 2.10   MPEG-7 basic signal parameters extracted from a music signal (cor anglais, 44.1 kHz)

notes and at the end of the audio segment which is terminated by a short silence. The interruptions and discontinuities of the AFF plot (the *pitch contour* of the audio segment) mostly correspond to the onsets of notes.

2.7 TIMBRAL DESCRIPTORS

The timbral descriptors aim at describing perceptual features of instrument sounds. *Timbre* refers to the features that allow one to distinguish two sounds that are equal in pitch, loudness and subjective duration. The underlying perceptual mechanisms are rather complex. They involve taking into account several perceptual dimensions at the same time in a possibly complex way. Timbre is thus a multi-dimensional feature that includes among others the spectral envelope, temporal envelope and variations of each of them. The MPEG-7 timbre description (Peeters *et al.*, 2000) relies on the experiments of (Krumhansl, 1989), (McAdams *et al.*, 1995) and (Lakatos, 2000). The seven timbral descriptors are of two types:

- The *temporal timbral* descriptors: log attack time (LAT) and temporal centroid (TC).
- The *spectral timbral* descriptors: harmonic spectral centroid (HSC), harmonic spectral deviation (HSD), harmonic spectral spread (HSS), harmonic spectral variation (HSV) and spectral centroid (SC).

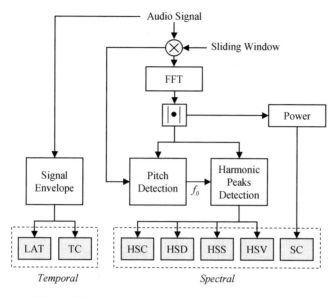

Figure 2.11 Extraction of the MPEG-7 timbral LLDs.

The calculation of each descriptor will be detailed in the following sections. The block diagram depicted in Figure 2.11 gives a first overview of the extraction of the temporal and spectral timbral descriptors.

It should be noted that these descriptors only make sense in the context of well-segmented sounds. They were originally designed to work with the high-level timbre description tools. However, their definition as MPEG-7 LLDs makes them available for other applications.

2.7.1 Temporal Timbral: Requirements

The temporal timbral descriptors are extracted from the signal envelope in the time domain. The signal envelope describes the energy change of the signal and is generally equivalent to the so-called ADSR (Attack, Decay, Sustain, Release) of a musical sound. Figure 2.12 gives a schematic representation of the envelope of a sound, showing its different phases and the corresponding time limits (expressed in the frame index domain).

The extraction of the signal envelope *Env* is not normative. A straightforward method is to compute frame by frame the RMS of the original signal $s(n)$:

$$Env(l) = \sqrt{\frac{1}{N_w} \sum_{n=0}^{N_w-1} s^2\left(lN_{hop} + n\right)} \quad (0 \leq l \leq L-1), \qquad (2.41)$$

where L is the total number of frames.

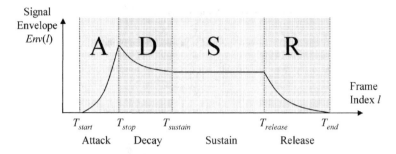

Figure 2.12   General shape of the ADSR envelope of a sound

The typical ADSR phases of a sound are:

- *Attack* is the length of time required for the sound to reach its initial maximum volume. It will be very short for a *percussive* sound.
- *Decay* is the time taken for the volume to reach a second volume level known as the sustain level.
- *Sustain* is the volume level at which the sound sustains after the decay phase. In most sounds is it lower than the attack volume, but it could be the same or even higher.
- *Release* is the time it takes the volume to reduce to zero.

A sound does not have to have all four phases. A woodblock, for example, only has an attack phase and a decay phase. An organ has an attack phase, a sustain phase and a release phase, but no decay phase.

2.7.2 Log Attack Time

The log attack time (LAT) is defined as the time it takes to reach the maximum amplitude of a signal from a minimum threshold time (McAdams, 1999). Its main motivation is the description of the onsets of single sound samples from different musical instruments.

In the MPEG-7 standard, LAT is defined as the logarithm (decimal base) of the duration from time T_{start} (see Figure 2.12) when the signal starts to time T_{stop} when it reaches its maximum value (for a percussive sound) or its sustained part (for a sustained sound, i.e. with no decay phase). It is defined as:

$$LAT = \log_{10}\left(T_{stop} - T_{start}\right). \tag{2.42}$$

Although the attack portion embodies a great deal of transitional information of the signal leading to a steady state, it is difficult to say where the attack portion ends and where the steady begins. The standard does not specify any

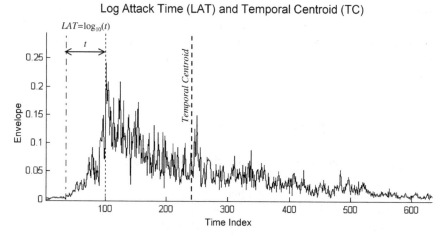

Figure 2.13   MPEG-7 LAT and TC extracted from the envelope of a dog bark sound (22.05 kHz)

method for precisely determining T_{start} and T_{stop}. A simple way of defining them could be:

- Estimate T_{start} as the time the signal envelope exceeds 2% of its maximal value.
- Estimate T_{stop} as the time the signal envelope reaches its maximal value.

The attack time feature has been used in wavetable music synthesis. The basic idea is to take an auditory snapshot of the signal – the attack and first few milliseconds of the state portion – and then loop the steady-state portion. Hence, this gives the listener the illusion that the whole signal is being played back, although only a fractional length of the signal has actually been used to render such an illusion. Today's popular music genres and electronic jazz music are very much dominated by this technology.

Figure 2.13 illustrates the extraction of LAT from a dog bark percussive sound.

2.7.3   Temporal Centroid

The TC is defined as the time average over the energy envelope of the signal. The resulting time-based centroid is:

$$TC = \frac{N_{hop}}{F_s} \frac{\sum_{l=0}^{L-1}(lEnv(l))}{\sum_{l=0}^{L-1}Env(l)}, \qquad (2.43)$$

where $Env(l)$ is the signal envelope defined in Equation (2.41). The multiplying factor N_{hop}/F_s is the frame sampling rate. This enables the conversion from the discrete frame index domain to the continuous time domain. The unit of the TC feature is the second. Figure 2.13 illustrates the extraction of the TC from a dog bark sound.

2.7.4 Spectral Timbral: Requirements

The spectral timbral features aim at describing the structure of harmonic spectra. Contrary to the previous spectral descriptors (the basic spectral descriptors of Section 2.5), they are extracted in a linear frequency space. They are designed to be computed using signal frames if instantaneous values are required, or larger analysis windows if global values are required. In the case of a frame-based analysis, the following parameters are recommended by the standard:

- Frame size: $L_w = 30$ ms.
- Hop size: $hopSize = 10$ ms.

If global spectral timbral features are extracted from large signal segments, the size of the analysis window should be a whole number of the local fundamental period. In that case, the recommended parameters are:

- Frame size: $L_w = 8$ fundamental periods.
- Hop size: $hopSize = 4$ fundamental periods.

In both cases, the recommended windowing function is the Hamming window.

The extraction of the spectral timbral descriptors requires the estimation of the fundamental frequency f_0 and the detection of the harmonic components of the signal. How these pre-required features should be extracted is again not part of the MPEG-7 standard. The following just provides some general definitions, along with indications of the classical estimation methods.

The schema of a pitch and harmonic peak detection algorithm is shown in Figure 2.14.

This detection algorithm consists of four main steps:

1. The first step is to extract by means of an FFT algorithm the spectrum $S(k)$ of the windowed signal defined in Equation (2.1). The amplitude spectrum $|S(k)|$ is then computed.
2. Estimation of the pitch frequency f_0 is then performed.
3. The third step consists of detecting the peaks in the spectrum.
4. Finally, each of the candidate peaks is analysed to determine if it is a harmonic peak or not.

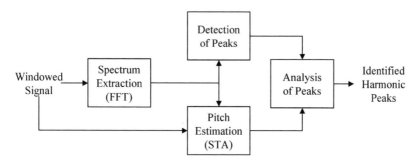

Figure 2.14 Block diagram of pitch and harmonic peak detection

As mentioned above, the estimation of the fundamental frequency f_0 can be performed, for instance, by searching the maximum of one of the two autocorrelation functions:

- The temporal autocorrelation function (TA method) defined in Equation (2.30).
- The spectro-temporal autocorrelation function (STA method) defined in Equation (2.38).

The estimated fundamental frequency is used for detecting the harmonic peaks in the spectrum. The harmonic peaks are located around the multiples of the fundamental frequency f_0:

$$f_h = hf_0 \quad (1 \leq h \leq N_H), \tag{2.44}$$

where N_H is the number of harmonic peaks. The frequency of the hth harmonic is just h times the fundamental frequency f_0, the first harmonic peak corresponding to f_0 itself ($f_1 = f_0$). Hence, the most straightforward method to estimate the harmonic peaks is simply to look for the maximum values of the amplitude spectrum around the multiples of f_0. This method is illustrated in Figure 2.15. The amplitude spectrum $|S(k)|$ of a signal whose pitch has been estimated at $f_0 = 300\,\text{Hz}$ is depicted in the $[0,1350\,\text{Hz}]$ range.

The harmonic peaks are searched within a narrow interval (grey bands in Figure 2.15) centred at every multiple of f_0. The FFT bin k_h corresponding to the hth harmonic peak is thus estimated as:

$$k_h = \underset{k \in [a_h, b_h]}{\text{argmax}} |S(k)|. \tag{2.45}$$

The search limits a_h and b_h are defined as:

$$a_h = floor\left[(h - nht)\frac{f_0}{\Delta F}\right]$$
$$b_h = ceil\left[(h + nht)\frac{f_0}{\Delta F}\right], \tag{2.46}$$

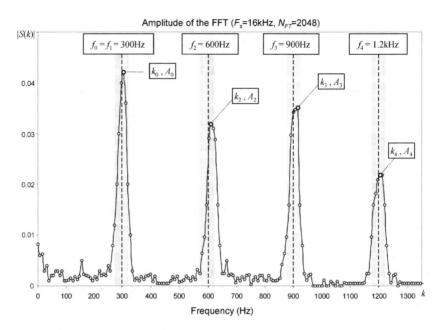

Figure 2.15 Localization of harmonic peaks in the amplitude spectrum

where $\Delta F = F_s/N_{FT}$ is the frequency interval between two FFT bins, and *nht* specifies the desired non-harmonicity tolerance ($nht = 0.15$ is recommended). The final set of detected harmonic peaks consists of the harmonic frequencies $f(k_h)$, estimated from k_h through Equation (2.5), and their corresponding amplitudes $A_h = |S(k_h)|$.

The detection of harmonic peaks is generally not that easy, due to the presence of many noisy components in the signal. This results in numerous local maxima in the spectrum. The above method is feasible when the signal has a clear harmonic structure, as in the example of Figure 2.15. Several other methods have been proposed to estimate the harmonic peaks in a more robust way (Park, 2000; Ealey *et al.*, 2001). As depicted in Figure 2.14, these methods consist of two steps: first the detection of spectral peaks, then the identification of the harmonic ones.

A first pass roughly locates possible peaks, where the roughness factor for searching peaks is controlled via a slope threshold: the difference between the magnitude of a peak candidate (a local maximum) and the magnitude of some neighbouring frequency bins must be greater than the threshold value. This threshold dictates the degree of "peakiness" that is allowed for a local maximum to be considered as a possible peak. Once every possible peak has been detected, the most prominent ones are selected. This time, the peaks are filtered by means of a second threshold, applied to the amplitude differences between neighbouring peak candidates.

After a final set of candidate peaks has been selected, the harmonic structure of the spectrum is examined. Based on the estimated pitch, a first pass looks for any broken harmonic sequence, analysing harmonic relationships among the currently selected peaks. In this pass, peaks that may have been deleted or missed in the initial peak detection and selection process are inserted. Finally, the first candidate peaks in the spectrum are used to estimate an "ideal" set of harmonics because lower harmonics are generally more salient and stable than the higher ones. The harmonic nature of each subsequent candidate peak is assessed by measuring its deviation from the ideal harmonic structure. The final set of harmonics is obtained by retaining those candidate peaks whose deviation measure is below a decision threshold.

The analysis of the harmonic structure of the spectrum is particularly useful for music and speech sounds. Pitched musical instruments display a high degree of harmonic spectral quality. Most tend to have quasi-integer harmonic relationships between spectral peaks and the fundamental frequency. In the voice, the spectral envelope displays mountain-like contours or valleys known as formants. The locations of the formants distinctively describe vowels. This is also evident in violins, but the number of valleys is greater and the formant locations change very little with time, unlike the voice, which varies substantially for each vowel.

2.7.5 Harmonic Spectral Centroid

The harmonic spectral centroid (HSC) is defined as the average, over the duration of the signal, of the amplitude-weighted mean (on a linear scale) of the harmonic peaks of the spectrum. The local expression $LHSC_l$ (i.e. for a given frame l) of the HSC is:

$$LHSC_l = \frac{\sum_{h=1}^{N_H} (f_{h,l} A_{h,l})}{\sum_{h=1}^{N_H} A_{h,l}}, \qquad (2.47)$$

where $f_{h,l}$ and $A_{h,l}$ are respectively the frequency and the amplitude of the hth harmonic peak estimated within the lth frame of the signal, and N_H is the number of harmonics that is taken into account.

The final HSC value is then obtained by averaging the local centroids over the total number of frames:

$$HSC = \frac{1}{L} \sum_{l=0}^{L-1} LHSC_l, \qquad (2.48)$$

where L is the number of frames in the sound segment. Similarly to the previous spectral centroid measure (the ASC defined in Section 2.5.2), the HSC provides a measure of the timbral sharpness of the signal.

Figure 2.16 gives graphical representations of the spectral timbral LLDs extracted from a piece of music (an oboe playing a single vibrato note, recorded at 44.1 kHz). Part (b) depicts the sequence of frame-level centroids $LHSC$ defined in Equation (2.47). The HSC is defined as the mean $LHSC$ across the entire audio segment.

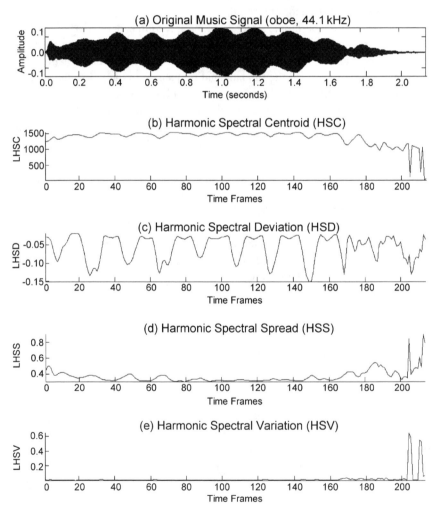

Figure 2.16 MPEG-7 spectral timbral descriptors extracted from a music signal (oboe, 44.1 kHz)

2.7.6 Harmonic Spectral Deviation

The harmonic spectral deviation (HSD) measures the deviation of the harmonic peaks from the envelopes of the local spectra. Within the lth frame of the signal, where N_H harmonic peaks have been detected, the spectral envelope $SE_{h,l}$ is coarsely estimated by interpolating adjacent harmonic peak amplitudes $A_{h,l}$ as follows:

$$SE_{h,l} = \begin{cases} 1/2(A_{h,l} + A_{h+1,l}) & \text{if } h = 1 \\ 1/3(A_{h-1,l} + A_{h,l} + A_{h+1,l}) & \text{if } 2 \leq h \leq N_H - 1. \\ 1/2(A_{h-1,l} + A_{h,l}) & \text{if } h = N_H \end{cases} \quad (2.49)$$

Then, a local deviation measure is computed for each frame:

$$LHSD_l = \frac{\sum\limits_{h=1}^{N_H} |\log_{10}(A_{h,l}) - \log_{10}(SE_{h,l})|}{\sum\limits_{h=1}^{N_H} \log_{10}(A_{h,l})}. \quad (2.50)$$

As before, the local measures are finally averaged over the total duration of the signal:

$$HSD = \frac{1}{L} \sum_{l=0}^{L-1} LHSD_l, \quad (2.51)$$

where L is the number of frames in the sound segment.

Figure 2.16 depicts the sequence of frame-level deviation values $LHSD$ defined in Equation (2.50). The HSD is defined as the mean $LHSD$ across the entire audio segment. This curve clearly reflects the spectral modulation within the vibrato note.

2.7.7 Harmonic Spectral Spread

The harmonic spectral spread (HSS) is a measure of the average spectrum spread in relation to the HSC. At the frame level, it is defined as the power-weighted RMS deviation from the local HSC $LHSC_l$ defined in Equation (2.47). The local spread value is normalized by $LHSC_l$ as:

$$LHSS_l = \frac{1}{LHSC_l} \sqrt{\frac{\sum\limits_{h=1}^{N_H} \left[(f_{h,l} - LHSC_l)^2 A_{h,l}^2\right]}{\sum\limits_{h=1}^{N_H} A_{h,l}^2}} \quad (2.52)$$

and then averaged over the signal frames:

$$HSS = \frac{1}{L} \sum_{l=0}^{L-1} LHSS_l, \tag{2.53}$$

where L is the number of frames in the sound segment.

Figure 2.16 depicts the sequence of frame-level spread values $LHSS$ defined in Equation (2.52). The HSS is defined as the mean $LHSS$ across the entire audio segment. The $LHSS$ curve reflects the vibrato modulation less obviously than the $LHSD$.

2.7.8 Harmonic Spectral Variation

The HSV (HSV) reflects the spectral variation between adjacent frames. At the frame level, it is defined as the complement to 1 of the normalized correlation between the amplitudes of harmonic peaks taken from two adjacent frames:

$$LHSV_l = 1 - \frac{\sum_{h=1}^{N_H} (A_{h,l-1} A_{h,l})}{\sqrt{\sum_{h=1}^{N_H} A_{h,l-1}^2} \sqrt{\sum_{h=1}^{N_H} A_{h,l}^2}}. \tag{2.54}$$

The local values are then averaged as before:

$$HSV = \frac{1}{L} \sum_{l=0}^{L-1} LHSV_l, \tag{2.55}$$

where L is the number of frames in the sound segment.

Figure 2.16 shows the sequence of frame-level spectral variation values $LHSV$ defined in Equation (2.54). The HSV is defined as the mean $LHSV$ across the entire audio segment. The local variation remains low across the audio segment (except at the end, where the signal is dominated by noise). This reflects the fact that the vibrato is a slowly varying modulation.

2.7.9 Spectral Centroid

The spectral centroid (SC) is not related to the harmonic structure of the signal. It gives the power-weighted average of the discrete frequencies of the estimated spectrum over the sound segment. For a given sound segment, it is defined as:

$$SC = \frac{\sum_{k=0}^{N_{FT}/2} f(k) P_s(k)}{\sum_{k=0}^{N_{FT}/2} P_s(k)}, \tag{2.56}$$

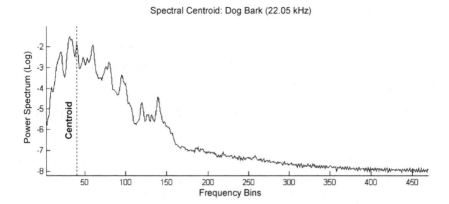

Figure 2.17   MPEG-7 SC extracted from the envelope of a dog bark sound

where P_s is the estimated power spectrum for the segment, $f(k)$ stands for the frequency of the kth bin and N_{FT} is the size of the DFT. One possibility to obtain P_s is to average the power spectra P_l for each of the frames (computed according to Equation (2.4)) across the sound segment.

This descriptor is very similar to the ASC defined in Equation (2.25), but is more specifically designed to be used in distinguishing musical instrument timbres. Like the two other spectral centroid definitions contained in the MPEG-7 standard (ASC in Section 2.5.2 and HSC in Section 2.7.5), it is highly correlated with the perceptual feature of the *sharpness* of a sound.

The spectral centroid (Beauchamp, 1982) is commonly associated with the measure of the *brightness* of a sound (Grey and Gordon, 1978). It has been found that increased loudness also increases the amount of high spectrum content of a signal thus making a sound brighter.

Figure 2.17 illustrates the extraction of the SC from the power spectrum of the dog bark sound of Figure 2.13.

2.8   SPECTRAL BASIS REPRESENTATIONS

The audio spectrum basis (ASB) and audio spectrum projection (ASP) descriptors were initially defined to be used in the MPEG-7 sound recognition high-level tool described in Chapter 3. The goal is the projection of an audio signal spectrum (high-dimensional representation) into a low-dimensional representation, allowing classification systems to be built in a more compact and efficient way. The extraction of ASB and ASP is based on normalized techniques which are part of the standard: the singular value decomposition (SVD) and the Independent Component Analysis (ICA). These descriptors will be presented in detail in Chapter 3.

2.9 SILENCE SEGMENT

The MPEG-7 *Silence* descriptor attaches the simple semantic label of *silence* to an audio segment, reflecting the fact that no significant sound is occurring in this segment. It contains the following attributes:

- *confidence*: this confidence measure (contained in the range $[0,1]$) reflects the degree of certainty that the detected silence segment indeed corresponds to a silence.
- *minDurationRef*: the *Silence* descriptor is associated with a *SilenceHeader* descriptor that encloses a *minDuration* attribute shared by other *Silence* descriptors. The value of *minDuration* is used to communicate a minimum temporal threshold determining whether a signal portion is identified as a silent segment. The *minDuration* element is usually applied uniformly to a complete segment decomposition as a parameter for the extraction algorithm. The *minDurationRef* attribute refers to the *minDuration* attribute of a *Silence-Header*.

The time information (start time and duration) of a silence segment is enclosed in the *AudioSegment* descriptor to which the *Silence* descriptor is attached.

The *Silence* Descriptor captures a basic semantic event occurring in audio material and can be used by an annotation tool; for example, when segmenting an audio stream into general sound classes, such as silence, speech, music, noise, etc. Once extracted it can help in the retrieval of audio events. It may also simply provide a hint not to process a segment. There exist many well-known silence detection algorithms (Jacobs *et al.*, 1999). The extraction of the MPEG-7 *Silence* Descriptor is non-normative and can be implemented in various ways.

2.10 BEYOND THE SCOPE OF MPEG-7

Many classical low-level features used for sound are not included in the foundation layer of MPEG-7 audio. In the following, we give a non-exhaustive list of the most frequently encountered ones in the audio classification literature. The last section focuses in more detail on the mel-frequency cepstrum coefficients.

2.10.1 Other Low-Level Descriptors

2.10.1.1 Zero Crossing Rate

The zero crossing rate (ZCR) is commonly used in characterizing audio signals. The ZCR is computed by counting the number of times that the audio waveform crosses the zero axis. This count is normalized by the length of the input signal $s(n)$ (Wang $et\ al.$, 2000):

$$ZCR = \frac{1}{2} \left(\sum_{n=1}^{N-1} |sign(s(n)) - sign(s(n-1))| \right) \frac{F_s}{N}, \qquad (2.57)$$

where N is the number of samples in $s(n)$, F_s is the sampling frequency and $sign(x)$ is defined as:

$$sign(x) = \begin{cases} 1 & \text{if } x > 0 \\ 0 & \text{if } x = 0 \\ -1 & \text{if } x < 0. \end{cases} \qquad (2.58)$$

Different definitions of zero crossing features have been used in audio signal classification, in particular for voiced/unvoiced speech, speech/music (Scheirer and Slaney, 1997) or music genre classification (Tzanetakis and Cook, 2002; Burred and Lerch 2004).

2.10.1.2 Spectral Rolloff Frequency

The spectral rolloff frequency can be defined as the frequency below which 85% of the accumulated magnitude of the spectrum is concentrated (Tzanetakis and Cook, 2002):

$$\sum_{k=0}^{K_{roll}} |S(k)| = 0.85 \sum_{k=0}^{N_{FT}/2} |S(k)|, \qquad (2.59)$$

where K_{roll} is the frequency bin corresponding to the estimated rolloff frequency. Other studies have used rolloff frequencies computed with other ratios, e.g. 92% in (Li $et\ al.$, 2001) or 95% in (Wang $et\ al.$, 2000).

The rolloff is a measure of spectral shape useful for distinguishing voiced from unvoiced speech.

2.10.1.3 Spectral Flux

The spectral flux (SF) is defined as the average variation of the signal amplitude spectrum between adjacent frames. It is computed as the averaged squared difference between two successive spectral distributions (Lu $et\ al.$, 2002):

$$SF = \frac{1}{LN_{FT}} \sum_{k=0}^{L-1} \sum_{k=0}^{N_{FT}-1} [\log (|S_1(k)| + \delta) - \log (|S_{l-1}(k)| + \delta)]^2, \qquad (2.60)$$

where $S_l(k)$ is the DFT of the lth frame, N_{FT} is the order of the DFT, L is the total number of frames in the signal and δ is a small parameter to avoid calculation overflow.

The SF is a measure of the amount of local spectral change. According to (Lu *et al.*, 2002), SF values of speech are higher than those of music. The SF feature has therefore been used for the separation of music from speech (Scheirer and Slaney, 1997; Burred and Lerch, 2004). In addition, environmental sounds generally present the highest SF values with important spectral change between consecutive frames.

2.10.1.4 Loudness

The loudness is a psycho-acoustical feature of audio sounds (Wold *et al.*, 1996; Allamanche *et al.*, 2001). It can be approximated by the signal's RMS level in decibels. It is generally calculated by taking a series of frames and computing the square root of the sum of the squares of the windowed sample values.

2.10.2 Mel-Frequency Cepstrum Coefficients

The mel-frequency cepstrum coefficients (MFCCs) can be used as an excellent feature vector for representing the human voice and musical signals (Logan, 2000). In particular, the MFCC parameterization of speech has proved to be beneficial for speech recognition (Davis and Mermelstein, 1980). As the MFCC representation is not part of the MPEG-7 standard, several works have made comparative studies using MFCC and MPEG-7-only LLDs in different kinds of audio segmentation and classification applications (Xiong *et al.*, 2003; Kim and Sikora, 2004).

Cepstral coefficient parameterization methods rely on the notion of *cepstrum* (Rabiner and Schafer, 1978). If we suppose that a signal $s(t)$ can be modelled as the convolution product of an excitation signal $e(t)$ and the impulse response of a filter $h(t) (s(t) = e(t)^* h(t))$, the cepstrum is a homomorphic transformation (Oppenheim *et al.*, 1968) that permits the separation of $e(t)$ and $h(t)$. The spectrum of $s(t)$ is obtained by taking the inverse Fourier transform (TF^{-1}) of the logarithm of the spectrum: that is, $TF^{-1} \circ \text{Log}|.| \circ TF(s(t))$.

The MFCCs are the most popular cepstrum-based audio features, even though there exist other types of cepstral coefficients (Angelini *et al.*, 1998), like the *linear prediction cepstrum coefficient* (LPCC), extracted from the linear prediction coefficient (LPC). MFCC is a perceptually motivated representation defined as the cepstrum of a windowed short-time signal. A non-linear *mel*-frequency scale is used, which approximates the behaviour of the auditory system.

The mel is a unit of pitch (i.e. the subjective impression of frequency). To convert a frequency f in hertz into its equivalent in mel, the following formula is used:

$$Pitch(\text{mel}) = 1127.0148 \log\left(1 + \frac{f(\text{Hz})}{700}\right). \tag{2.61}$$

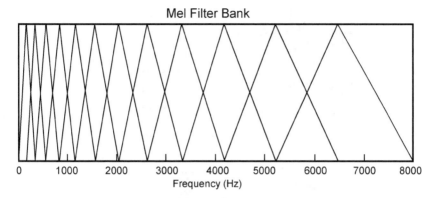

Figure 2.18 Mel-spaced filter bank

The *mel scale* is a scale of pitches judged by listeners to be equal in distance one from another. The reference point between this scale and normal frequency measurement is defined by equating a 1000 Hz tone, 40 dB above the listener's threshold, with a pitch of 1000 mels. Below about 500 Hz the mel and hertz scales coincide; above that, larger and larger intervals are judged by listeners to produce equal pitch increments.

The MFCCs are based on the extraction of the signal energy within critical frequency bands by means of a series of triangular filters whose centre frequencies are spaced according to the mel scale. Figure 2.18 gives the general shape of such a mel-spaced filter bank in the [0 Hz,8 kHz] frequency range. The non-linear mel scale accounts for the mechanisms of human frequency perception, which is more selective in the lower frequencies than in the higher ones.

The extraction of MFCC vectors is depicted in Figure 2.19.

The input signal $s(n)$ is first divided into overlapping frames of N_w samples. Typically, frame duration is between 20 and 40 ms, with a 50% overlap between adjacent frames. In order to minimize the signal discontinuities at the borders of each frame a windowing function is used, such as the Hanning function defined as:

$$w(n) = \frac{1}{2}\left\{1 - \cos\left[\frac{2\pi}{N_w}\left(n + \frac{1}{2}\right)\right]\right\} \quad (0 \leq n \leq N_w - 1). \tag{2.62}$$

An FFT is applied to each frame and the absolute value is taken to obtain the magnitude spectrum. The spectrum is then processed by a mel-filter bank such as the one depicted in Figure 2.18. The log-energy of the spectrum is measured within the pass-band of each filter, resulting in a reduced representation of the spectrum.

The cepstral coefficients are finally obtained through a Discrete Cosine Transform (DCT) of the reduced log-energy spectrum:

$$c_i = \sum_{j=1}^{N_f}\left\{\log(E_j)\cos\left[i\left(j - \frac{1}{2}\right)\frac{\pi}{N_f}\right]\right\} \quad (1 \leq i \leq N_c). \tag{2.63}$$

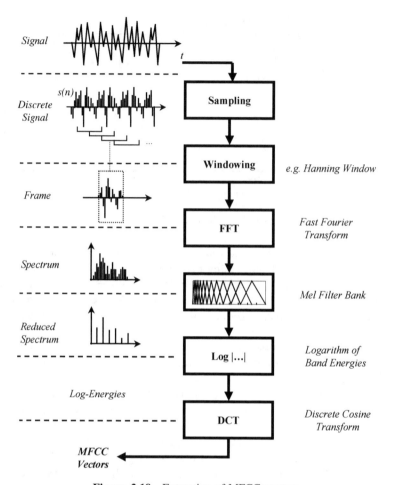

Figure 2.19 Extraction of MFCC vectors

where c_i is the ith-order MFCC, E_j is the spectral energy measured in the critical band of the jth mel filter and N_f is the total number of mel filters (typically $N_f = 24$). N_c is the number of cepstral coefficients c_i extracted from each frame (typically $N_c = 12$). The global log-energy measured on the whole frame spectrum – or, equivalently, the c_0 MFCC calculated according to the formula of Equation (2.63) with $i = 0$ – is generally added to the initial MFCC vector. The extraction of an MFCC vector from the reduced log-energy spectrum is depicted in Figure 2.20.

The estimation of the derivative and acceleration of the MFCC features are usually added to the initial vector in order to take into account the temporal changes in the spectra (which play an important role in human perception). One way to capture this information is to use *delta coefficients* that measure the change in coefficients over time. These additional coefficients result from

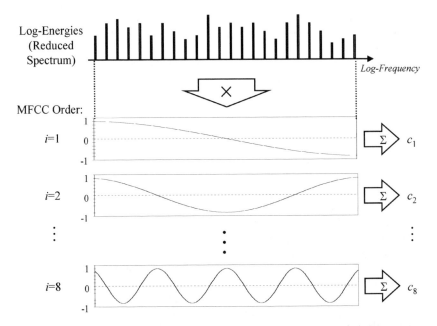

Figure 2.20 Extraction of an eighth-order MFCC vector from a reduced log-energy spectrum

a linear regression over a few adjacent frames. Typically, the two previous and the two following frames are used, for instance, as follows:

$$\Delta c_i(l) = -c_i(l-2) - \frac{1}{2}c_i(l-1) + \frac{1}{2}c_i(l+1) + c_i(l+2) \tag{2.64}$$

and:

$$\Delta\Delta c_i(l) = c_i(l-2) - \frac{1}{2}c_i(l-1) - c_i(l) - \frac{1}{2}c_i(l+1) + c_i(l+2), \tag{2.65}$$

where $c_i(l)$ is the ith-order MFCC extracted from the lth frame of the signal. The $\Delta c_i(l)$ and $\Delta\Delta c_i(l)$ coefficients are the estimates of the derivative and acceleration of coefficient c_i at frame instant l, respectively. Together with the cepstral coefficients $c_i(l)$, the Δ and $\Delta\Delta$ coefficients form the final MFCC vector extracted from frame l.

REFERENCES

Allamanche E., Herre J., Helmuth O., Fröba B., Kasten T. and Cremer M. (2001) "Content-based Identification of Audio Material Using MPEG-7 Low Level Description", *International Symposium Music Information Retrieval*, Bloomington, IN, USA, October.

Angelini B., Falavigna D., Omologo M. and De Mori R. (1998) "Basic Speech Sounds, their Analysis and Features", in *Spoken Dialogues with Computers*, pp. 69–121, Academic Press, London.

Beauchamp J. W. (1982) "Synthesis by Spectral Amplitude and 'Brightness' Matching Analyzed Musical Sounds", *Journal of Audio Engineering Society*, vol. 30, no. 6, pp. 396–406.

Burred J. J. and Lerch A. (2003) "A Hierarchical Approach to Automatic Musical Genre Classification", *6th International Conference on Digital Audio Effects (DAFX)*, London, UK, September.

Burred J. J. and Lerch A. (2004) "Hierarchical Automatic Audio Signal Classification", *Journal of the Audio Engineering Society*, vol. 52, no. 7/8, pp. 724–739.

Cho Y. D., Kim M. Y. and Kim S. R. (1998) "A Spectrally Mixed Excitation (SMX) Vocoder with Robust Parameter Determination", *ICASSP '98*, vol. 2, pp. 601–604, Seattle, WA , USA, May.

Davis S. B. and Mermelstein P. (1980) "Comparison of Parametric Representations for Monosyllabic Word Recognition in Continuously Spoken Sentences", *IEEE Transactions on Acoustics, Speech, and Signal Processing*, vol. 28, no. 4, pp. 357–365.

Ealey D., Kelleher H. and Pearce D. (2001) "Harmonic Tunnelling: Tracking Non-Stationary Noises during Speech", *Eurospeech 2001*, Aalborg, Denmark, September.

Gold B. and Morgan N. (1999) *Speech and Audio Signal Processing: Processing and Perception of Speech and Music*, John Wiley & Sons, Inc., New York.

Grey J. M. and Gordon J. W. (1978) "Perceptual Effects of Spectral Modifications on Musical Timbres", *Journal of Acoustical Society of America*, vol. 63, no. 5, pp. 1493–1500.

ISO/IEC (2001) *Information Technology - Multimedia Content Description Interface - Part 4: Audio*, FDIS 15938-4:2001(E), June.

Jacobs S., Eleftheriadis A. and Anastassiou D. (1999) "Silence Detection for Multimedia Communication Systems", *Multimedia Systems*, vol. 7, no. 2, pp. 157–164.

Kim H.-G. and Sikora T. (2004) "Comparison of MPEG-7 Audio Spectrum Projection Features and MFCC Applied to Speaker Recognition, Sound Classification and Audio Segmentation", *ICASSP'2004*, Montreal, Canada, May.

Krumhansl C. L. (1989) "Why is musical timbre so hard to understand?" in *Structure and perception of electroacoustic sound and music*, pp. 43–53, Elsevier, Amsterdam.

Lakatos S. (2000) "A Common Perceptual Space for Harmonic and Percussive Timbres", *Perception and Psychophysics*, vol. 62, no. 7, pp. 1426–1439.

Li D., Sethi I. K., Dimitrova N. and McGee T. (2001) "Classification of General Audio Data for Content-based Retrieval", *Pattern Recognition Letters, Special Issue on Image/Video Indexing and Retrieval*, vol. 22, no. 5.

Li S. Z. (2000) "Content-based Audio Classification and Retrieval using the Nearest Feature Line Method", *IEEE Transactions on Speech and Audio Processing*, vol. 8, no. 5, pp. 619–625.

Logan B. (2000) "Mel Frequency Cepstral Coefficients for Music Modeling", *International Symposium on Music Information Retrieval (ISMIR)*, Plymouth, MA, October.

Lu L., Zhang H.-J. and Jiang H. (2002) "Content Analysis for Audio Classification and Segmentation", *IEEE Transactions on Speech and Audio Processing*, vol. 10, no. 7, pp. 504–516.

Manjunath B. S., Salembier P. and Sikora T. (2002) *Introduction to MPEG-7*, John Wiley & Sons, Ltd, Chicherter.

McAdams S. (1999) "Perspectives on the Contribution of Timbre to Musical Structure", *Computer Music Journal*, vol. 23, no. 3, pp. 85–102.

McAdams S., Winsberg S., Donnadieu S., De Soete G. and Krimphoff J. (1995) "Perceptual Scaling of Synthesized Musical Timbres: Common Dimensions, Specificities, and Latent Subject Classes", *Psychological Research*, no. 58, pp. 177–192.

Moorer J. (1974) "The Optimum Comb Method of Pitch Period Analysis of Continuous Digitized Speech", *IEEE Transactions on Acoustics, Speech, and Signal Processing*, vol. 22, no. 5, pp. 330–338.

Oppenheim A. V., Schafer R. W. and Stockham T. G. (1968) "Nonlinear Filtering of Multiplied and Convolved Signals", *IEEE Proceedings*, vol. 56, no. 8, pp. 1264–1291.

Park T. H. (2000) "Salient Feature Extraction of Musical Instrument Signals", Thesis for the Degree of Master of Arts in Electro-Acoustic Music, Dartmouth College.

Peeters G., McAdams S. and Herrera P. (2000) "Instrument Sound Description in the Context of MPEG-7", *ICMC'2000 International Computer Music Conference*, Berlin, Germany, August.

Rabiner L. R. and Schafer R. W. (1978) *Digital Processing of Speech Signals*, Prentice Hall, Englewood Cliffs, NJ.

Scheirer E. and Slaney M. (1997) "Construction and Evaluation of a Robust Multifeature Speech/Music Discriminator", *ICASSP '97*, vol. 2, pp. 1331–1334, Munich, Germany, April.

Tzanetakis G. and Cook P. (2002) "Musical Genre Classification of Audio Signals", *IEEE Transactions on Speech and Audio Processing*, vol. 10, no. 5, pp. 293–302.

Wang Y., Liu Z. and Huang J.-C. (2000) "Multimedia Content Analysis Using Both Audio and Visual Cues", *IEEE Signal Processing Magazine*, vol. 17, no. 6, pp. 12–36.

Wold E., Blum T., Keslar D. and Wheaton J. (1996) "Content-Based Classification, Search, and Retrieval of Audio", *IEEE MultiMedia*, vol. 3, no. 3, pp. 27–36.

Xiong Z., Radhakrishnan R., Divakaran A. and Huang T. S. (2003) "Comparing MFCC and MPEG-7 Audio Features for Feature Extraction, Maximum Likelihood HMM and Entropic Prior HMM for Sports Audio Classification", *IEEE International Conference on Acoustics, Speech and Signal Processing (ICASSP'03)*, vol. 5, pp. 628–631, Hong Kong, April.

3

Sound Classification and Similarity

3.1 INTRODUCTION

Many audio analysis tasks become possible based on sound similarity and sound classification approaches. These include:

- the segmentation of audio tracks into basic elements, such as speech, music, sound or silence segments;
- the segmentation of speech tracks into segments with speakers of different gender, age or identity;
- the identification of speakers and sound events (such as specific persons, explosions, applause, or other important events);
- the classification of music into genres (such as rock, pop, classic, etc.);
- the classification of musical instruments into classes.

Once the various segments and/or events are identified, they can be used to index audio tracks. This provides powerful means for understanding semantics in audiovisual media and for building powerful search engines that query based on semantic entities.

Spectral features of sounds (i.e. the ASE feature described in Section 2.5.1) are excellent for describing sound content. The specific spectral feature of a sound – and more importantly the specific time variation of the feature – can be seen as a fingerprint. This fingerprint allows us to distinguish one sound from another.

Using a suitable measure it is possible to calculate the level of *sound similarity*. One application might be to feed the sound fingerprint of a specific violin instrument into a sound similarity system. The response of the system is a list with the most similar violins fingerprinted in the database, ranked according to

MPEG-7 Audio and Beyond: Audio Content Indexing and Retrieval   H.-G. Kim, N. Moreau and T. Sikora
© 2005 John Wiley & Sons, Ltd

the level of similarity. We may be able to understand whether the example violin is of rather good or bad quality.

The purpose of *sound classification* on the other hand is to understand whether a particular sound belongs to a certain class. This is a recognition problem, similar to voice, speaker or speech recognition. In our example above this may translate to the question whether the sound example belongs to a violin, a trumpet, a horn, etc.

Many classification systems can be partitioned into components such as the ones shown in Figure 3.1.

In this figure:

1. A segmentation stage isolates relevant sound segments from the background (i.e. the example violin sound from background noise or other sounds).
2. A feature extraction stage extracts properties of the sound that are useful for classification (the feature vector, fingerprint). For both the sound similarity and sound classification tasks, it is vital that the feature vectors used are rich enough to describe the content of the sound sufficiently. The MPEG-7 standard sound classification tool relies on the audio spectrum projection (ASP) feature vector for this purpose. Another well-established feature vector is based on MFCC.

   It is important that the feature vector is of a manageable size. In practice it is often necessary to reduce the size of the feature vector. A dimension reduction stage maps the feature vector onto another feature vector of lower dimension. MPEG-7 employs singular value decomposition (SVD) or independent component analysis (ICA) for this purpose. Other well-established techniques include principal component analysis (PCA) and the discrete cosine transform (DCT).
3. A classifier uses the reduced dimension feature vector to assign the sound to a category. The sound classifiers are often based on statistical models. Examples of such classifiers include Gaussian mixture models (GMMs), hidden Markov models (HMMs), neural networks (NNs) and support vector machines (SVMs).

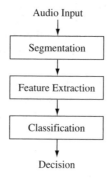

Figure 3.1 General sound classification system

The figure implies that the classification problem can be seen as a batch process employing various stages independently. In practice many systems employ feedback from and to various stages of the process; for instance, when segmenting speech parts in an audio track it is often useful to perform classification at the same time.

The choice of the feature vector and the choice of the classifier are critical in the design of sound classification systems. Often prior knowledge plays a major role when selecting such features. It is worth mentioning that in practice many of the feature vectors described in Chapter 2 may be combined to arrive at a "large" compound feature vector for similarity measure or classification.

It is usually necessary to train the classifier based on sound data. The data collection can amount to a surprisingly large part of the costs and time when developing a sound classification system. The process of using a collection of sound data to determine the classifier is referred to as training the classifiers and choosing the model.

The purpose of this chapter is to provide an overview of the diverse field of sound classification and sound similarity. Feature dimensionality reduction and training of the classifier model are discussed in Section 3.2. Section 3.3 introduces various classifiers and their properties. In Section 3.4 we use the MPEG-7 standard as a starting point to explain the practical implementation of sound classification systems. The performance of the MPEG-7 system is then compared with the well-established MFCC feature extraction method. Section 3.5 introduces the MPEG-7 system for indexing and similarity retrieval and Section 3.6 provides simulation results of various systems for sound classification.

3.2 DIMENSIONALITY REDUCTION

Removal of the statistical dependencies of observations is used in practice to reduce the size of feature vectors while retaining as much important perceptual information as possible. We may choose one of the following methods: singular value decomposition (SVD) (Golub and Van Loan, 1993), principal component analysis (PCA) (Jollife, 1986), independent component analysis (ICA) (Hyvärinen *et al.*, 2001) or non-negative matrix factorization (NMF) (Lee and Seung, 1999, 2001).

3.2.1 Singular Value Decomposition (SVD)

Let X be the feature matrix, in the form of an $L \times F$ time–frequency matrix. In this example, the vertical dimension represents time (i.e. each row corresponds to a time frame index $l(1 \leq l \leq L)$) and the horizontal dimension represents the spectral coefficients (i.e. each column corresponds to a logarithmic frequency range index $f(1 \leq f \leq F)$).

SVD is performed on the feature matrix of all the audio frames from all training examples in the following way:

$$X = UDV^T, \tag{3.1}$$

where X is factored into the matrix product of three matrices: the $L \times L$ row basis U matrix, the $L \times F$ diagonal singular value matrix D and the $F \times F$ transposed column basis functions V.

In order to perform dimensionality reduction, the size of the matrix V is reduced by discarding $F - E$ of the columns of V. The resulting matrix V_E has the dimensions $F \times E$. To calculate the proportion of information retained for E basis functions we use the singular values contained in matrix D:

$$I(E) = \sum_{i=1}^{E} D(i, i) \Big/ \sum_{j=1}^{F} D(j, j), \tag{3.2}$$

where $I(E)$ is the proportion of information retained for E basis functions and F is the total number of basis functions, which is also equal to the number of spectral bins.

The SVD transformation produces decorrelated, dimension-reduced bases for the data, and the right singular basis functions are cropped to yield fewer basis functions.

3.2.2 Principal Component Analysis (PCA)

The purpose of PCA is to derive a relatively small number of decorrelated linear combinations of a set of random zero-mean variables, while retaining as much of the information from the original variables as possible. PCA decorrelates the second-order moments corresponding to low-frequency properties and extracts orthogonal principal components of variations. By projecting onto these highly varying subspaces, the relevant statistics can be approximated by a smaller dimension system.

Before applying a PCA algorithm on matrix X, centring is performed. First, the columns are centred by subtracting the mean value from each one:

$$\hat{X}(f, l) = X(f, l) - \mu_f \tag{3.3}$$

$$\mu_f = \frac{1}{L} \sum_{l=1}^{L} X(f, l), \tag{3.4}$$

where μ_f is the mean of the column f. Next, the rows are standardized by removing any DC offset and normalizing the variance:

$$\mu_l = \frac{1}{F} \sum_{f=1}^{F} \hat{X}(f, l) \tag{3.5}$$

$$\chi_l = \sum_{f=1}^{F} \hat{X}^2(f, l) \tag{3.6}$$

$$\Gamma_l = \sqrt{(\chi_l - F\mu_l^2)/(F - 1)} \tag{3.7}$$

$$\hat{X}(f, l) = \frac{\hat{X}(f, l) - \mu_l}{\Gamma_l}, \tag{3.8}$$

where μ_l and Γ_l are respectively the mean and standard deviation of row l, and χ_l is the energy of the $\hat{X}(f, l)$.

Using PCA, the columns are linearly transformed to remove any linear correlations between the dimensions. PCA can be performed via eigenvalue decomposition of the covariance matrix:

$$C = VDV^T = E\left\{\hat{X}\hat{X}^T\right\} \tag{3.9}$$

$$C_P = D^{-1/2}V^T, \tag{3.10}$$

where V is the matrix of orthogonal eigenvectors and D is a diagonal matrix with the corresponding eigenvalues. In order to perform dimension reduction, we reduce the size of the matrix C_P by throwing away $F - E$ of the columns of C_P corresponding to the smallest eigenvalues of D. The resulting matrix C_E has the dimensions $F \times E$.

3.2.3 Independent Component Analysis (ICA)

ICA defines a generative model for the observed multivariate data, which is typically estimated based on a large set of training data. In the model, the data variables are assumed to be linear mixtures of some unknown latent variables, and the mixing system is also unknown. The latent variables are assumed to be non-Gaussian and mutually independent. They are called the independent components of the observed data. These independent components, also called sources or factors, can be found by ICA.

ICA is a statistical method which not only decorrelates the second-order statistics but also reduces higher-order statistical dependencies. Thus, ICA produces mutually uncorrelated bases.

The independent components of matrix X can be thought of as a collection of statistically independent bases for the rows (or columns) of X. The $L \times F$ matrix X is decomposed as:

$$X = WS + N, \tag{3.11}$$

where S is the $P \times F$ source signal matrix, W is the $L \times P$ mixing matrix (also called the matrix of spectral basis functions) and N is the $L \times F$ matrix of noise signals. Here, P is the number of independent sources. The above decomposition can be performed for any number of independent components and the sizes of W and S vary accordingly.

To find a statistically independent basis using the basis functions, the well-known ICA algorithms, such as INFOMAX, JADE or FastICA, can be used. From several ICA algorithms we use a combination of PCA and the FastICA algorithm (Hyvärinen, 1999) in the following to perform the decomposition.

After extracting the reduced PCA basis C_E, a further step consisting of basis rotation in the direction of maximal statistical independence is needed for applications that require maximum independence of features. This whitening, which is closely related to PCA, is done by multiplying the $F \times E$ transformation matrix C_E by the normalized $L \times F$ feature matrix $\hat{X}$:

$$\check{X} = \hat{X} C_E. \tag{3.12}$$

The input $\check{X}$ is then fed to the FastICA algorithm, which maximizes the information in the following six steps:

Step 1. Initialize spectrum basis W_i to small random values, where i is the number of independent components.

Step 2. Apply Newton's method:

$$W_i = E\left\{ \check{X} g\left(W_i^T \check{X} \right) \right\} - E\left\{ g'\left(W_i^T \check{X} \right) \right\} W_i, \tag{3.13}$$

where g is the derivative of the non-quadratic function.

Step 3. Normalize the spectrum basis approximation W_i as:

$$W_i = \frac{W_i}{\| W_i \|}. \tag{3.14}$$

Step 4. Decorrelate using the Gram–Schmidt orthogonalization:

$$W_i = W_i - \sum_{j=1}^{i-1} W_i^T W_j W_j. \tag{3.15}$$

After every iteration step, subtract from W_i the projections $W_i^T W_j W_j$, $j = 1, \ldots, i$, of the previously estimated i vectors.

Step 5. Renormalize the spectrum basis approximation as:

$$W_i = \frac{W_i}{\|W_i\|}. \tag{3.16}$$

Step 6. If not converged, go back to step 2.

The purpose of the Gram–Schmidt decorrelation/orthogonalization performed in the algorithm is to avoid finding the same component more than once. When the tolerance becomes close to zero, Newton's method will usually keep converging towards the optimum. By turning off the decorrelation when almost converged, the orthogonality constraint is loosened. Steps 1–6 are executed until convergence. Then the iteration performing only the Newton step and normalization is carried out until convergence $W_i W_i^T = 1$. With this modification the true maximum is found.

3.2.4 Non-Negative Factorization (NMF)

NMF has been recently proposed as a new method for dimensionality reduction. NMF is a subspace method which finds a linear data representation with the non-negativity constraint instead of the orthogonality.

PCA and ICA are holistic representations because basis vectors are allowed to be combined with either positive or negative coefficients. Due to the holistic nature of the method, the resulting components are global interpretations, and thus PCA and ICA are unable to extract basis components manifesting localized features. The projection coefficients for the linear combinations in the above methods can be either positive or negative, and such linear combinations generally involve complex cancellations between positive and negative numbers. Therefore, these representations lack the intuitive meaning of adding parts to form a whole. NMF imposes the non-negativity constraints in the learning basis. For this reasons, NMF is considered as a procedure for learning a parts-based representation. NMF preserves much of the structure of the original data and guarantees that both basis and weights are non-negative. It is conceptually simpler than PCA or ICA, but not necessarily more computationally efficient. Within this context, it was first applied for generating parts-based representations from still images and later was evaluated in audio analysis tasks, such as general sound classification (Cho *et al.*, 2003) and polyphonic music transcription (Smaragdis and Brown, 2003).

Given a non-negative $L \times F$ matrix X, NMF consists of finding the non-negative $L \times P$ matrix G and the $P \times F$ matrix H such that:

$$|X| = GH, \tag{3.17}$$

where the columns of H are the basis signals, matrix G is the mixing matrix, and P ($P < L$ and $P < F$) is the number of non-negative components.

Several algorithms have been proposed to perform NMF. Here, the multiplicative divergence update rules are described. The divergence of two matrixes A and B is defined as:

$$D(A \parallel B) = \sum_{ij} \left(A_{ij} \log \frac{A_{ij}}{B_{ij}} - A_{ij} + B_{ij} \right). \tag{3.18}$$

The algorithm iterates the update of the factor matrices in such a way that the divergence $D(|X| \parallel GH)$ is minimized. Such a factorization can be found using the update rules:

$$G_{ia} \leftarrow G_{ia} \frac{\sum_{\mu} H_{a\mu} X_{i\mu} / (GH)_{i\mu}}{\sum_{\nu} H_{a\nu}} \tag{3.19}$$

$$H_{a\mu} \leftarrow H_{a\mu} \frac{\sum_{i} G_{ia} X_{i\mu} / (GH)_{i\mu}}{\sum_{k} G_{ka}} \tag{3.20}$$

More details about the algorithm can be found in (Cho *et al.*, 2003).

In our case, X is the $L \times F$ feature matrix, and thus factorization yields the matrices G_E and H_E of size $L \times E$ and $E \times F$, respectively, where E is the desired dimension-reduced bases.

3.3 CLASSIFICATION METHODS

Once feature vectors are generated from audio clips, and if required reduced in dimension, these are fed into classifiers.

The MPEG-7 audio LLDs and some other non-MPEG-7 low-level audio features are described in Chapter 2. They are defined in the temporal and/or the spectral domain. The model-based classifiers that have been most often used for audio classification include Gaussian mixture model (GMM) (Reynolds, 1995) classifiers, neural network (NN) (Haykins, 1998) classifiers, hidden Markov model (HMM) (Rabiner and Jung, 1993) classifiers, and support vector machines (SVMs) (Cortes and Vaprik, 1995). The basic concepts of these model-based classifiers are introduced in this section.

3.3.1 Gaussian Mixture Model (GMM)

GMMs have been widely used in the field of speech processing, mostly for speech recognition, speaker identification and voice conversion. Their capability to model arbitrary probability densities and to represent general spectral features motivates their use. The GMM approach assumes that the density of an observed process can be modelled as a weighted sum of component densities given by:

$$p(x|\lambda) = \sum_{m=1}^{M} c_m b_m(x),$$ (3.21)

where x is a d-dimensional random vector, M is a number of mixture components, and $b_m(x)$ is a Gaussian density, parameterized by a mean vector μ_m and the covariance matrix Σ_m:

$$b_m(x) = \frac{1}{(2\pi)^{d/2}|\Sigma_m|^{1/2}} \exp\left\{-\frac{1}{2}\left[(x - \mu_m)^T \Sigma_m^{-1}(x - \mu_m)\right]\right\}$$ (3.22)

The parameters of the sound model are denoted as $\lambda = \{c_m, \mu_m, \Sigma_m\}$, $m = 1, \ldots, M$.

A useful algorithm for estimating the parameters of a GMM that maximize the likelihood of a set of n data vectors is the expectation maximization algorithm. This algorithm works by iteratively updating the parameters according (in the case of diagonal covariance matrices) to the following equations:

$$\mu_m^{new} = \frac{\sum_{i=1}^{n} p(m|x_i, \lambda) x_i}{\sum_{i=1}^{n} p(m|x_i, \lambda)}$$ (3.23)

$$\Sigma_m^{new} = \frac{\sum_{i=1}^{n} p(m|x_i, \lambda)(x_i - \mu_m)^T (x_i - \mu_m)}{\sum_{i=1}^{n} p(m|x_i, \lambda)}$$ (3.24)

$$c_m^{new} = \frac{1}{n} \sum_{i=1}^{n} p(m|x_i, \lambda)$$ (3.25)

where the value $p(m|x_i, \lambda)$ can be computed as:

$$p(m|x_i, \lambda) = \frac{c_m b_m(x_i)}{\sum_{j=1}^{M} c_j g_j(x_i)}$$ (3.26)

For a group of K sounds represented by GMMs $\lambda_1, \lambda_2, \ldots, \lambda_K$, the objective of recognition (classification) is to find the model which has the maximum a posteriori probability for a given L observation sequence $X = x_1, x_2, \ldots, x_L$:

$$\hat{K} = \underset{1 \leq k \leq K}{\arg\max} P_r(\lambda_k|X) = \underset{1 \leq k \leq K}{\arg\max} \frac{p(X|\lambda_k)P_r(\lambda_k)}{p(X)},$$ (3.27)

where $p(X)$ is the same for all sound models, and assuming that the $P_r(\lambda_k)$ are equal for each sound, the classification rule simplifies to:

$$\hat{K} = \operatorname*{argmax}_{1 \leq k \leq K} p(X|\lambda_k). \tag{3.28}$$

Using logarithms and the independence between observations, the sound recognition system computes:

$$\hat{K} = \operatorname*{argmax}_{1 \leq k \leq K} \sum_{l=1}^{L} \log p(x_l|\lambda_k). \tag{3.29}$$

GMMs have the following advantages and disadvantages.

Advantages
- GMMs are computationally inexpensive. They are based on a well-understood statistical model. I.e for text-independent speech recognition tasks they are insensitive to the temporal aspects of the speaker (modelling only the underlying distribution of acoustic observations from a speaker).

Disadvantages
- Higher-level information about the sound conveyed in the temporal audio signal is not used. The modelling and exploitation of such higher-level information may benefit speech recognition in the future. To date, large vocabulary or phoneme recognizers only compute likelihood values, without explicit use of any higher-level information such as speaker-dependent word usage or speaking style.

3.3.2 Hidden Markov Model (HMM)

An HMM is a statistical method, widely used in the pattern classification field. Very successful applications based on HMM include speech recognition, speaker verification and handwriting recognition. HMMs are used to model processes with time varying characteristics. After the models are trained it is useful to analyse and study the models more closely.

An HMM can be described as:

- A set of N_S states $\{S_i\}$.
- A set of state transition probabilities $\{a_{ij}\}$, where a_{ij} is the probability of transition from state S_i to sate S_j.
- A set of d-dimensional probability density functions $\{b_j(x)\}$, where b_j is the density function of state S_j.
- A set of initial state probabilities $\{\pi_i\}$, where π_i is the probability that S_i is the initial state.

The system starts at time 0 in a state S_i with a probability π_i. When in a state S_i at time l the system moves at time $l+1$ to state S_j with a probability a_{ij} and so on, generating a sequence of L observation vectors x_l. An HMM is completely specified by the three sets $\{a_{ij}\}$, $\{b_j\}$ and $\{\pi_i\}$. Continuous HMMs generally set $b_j(x)$ to a multivariate Gaussian distribution with mean μ_j and covariance matrix $\sum_j$, giving $b_j = \{\mu_j, \sum_j\}$ for each state.

Two useful algorithms for HMMs are the Baum–Welch and the Viterbi algorithms. The Baum–Welch algorithm finds the parameters $\theta = \left[\{a_{ij}\}, \{b_j\}, \{\pi_i\}\right]$ of an HMM that maximize the likelihood of a sequence of observation vectors. The Viterbi algorithm finds the most likely sequence of states given the model and the observations.

HMMs have the following advantages and disadvantages.

Advantages
- Rich mathematical framework: HMMs are based on a flexible statistical theory.
- Efficient learning and decoding algorithms: these algorithms handle sequences of observations probabilistically and do not require explicit hand segmentation of the basic sound units. They can be implemented very efficiently even for large systems.
- Easy integration of multiple knowledge sources: different levels of constraints can be incorporated within the HMM framework as long as these are expressed in terms of the same statistical formalism.
- Effective sound similarity capabilities: the state path generated by the selected model is used to compute a sound model state histogram. Distances are calculated between the query histogram and a pre-computed database of histograms using the sum of square errors distance metrics. These distances are used to sort the results in ascending order thereby yielding the best matches for the given audio query.

Disadvantages
- Poor discrimination: estimation of the parameters of HMMs is based on likelihood maximization. This means that only correct models receive training information; incorrect models do not get any feedback.
- First-order Markov assumption: current observations and state transitions are dependent only on the previous state. All other history is neglected.
- Independence assumptions: consecutive feature vectors are assumed to be statistically independent.
- Distributional assumptions required: for example, modelling acoustic observations by a mixture of Gaussians with diagonal covariance matrices requires uncorrelated feature coefficients.
- Assumption of exponential state duration distributions: this assumption is an integral part of first-order HMMs. It can only be circumvented by applying explicit state duration modelling; that is, imposing external duration distributions such as a gamma distribution.

3.3.3 Neural Network (NN)

An NN classifier is an artificial intelligence network with parallel processing units working together. NNs are well suited to discriminative objective functions (e.g. mean squared error). The probabilities are optimized to maximize discrimination between sound classes, rather than to match most closely the distributions within each class. It can be argued that such a training is conservative of parameters, since the parameters of the estimate are trained to split the space between classes, rather than to represent the volumes that compose the division of space constituting each class. For these reasons, NNs have been studied for many years in the hope of achieving human-like performance in the fields of speech and image recognition.

Various NNs, such as Kohonen self-organizing maps (SOMs), the multi-layer perceptron (MLP), time-delay neural network (TDNN) and hidden control neural network (HCNN), have been used for speech recognition. Among these, MLPs are the most common NN architecture used for speech recognition and sound classification.

Typically, MLPs are feedforward nets with an input layer (consisting of the input variables), zero or more hidden (intermediate) layers and an output layer, as shown in Figure 3.2.

The number of neurons in the output layer is determined by the number of audio classes to classify. Each layer computes a set of linear discriminant functions (via a weight matrix) followed by a non-linear function, which is often a sigmoid function:

$$sig(x) = \frac{1}{1 + \exp(-x)}, \tag{3.30}$$

where x is the input vector.

This non-linear function performs a different role for the hidden and the output units. For the hidden units, it serves to generate high-order moments of the input; this can be done effectively by many non-linear functions, not just by sigmoids.

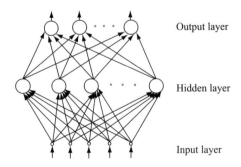

Figure 3.2   MLP architecture

The activation function of the neurons in the hidden layer is selected to be a hyperbolic tangent function. There is no activation function in the output layer. MLPs with enough hidden units can provide arbitrary mappings between input and output. MLP parameters (the elements of the weight matrices) are trained to associate a desired output vector with an input vector. This is achieved via the error back propagation (EBP) algorithm, which uses an iterative gradient algorithm designed to minimize the mean square error between the actual output of a multi-layer feedforward perceptron and the desired output. It requires continuous differentiable non-linearities. Although the standard back propagation (BP) algorithm is a common learning algorithm for MLP networks, it converges slowly and typically into local minima. Some fast learning algorithms have been proposed in the past to train feedforward NNs, such as the conjugate gradient algorithm, the quasi-Newton algorithm or the Levenberg–Marquadt algorithm. The last is usually more efficient than the conjugate gradient or quasi-Newton algorithms.

NNs have the following advantages and drawbacks.

Advantages
- Few parameters.
- Excellent performance.

Disadvantages
- Slow training procedure.
- The network must be retrained when a new sound class is added to the system.

3.3.4 Support Vector Machine (SVM)

SVMs have been used in a variety of classification tasks, such as isolated handwritten digit recognition, speaker identification, object recognition, face detection and vowel classification.

Recently SVMs have also been introduced for the classification and segmentation of audio streams or audio clips. Advantages of SVMs for audio classification are:

- A set of training data is often available and can be used to train a classifier.
- Once trained, the computation in an SVM depends on a usually small number of supporting vectors and is fast.
- The distribution of audio data in the feature space is complicated and different classes may have overlapping or interwoven areas in feature space. A kernel-based SVM is well suited to handle such a situation.

Given a set of training vectors belonging to two separate classes, $(x_1, y_1), \ldots, (x_l, y_l)$, where $x_i \in R^n$ and $y_i \in \{-1, +1\}$, we want to find a hyperplane $wx + b = 0$ to separate the data. Of all the boundaries determined by w and b, the one that maximizes the margin will generalize better than other possible separating hyperplanes. The linear classifier is termed the optimal separating hyperplane. The optimization condition relies upon finding the plane that maximizes the distance between the hyperplane and the closest sample:

$$d(w, b) = \min_{\{x_i | y_i = 1\}} \frac{wx_i + b}{|w|} - \max_{\{x_i | y_i = -1\}} \frac{wx_i + b}{|w|} \qquad (3.31)$$

and the appropriate minimum and maximum values are ± 1. Distance is needed to maximize:

$$d(w, b) = \frac{1}{w} - \frac{-1}{w} = \frac{2}{w} \qquad (3.32)$$

The pair of hyperplanes gives the maximum margin by minimizing $|w|^2/2$ subject to the constraints $y_i((wx_i) + b) \geq 1$.

The solution to the optimization problem of SVMs is given by the saddle point of the Lagrange function:

$$L(w, b, \alpha) = \frac{1}{2}\|w\|^2 - \sum_{i=1}^{l} \alpha_i\{y_i[(wx_i) + b] - 1\}, \qquad (3.33)$$

with Lagrange multipliers α_i.

While $L(w, b, \alpha)$ is minimized with respect to w and b, the derivatives of $L(w, b, \alpha)$ with respect to all the α_i vanish, all subject to the constraints $\alpha_i \geq 0$.

The solution is given by:

$$\bar{w} = \sum_{i=1}^{l} \bar{\alpha}_i y_i x_i, \quad \bar{b} = -\frac{1}{2}\bar{w}[x_r + x_s], \qquad (3.34)$$

where x_r and x_s are any two support vectors which belong to class $y_r = 1$ and $y_s = -1$. The samples in the input space cannot be separated by any linear hyperplane, but can be linearly separated in the non-linear mapped feature space. Note that the feature space of the SVMs is different from the audio feature space. SVMs can realize non-linear discrimination $f(x)$ by kernel mapping $K(\cdot, \cdot)$:

$$f(x) = \mathrm{sgn}\left(\sum_{i=1}^{l} \bar{\alpha}_i y_i K(x_i, x) + b\right) \sum_{i=1}^{N} \alpha_i t_i K(x, x_i) + b, \qquad (3.35)$$

where the y_i are the target values, $\sum_{i=1}^{l} \bar{\alpha}_i y_i = 0$, and $\bar{\alpha}_i > 0$.

The kernel $K(\cdot, \cdot)$ is constructed to have certain properties (the Mercer condition), so that $K(\cdot, \cdot)$ can be expressed as:

$$K(x, y) = \Phi(x)\Phi(y), \qquad (3.36)$$

where $\Phi(x)$ is a mapping from the input space to a possibly infinite dimensional space.

There are three kernel functions for the nonlinear mapping:

1. Polynomial $K(x, y) = ((xy + 1))^z$, where parameter z is the degree of the polynomial.
2. Gaussian radial basis functions $K(x, y) = \exp\{-[(x - y)^2/2\sigma^2]\}$, where the parameter σ is the standard deviation of the Gaussian function.
3. MLP function $K(x, y) = \tanh(scale(xy) - offset)$, where $scale$ and $offset$ are two given parameters.

SVMs are classifiers for multi-dimensional data that essentially determine a boundary curve between two classes. The boundary can be determined only with vectors in boundary regions called the margin of two classes in a training data set. SVMs, therefore, need to be relearned only when vectors in boundaries change. From the training examples SVM finds the parameters of the decision function which can classify two classes and maximize the margin during a learning phase. After learning, the classification of unknown patterns is predicted.

SVMs have the following advantages and drawbacks.

Advantages
- The solution is unique.
- The boundary can be determined only by its support vectors. An SVM is robust against changes of all vectors but its support vectors.
- SVM is insensitive to small changes of the parameters.
- Different SVM classifiers constructed using different kernels (polynomial, radial basis function (RBF), neural net) extract the same support vectors.
- When compared with other algorithms, SVMs often provide improved performance.

Disadvantages
- Very slow training procedure.

3.4   MPEG-7 SOUND CLASSIFICATION

The MPEG-7 standard (Casey, 2001; Manjunath *et al.*, 2001) has adopted a generalized sound recognition framework, in which dimension-reduced, decorrelated log-spectral features, called the audio spectrum projection (ASP), are used to train HMM for classification of various sounds such as speech, explosions, laughter, trumpet, cello, etc. The feature extraction of the MPEG-7 sound recognition framework is based on the projection of a spectrum onto a low-dimensional subspace via reduced rank spectral basis functions called the audio spectrum basis (ASB). To attain a good performance in this framework, a balanced trade-off

between reducing the dimensionality of data and retaining maximum information content must be performed, as too many dimensions cause problems with
classification while dimensionality reduction invariably introduces information
loss. The tools provide a unified interface for automatic indexing of audio using
trained sound class models in a pattern recognition framework.

The MPEG-7 sound recognition classifier is performed using three steps:
audio feature extraction, training of sound models, and decoding. Figure 3.3
depicts the procedure of the MPEG-7 sound recognition classifier. Each classified
audio piece will be individually processed and indexed so as to be suitable for
comparison and retrieval by the sound recognition system.

3.4.1 MPEG-7 Audio Spectrum Projection (ASP) Feature Extraction

As outlined, an important step in audio classification is feature extraction. An
efficient representation should be able to capture sound properties that are the

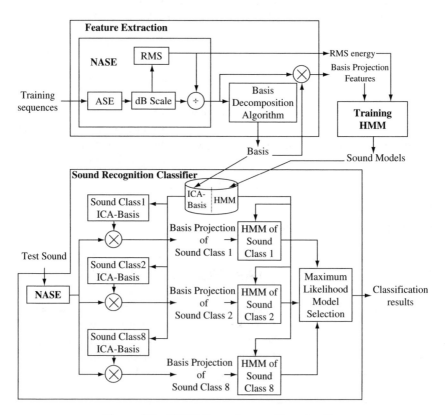

Figure 3.3 MPEG-7 sound recognition classifier

most significant for the task, robust under various environments and general enough to describe various sound classes.

Environmental sounds are generally much harder to characterize than speech and music sounds. They consist of multiple noisy and textured components, as well as higher-order structural components such as iterations and scatterings.

The purpose of MPEG-7 feature extraction is to obtain from the audio source a low-complexity description of its content. The MPEG-7 audio group has proposed a feature extraction method based on the projection of a spectrum onto a low-dimensional representation using decorrelated basis functions (Casey, 2001; Kim *et al.*, 2004a, 2004b; Kim and Sikora, 2004a, 2004b, 2004c). The starting point is the calculation of the audio spectrum envelope (ASE) descriptor outlined in Chapter 2.

Figure 3.3 shows the four steps of the feature extraction in the dimensionality reduction process:

- ASE via short-time Fourier transform (STFT);
- normalized audio spectrum envelope (NASE);
- basis decomposition algorithm – such as SVD or ICA;
- basis projection, obtained by multiplying the NASE with a set of extracted basis functions.

ASE

First, the observed audio signal $s(n)$ is divided into overlapping frames. The ASE is then extracted from each frame. The ASE extraction procedure is described in Section 2.5.1. The resulting log-frequency power spectrum is converted to the decibel scale:

$$ASE_{dB}(l, f) = 10 \log_{10}(ASE(l, f)), \qquad (3.37)$$

where f is the index of an ASE logarithmic frequency range, l is the frame index.

NASE

Each decibel-scale spectral vector is normalized with the RMS energy envelope, thus yielding a normalized log-power version of the ASE called NASE. The full-rank features for each frame l consist of both the RMS-norm gain value R_l and the NASE vector $X(l, f)$:

$$R_l = \sqrt{\sum_{f=1}^{F}(ASE_{dB}(l, f))^2}, \quad 1 \le f \le F \qquad (3.38)$$

and:

$$X(l, f) = \frac{ASE_{dB}(l, f)}{R_l}, \quad 1 \le l \le L \tag{3.39}$$

where F is the number of ASE spectral coefficients and L is the total number of frames.

Much of the information is disregarded due to the lower frequency resolution when reducing the spectrum dimensionality from the size of the STFT to the F frequency bins of NASE.

To help the reader visualize the kind of information that the NASE vectors $X(l, f)$ convey, three-dimensional (3D) plots of the NASE of a male and a female speaker reading the sentence "*Handwerker trugen ihn*" are shown in Figure 3.4. In order to make the images look smoother, the frequency channels are spaced with 1/16-octave bands instead of the usual 1/4-octave bands. The reader should note that recognizing the gender of the speaker by visual inspection of the plots is easy. Compared with the female speaker, the male speaker produces more energy at the lower frequencies and less at the higher frequencies.

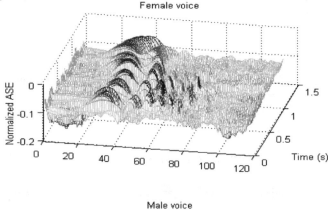

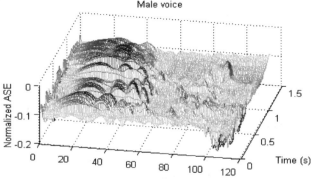

Figure 3.4 The 3D plots of the normalized ASE of a male speaker and a female speaker

Dimensionality Reduction Using Basis Decomposition

In order to achieve a trade-off between further dimensionality reduction and information loss, the ASB and ASP of MPEG-7 low-level audio descriptors are used. To obtain the ASB, SVD or ICA may be employed.

ASP

The ASP Y is obtained by multiplying the NASE matrix with a set of basis functions extracted from several basis decomposition algorithms:

$$Y = \begin{cases} XV_E & \text{for } SVD \\ XC_E & \text{for } PCA \\ XC_EW & \text{for } FastICA \\ |X|H_E^T & \text{for } NMF \text{ (not MPEG-7 compliant).} \end{cases} \tag{3.40}$$

After extracting the reduced SVD basis V_E or PCA basis C_E, ICA is employed for applications that require maximum decorrelation of features, such as the separation of the source components of a spectrogram. A statistically independent basis W is derived using an additional ICA step after SVD or PCA extraction.

The ICA basis W is the same size as the reduced SVD basis V_E or PCA basis C_E. The basis function C_EW obtained by PCA and ICA is stored in the MPEG-7 basis function database for the classification scheme.

The spectrum projection features and RMS-norm gain values are used as input to the HMM training module.

3.4.2 Training Hidden Markov Models (HMMs)

In order to train a statistical model on the basis projection features for each audio class, the MPEG-7 audio classification tool uses HMMs, which consist of several states. During training, the parameters for each state of an audio model are estimated by analysing the feature vectors of the training set. Each state represents a similarly behaving portion of an observable symbol sequence process. At each instant in time, the observable symbol in each sequence either stays at the same state or moves to another state depending on a set of state transition probabilities. Different state transitions may be more important for modelling different kinds of data. Thus, HMM topologies are used to describe how the states are connected. That is, in TV broadcasts, temporal structures of video sequences require the use of an ergodic topology, where each state can be reached from any other state and can be revisited after leaving. In sound classification, five-state left–right models are suitable for isolated sound recognition. A left–right HMM with five states is trained for each sound class.

Figure 3.5 illustrates the training process of an HMM for a given sound class i.

The training audio data is first projected onto the basis function corresponding to sound class i. The HMM parameters are then obtained using the well-known Baum–Welch algorithm. The procedure starts with random initial values for all of the parameters and optimizes the parameters by iterative re-estimation. Each iteration runs through the entire set of training data in a process that is repeated until the model converges to satisfactory values. Often parameters converge after three or four training iterations.

With the Baum–Welch re-estimation training patterns, one HMM is computed for each class of sound that captures the statistically most regular features of the sound feature space. Figure 3.6 shows an example classification scheme consisting of dogs, laughter, gunshot and motor classes. Each of the resulting HMMs is stored in the MPEG-7 sound classifier.

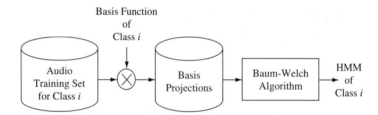

Figure 3.5 HMM training for a given sound class i

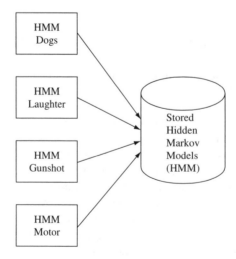

Figure 3.6 Example classification scheme using HMMs

3.4.3 Classification of Sounds

Sounds are modelled according to category labels and represented by a set of HMM parameters. Automatic classification of audio uses a collection of HMM, category labels and basis functions. Automatic audio classification finds the best-match class for an input sound by presenting it to a number of HMM and selecting the model with the maximum likelihood score.

Here, the Viterbi algorithm is used as the dynamic programming algorithm applied to the HMM for computing the most likely state sequence for each model in the classifier given a test sound pattern. Thus, given a sound model and a test sound pattern, a maximum accumulative probability can be recursively computed at every time frame according to the Viterbi algorithm.

Figure 3.3 depicts the recognition module used to classify an audio input based on pre-trained sound class models (HMMs). Sounds are read from a media source format, such as WAV files. Given an input sound, the NASE features are extracted and projected against each individual sound model's set of basis functions, producing a low-dimensional feature representation. Then, the Viterbi algorithm (outlined in more detail in Chapter 4) is applied to align each projection on its corresponding sound class HMM (each HMM has its own representation space). The HMM yielding the best maximum likelihood score is selected, and the corresponding optimal state path is stored.

3.5 COMPARISON OF MPEG-7 AUDIO SPECTRUM PROJECTION VS. MFCC FEATURES

Automatic classification of audio signals has a long history originating from speech recognition. MFCCs are the state-of-the-art dominant features used for speech recognition. They represent the speech amplitude spectrum in a compact form by taking into account perceptual and computational considerations. Most of the signal energy is concentrated in the first coefficients. We refer to Chapter 4 for a detailed introduction to speech recognition.

In the following we compare the performance of MPEG-7 ASP features based on several basis decomposition algorithms vs. MFCCs. The processing steps involved in both methods are outlined in Table 3.1.

As outlined in Chapter 2, the first step of MFCC feature extraction is to divide the audio signal into frames, usually by applying a Hanning windowing function at fixed intervals. The next step is to take the Fourier transform of each frame. The power spectrum bins are grouped and smoothed according to the perceptually motivated mel-frequency scaling. Then the spectrum is segmented into critical bands by means of a filter bank that typically consists of overlapping triangular filters. Finally, a DCT applied to the logarithm of the filter bank outputs results in vectors of decorrelated MFCC features. The block diagram of the sound classification scheme using MFCC features is shown in Figure 3.7.

Table 3.1   Comparison of MPEG-7 ASP and MFCCs

Steps	MFCCs	MPEG-7 ASP
1	Convert to frames	Convert to frames
2	For each frame, obtain the amplitude spectrum	For each frame, obtain the amplitude spectrum
3	Mel-scaling and smoothing	Log-scale octave bands
4	Take the logarithm	Normalization
5	Take the DCT	Perform basis decomposition using PCA, ICA, or NMF for projection features

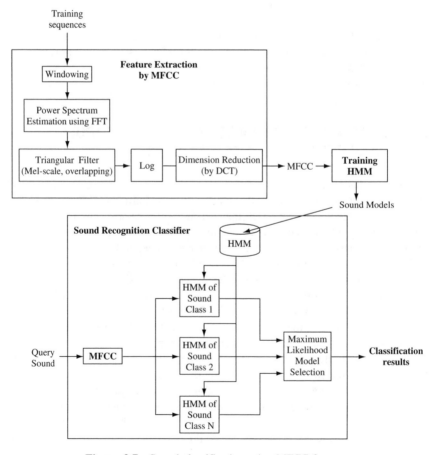

Figure 3.7   Sound classification using MFCC features

Both MFCC and MPEG-7 ASP are short-term spectral-based features. There are some differences between the MPEG-7 ASP and the MFCC procedures.

Filter Bank Analysis

The filters used for MFCC are triangular to smooth the spectrum and emphasize perceptually meaningful frequencies (see Section 2.10.2). They are equally spaced along the mel-scale. The mel-frequency scale is often approximated as a linear scale from 0 to 1 kHz, and as a logarithmic scale beyond 1 kHz. The power spectral coefficients are binned by correlating them with each triangular filter.

The filters used for MPEG-7 ASP are trapezium-shaped or rectangular filters and they are distributed logarithmically between 62.5 Hz (*lowEdge*) and 16 kHz (*highEdge*). The *lowEdge–highEdge* range has been chosen to be an 8-octave interval, logarithmically centred on 1 kHz. The spectral resolution r can be chosen between 1/16 of an octave and 8 octaves, from eight possible values as described in Section 2.5.1.

To help the reader visualize the kind of information that the MPEG-7 ASP and MFCC convey, the results of different steps between both feature extraction methods are depicted in Figure 3.8–3.13. The test sound is that of a typical automobile horn being honked once for about 1.5 seconds. Then the sound decays for roughly 200 ms. For the visualization the audio data was digitized at 22.05 kHz using 16 bits per sample. The features were derived from sound frames of length 30 ms with a frame rate of 15 ms. Each frame was windowed using a Hamming window function and transformed into the frequency domain using a 512-point FFT. The MPEG-7 ASP uses octave-scale filters, while MFCC uses mel-scale filters.

MPEG-7 ASP features are derived from 28 subbands that span the logarithmic frequency band from 62.5 Hz to 8 kHz. Since this spectrum contains 7 octaves, each subband spans a quarter of an octave. MFCCs are calculated from 40 subbands (17 linear bands between 62.5 Hz and 1 kHz, 23 logarithmic bands between 1 kHz and 8 kHz). The 3-D plots and the spectrogram image of subband energy outputs for MFCC and MPEG-7 ASP are shown in Figure 3.8 and Figure 3.9, respectively.

Compared with the ASE coefficients, the output of MFCC triangular filters yields more significant structure in the frequency domain for this example.

Normalization

It is well known that the perceived loudness of a signal has been found to be approximately logarithmic. Therefore, the smoothed amplitude spectrum of the triangular filtering for MFCC is normalized by the natural logarithmic operation, while 30 ASE coefficients for each frame of MPEG-7 ASP are converted to the decibel scale and each decibel-scale spectral vector is normalized with the RMS energy envelope, thus yielding a NASE.

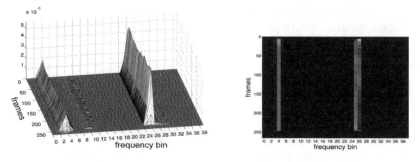

Figure 3.8   Mel-scaling and smoothing

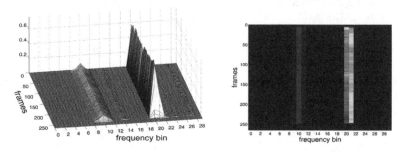

Figure 3.9   ASE

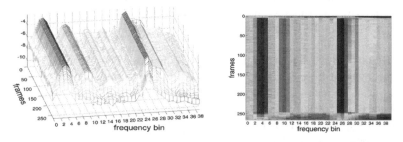

Figure 3.10   Logarithm of amplitude spectrum

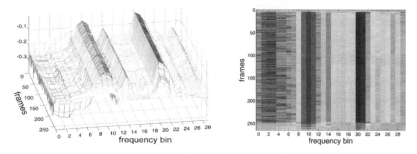

Figure 3.11   NASE

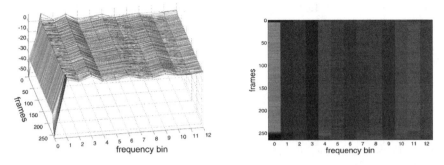

Figure 3.12 MFCC features

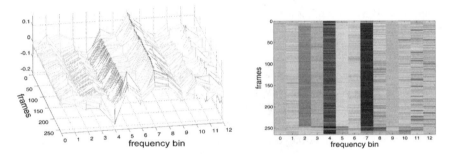

Figure 3.13 ASP features

Compared with the NASE depicted in Figure 3.11, the logarithm of the MFCC amplitude spectrum of Figure 3.10 produces more energy at the lower frequency bin.

Basis Representation for Dimension Reduction

The components of the Mel-spectral vectors calculated for each frame are highly correlated. Features are typically modelled by mixtures of Gaussian densities. Therefore, in order to reduce the number of parameters in the system, the cepstral coefficients are calculated using a DCT which attempts to decorrelate the frequency-warped spectrum. The 3-D plots and the spectrogram due to the DCT for MFCC are depicted in Figure 3.12, where the DCT is taken to obtain 13 cepstral features for each frame. MFCC basis vectors are the same for all audio classes. This is because it assumes that the probabilities of the basis functions by the DCT are all equal.

MPEG-7 audio features of the same example are different. Since each PCA space is derived from the training examples of each training class, each class has its own distinct PCA space. The ICA algorithm, however, uses a non-linear technique to perform the basis rotation in the directions of maximal statistical independence.

As a result, the ASP features generated via FastICA have more peaks on average due to larger variances. The 3-D plots and spectrogram image of the ASP feature are shown in the Figure 3.13, where 13 PCA basis components are used so that the number of MPEG-7 features is the same as that of the MFCC features.

3.6 INDEXING AND SIMILARITY

The structure of an audio indexing and retrieval system using MPEG-7 ASP descriptors is illustrated in Figure 3.14.

The audio indexing module extracts NASE features from a database of sounds. An HMM and a basis function were trained beforehand for each predefined sound class. A classification algorithm finds the most likely class for a given input sound by presenting it to each of the HMM (after projection on the corresponding basis functions) and by using the Viterbi algorithm. The HMM with the highest maximum likelihood score is selected as the representative class for the sound.

The algorithm also generates the optimal HMM state path for each model given the input sound. The state path corresponding to the most likely class is stored as an MPEG-7 descriptor in the sound indexing database. It will be used as an index for further query applications.

The audio retrieval is based on the results of the audio indexing. For a given query sound, the extracted audio features are used to run the sound classifier as

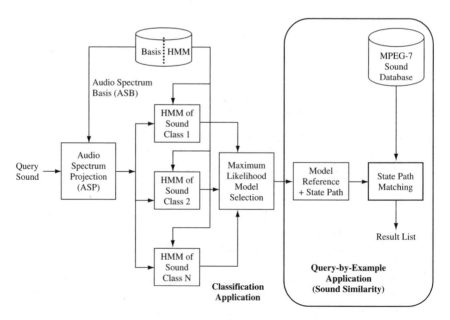

Figure 3.14 Structure of audio indexing and retrieval system

described above. The resulting state path corresponding to the most likely sound class is then used in a matching module to determine the list of the most similar sounds.

3.6.1   Audio Retrieval Using Histogram Sum of Squared Differences

In addition to classification, it is often useful to obtain a measure of how close two given sounds are in some perceptual sense. It is possible to leverage the internal hidden variables generated by an HMM in order to compare the evolution of two sounds through the model's state space. An input sound is indexed by selecting the HMM yielding the maximum likelihood score and storing the corresponding optimal HMM state path, which was obtained using the Viterbi algorithm. This state path describes the evolution of a sound through time with a sequence of integer state indices.

The MPEG-7 standard proposes a method for computing the similarity between two state paths generated by the Viterbi algorithm. This method, based on the sum of squared differences between "state path histograms", is explained in the following.

A normalized histogram can be generated from the state path obtained at the end of the classification procedure. Frequencies are normalized to values in the range [0–1] obtained by dividing the number of samples associated with each state of the HMM by the total number of samples in the state sequence:

$$hist(j) = \frac{N(j)}{\sum_{i=1}^{N_s} N(i)}, \quad 1 \leq j \leq N_s \tag{3.41}$$

where N_s is the number of states in the HMM and $N(j)$ is the number of samples for state j in the given state path.

A similarity measure between two state paths a and b is computed as the absolute difference between each relative frequency summed over state indices. This gives the Euclidean distance between the two sounds indexed by a and b:

$$\delta(a, b) = \sum_{j=1}^{N_s} \sqrt{\left[hist_a(j) - hist_b(j) \right]^2} \tag{3.42}$$

3.7   SIMULATION RESULTS AND DISCUSSION

In order to illustrate the performance of the MPEG-7 ASP features and MFCC, the feature sets are applied to speaker recognition, sound classification, musical instrument classification and speaker-based segmentation (Kim *et al.*, 2003, 2004a, 2004b; Kim and Sikora, 2004a, 2004b, 2004c).

3.7.1   Plots of MPEG-7 Audio Descriptors

To help the reader visualize the kind of information that the MPEG-7 ASP features convey, several results of four of the ASE and ASP descriptors are depicted in Figures 3.15–3.18.

Figure 3.15 compares the MPEG-7 NASE features of "horn" to a "telephone ringing" sound. Note that the harmonic nature of the honk, shown by the almost time-independent spectral peaks of the NASE $X(f, l)$, is readily visible.

The decay of the sound at the end can also be seen as the higher frequencies decay and the lower frequencies seem to grow in strength. The lower frequencies becoming stronger may seem out of place, but this phenomenon is actually due to the normalization. As the sound in general becomes quieter, the levels at the different frequencies become more even and all are boosted by the normalization, even the low ones.

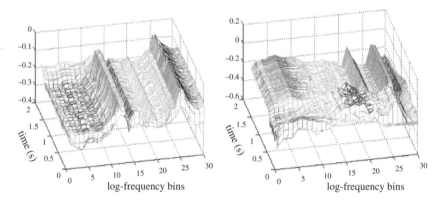

Figure 3.15   NASE of: left, an automobile horn; right, an old telephone ringing

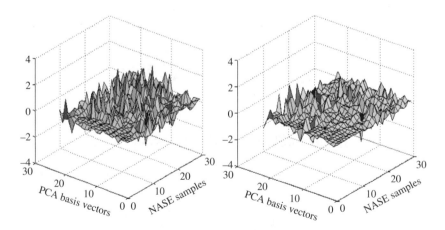

Figure 3.16   PCA basis vectors of: left, horns; and right, a telephone ringing

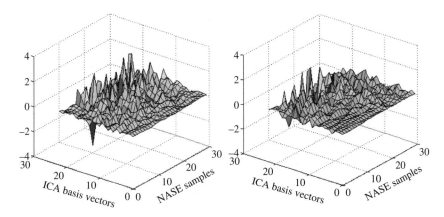

Figure 3.17 FastICA basis vectors of: left, horns; and right, a telephone ringing

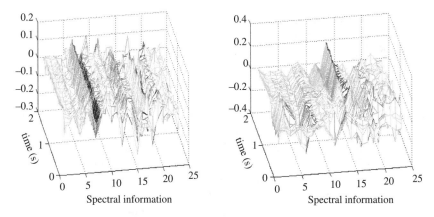

Figure 3.18 Projection of NASE onto basis vectors of: left, an automobile horn; and right, an old telephone ringing

The NASE $X(f, l)$ of an old telephone being rung once is depicted on the right of Figure 3.15. The first 0.7 seconds consist of the noise-like sound of the manual cranking necessary for old-fashioned telephones, while the rest of the sound consists of the harmonic sound of the bells ringing out. Distinguishing between the harmonic and noise-like parts of sounds is easy by visual inspection of the NASE.

While this visual interpretation of the NASE is rather easy, visual interpretation of the bases C_E in Figure 3.16 is not so straightforward. Each of these bases is a matrix, which can be thought as a linear transformation between a spectral domain containing correlated information (NASE) and PCA basis vectors, in which the correlations in the information are reduced.

However, since we do not know exactly how the correlations are being reduced in each case, the bases are difficult to interpret. For instance, one can see in the

PCA bases that the first basis vectors calculated are rather simple and have small variances, while the last basis vectors that are calculated tend to be complicated, have larger variances and be less well behaved in general. It becomes more and more difficult to find meaningful basis vectors. Much of the information has already been extracted. The PCA algorithm also tends to find basis vectors that have large amplitudes, but not necessarily those that convey more information.

The FastICA algorithm, however, uses a non-linear technique to help decorrelate the NASE. As a result, the bases generated via FastICA have more peaks on average due to larger variances. The FastICA bases $C_E W$ are shown on the left of Figure 3.17 for horns and on the right for telephone sounds.

The projections $Y = X C_E W$, on the other hand, look like versions of the NASE where the frequency information is scrambled by the basis. As can be verified on the left and the right of Figure 3.18, telling apart the harmonic and noise-like parts of the sounds is still possible.

3.7.2 Parameter Selection

The dimension-reduced audio spectrum basis (ASB) functions are used to project the high-dimensional spectrum into a low-dimensional representation contained by the ASP. The reduced representation should be well suited for use with probability model classifiers. The projection onto well-chosen bases increases recognition performance considerably. In order to perform a trade-off between dimensionality reduction and information content maximization, basis parameters in PCA and ICA of the feature extraction need to be selected with care.

For the MPEG-7 ASP feature extraction, we created 12 sound classes (trumpet, bird, dog, bell, telephone, baby, laughter, gun, motor, explosion, applause, footstep) containing 40 training and 20 different testing sound clips, which were recorded at 22 kHz and 16 bits and which ranged from 1 to 3 seconds long. Figure 3.19 shows the recognition rates according to the MPEG-7 ASP based on the PCA/FastICA method vs. the reduced dimension E.

The parameter with the most drastic impact turned out to be the horizontal dimension E of the basis matrix C_E from PCA. If E is too small, the matrix C_E reduces the data too much, and the HMM do not receive enough information. However, if E is too large, then the extra information extracted is not very important and is better ignored.

As can be seen in Figure 3.19, the best recognition rate of 96% for the classification of 12 sound classes resulted when E was 23. In other experiments we found the optimal E to be as small as 16. One needs to be careful about choosing E and to test empirically to find the optimal value.

For each predefined sound class, the training module builds a model from a set of training sounds using HMMs which consist of several states. The statistical behaviour of an observed symbol sequence in terms of a network of states, which represents the overall process behaviour with regard to movement between

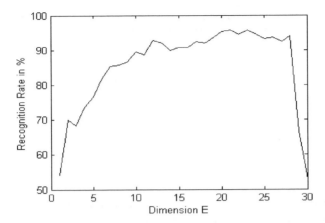

Figure 3.19 Classification rates of 12 sound classes due to FastICA method vs. the reduced dimension E

states of the process, describes the inherent variations in the behaviour of the observable symbols within a state. An HMM topology consists of the number of states with varied connections between states which depend on the occurrence of the observable symbol sequences being modelled. To determine the HMM topology it is necessary to decide on the types of HMM (such as ergodic, left–right, or some others) and to decide on the number of states and the connections between them.

We investigated the effects of different HMM topologies and differing numbers of states on the sound recognition rates. Figure 3.20 shows a few common HMM topologies.

Table 3.2 depicts the classification results for different HMM topologies given the features with $E = 24$. The number of states includes two non-emitting states, so seven states implies that only five non-emitting states were used. Total sound recognition rates are obtained by the maximum likelihood score among the 12 competing sound models.

From Table 3.2, we depict that the HMM classifier yields the best performance for our task when the number of states is 7 and topology is ergodic. The

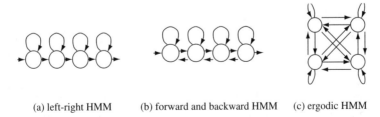

(a) left-right HMM   (b) forward and backward HMM   (c) ergodic HMM

Figure 3.20 Illustration of three HMM topologies with four emitting states

Table 3.2   Total sound recognition rate (%) of 12 sound classes for three HMMs

HMM topology	Number of states				
	4	5	6	7	8
Left–right HMM	77.3	75.9	78.1	78.8	77.5
Forward and backward HMM	61.8	78.1	73	76.7	75.9
Ergodic HMM	58.6	75.5	80.1	84.3	81.9

corresponding classification accuracy is 84.3%. Three iterations were used to train the HMMs.

It is obvious from the problems discussed that different applications and recognition tasks require detailed experimentation with various parameter settings and dimensionality reduction techniques. Figure 3.21 depicts a typical custom-designed user interface for this purpose.

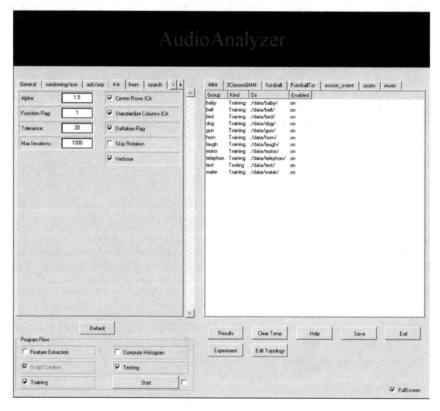

Figure 3.21   Input interface of the audio classification system using MPEG-7 audio features (TU-Berlin)

3.7.3 Results for Distinguishing Between Speech, Music and Environmental Sound

Automatic discrimination of speech, music and environmental sound is important in many multimedia applications, i.e. (1) radio receivers for the automatic monitoring of the audio content of FM radio channels, (2) disabling the speech recognizer during the non-speech portion of the audio stream in automatic speech recognition of broadcast news, (3) distinguishing speech and environmental sounds from music for low-bit-rate audio coding.

For the classification of speech, music and environmental sounds we collected music audio files from various music CDs. The speech files were taken from audio books, panel discussion TV programmes and the TIMIT database.[1] Environmental sounds were selected from various categories of CD movie sound tracks; 60% of the data was used for training and the other 40% for testing.

We compared the classification results of MPEG-7 ASP based on a PCA or ICA basis vs. MFCC. Table 3.3 shows the experimental results. Total recognition rates are obtained by the maximum likelihood score between the three sound classes. In our system, the best accuracy of 84.9% was obtained using an MPEG-7 ASP based on an ICA basis.

Figure 3.22 shows an analysis program for on-line audio classification. The audio recordings are classified and segmented into basic types, such as speech, music, several types of environmental sounds, and silence.

For the segmentation/classification we use four MPEG-7 LLDs, such as power, spectrum centroid, fundamental frequency and harmonic ratio. Also, four non-MPEG-7 audio descriptors' features including high zero crossing rate, low short-time energy ratio, spectrum flux and band periodicity are applied to segment the audio stream. In the implementation we compared the segmentation results using MPEG-7 audio descriptors vs. non-MPEG-7 audio descriptors. The

Table 3.3 Total classification accuracies (%) between speech, music and environmental sounds

Feature extraction methods	Feature dimension		
	7	13	23
PCA-ASP	78.6	81.5	80.3
ICA-ASP	82.5	84.9	79.9
MFCC	76.3	84.1	77.8

PCA-ASP: MPEG-7 ASP based on PCA basis.
ICA-ASP: MPEG-7 ASP based on ICA basis.
MFCC: mel-scale frequency cepstral coefficients.

[1] See LDC (Linguistic Data Consortium): http://www.ldc.upenn.edu.

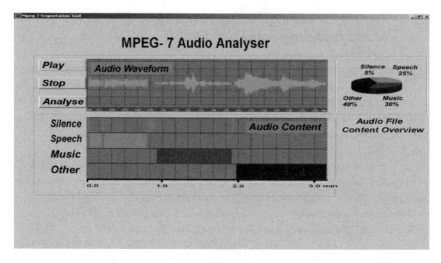

Figure 3.22 Demonstration of an on-line audio classification system between speech, music, environmental sound and silence (TU- Berlin)

experimental results show that the classification/segmentation using non-MPEG-7 audio descriptors is more robust, and can perform better and faster than the MPEG-7 audio descriptors.

3.7.4 Results of Sound Classification Using Three Audio Taxonomy Methods

Sound classification is useful for film/video indexing, searching and professional sounds archiving. Our goal was to identify classes of sound based on MPEG-7 ASP and MFCC.

To test the sound classification system, we built sound libraries from various sources. This included a speech database collected for speaker recognition, and the "Sound Ideas" general sound effects library (SoundIdeas: http://www.sound-ideas.com). We created 15 sound classes: 13 sound classes from the sound effects library and 2 from the collected speech database; 70% of the data was used for training and the other 30% for testing.

For sound classification, we used three different taxonomy methods: a direct approach, a hierarchical approach without hints and a hierarchical approach with hints.

In the direct classification scheme, only one decision step is taken to classify the input audio into one of the various classes of the taxonomy. This approach is illustrated in Figure 3.23(a).

For the direct approach, we used a simple sound recognition system to generate the classification results. Each input sound is tested on all of the sound

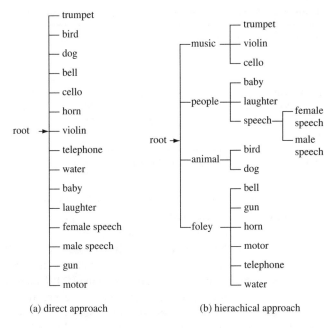

(a) direct approach   (b) hierachical approach

Figure 3.23   Classification using a direct and hierarchical approach

models, and the highest maximum likelihood score is used to determine the test clip's recognized sound class. This method is more straightforward, but would cause problems when there are too many classes. For the hierarchical approach we organize the database of sound classes using the hierarchy shown in Figure 3.23(b). Because we modelled the database in this fashion, we decided to use the same hierarchy for recognition. That is, we create additional bases and HMMs for the more general classes *animal*, *foley*, *people* and *music*. For each test sound, a path is found from the root down to a leaf node with testing occurring at each level in the hierarchy.

In certain systems, such as hierarchical classification with hints, it would be feasible to assume that additional information is available. For instance, it would be possible to have a recording of human speech but not be able to tell the gender of the speaker by ear. The hint *speech* can be given, so that the program can determine the gender of the speaker with possibly higher accuracy. In our hint experiments, each sound clip is assigned a hint, so that only one decision per clip needed to be made by the sound recognition program.

We performed experiments with different feature dimensions of the different feature extraction methods. The results of sound classification for the direct approach are shown in Table 3.4. Total sound recognition rates are obtained by the maximum likelihood score among the 15 competing sound models.

For the 15 sound classes MPEG-7 ASP projected onto a PCA basis provides a slightly better recognition rate than ASP projected onto a FastICA basis at

Table 3.4 Total classification accuracies (%) of 15 sound classes

Feature extraction methods	Feature dimension		
	7	13	23
PCA-ASP	82.9	90.2	95.0
ICA-ASP	81.7	91.5	94.6
NMF-ASP	74.5	77.2	78.6
MFCC	90.5	93.2	94.2

NMF-ASP: MPEG-7 ASP based on NMF basis.

dimensions 7 and 23, while slightly worse at dimension 13. Recognition rates using MPEG-7 confirm that ASP results appear to be significantly lower than the recognition rate of MFCC with the dimensions 7 and 13.

For performing NMF of the audio signal we had two choices: *NMF method 1*: The NMF basis was extracted from the NASE matrix. The ASP features projected onto the NMF basis were directly applied to the HMM sound classifier. *NMF method 2*: The audio signal was transformed to the spectrogram. NMF component parts were extracted from spectrogram image patches. Basis vectors computed by NMF were selected according to their discrimination capability. Sound features were computed from these reduced vectors and fed into the HMM classifier. This process is well described in (Cho *et al.*, 2003).

The ASP projected onto NMF derived from the absolute NASE matrix using *NMF method 1* yields the lowest recognition rate, while *NMF method 2* with a 95 ordered basis according to the spectrogram image patches provides a 95.8% recognition rate. Disadvantages are its computational complexity and its large memory requirements.

Table 3.5 describes the recognition results of several sounds with different classification structures. The total recognition rates are obtained by the maximum likelihood score among the 15 competing sound models. The MPEG-7 ASP

Table 3.5 Total classification accuracies (%) of 15 sound classes using different sound classification structures

Feature extraction methods	Feature dimension (13)		
	A	B	C
PCA-ASP	90.23	75.83	97.05
ICA-ASP	91.51	76.67	97.08
MFCC	93.24	86.25	96.25

A: direct approach.
B: hierarchical classification without hints.
C: hierarchical classification with hints.

features yield a 91.51% recognition rate in the classification using a direct approach A. This recognition rate appears to be significantly lower than the 93.24% recognition rate obtained with MFCC.

For classification using the hierarchical approach without hints B, the MFCC features yield a significant recognition improvement over the MPEG-7 ASP features. However, the recognition rate is lower compared with the direct approach. Many of the errors were due to problems with recognition in the highest layer – sound samples in different branches of the tree were too similar. For example, some dog sounds and horn sounds were difficult to tell apart with the human ear. Thus, a hierarchical structure for sound recognition does not necessarily improve recognition rates if sounds in different general classes are too similar unless some sort of additional information (e.g. a hint) is available. The hierarchical classification with hints C yields overall the highest recognition rate. Especially, the recognition rate of the MPEG-7 ASP is slightly better than the recognition rate of the MFCC features, because some male and female speeches are better recognized by the MPEG-7 ASP than by MFCC.

Figure 3.24 shows a typical graphical user interface for sound recognition. The underlying MPEG-7 sound classification tool is used to search a large database of sound categories and find the best matches to the selected query sound using state-path histograms. For the classification of environmental sounds, different models are constructed for a fixed set of acoustic classes, such as applause, bell,

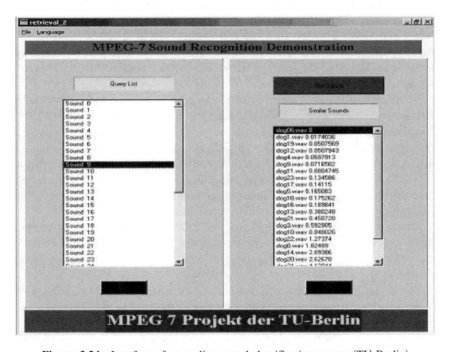

Figure 3.24 Interface of an on-line sound classification system (TU-Berlin)

footstep, laughter, bird's cry, and so on. The MPEG-7 ASP feature extraction is performed on a query sound as shown on the left of Figure 3.24. The model class and state path are stored and these results are compared against the state paths stored in a pre-computed sound index database. The matching module finds the recognized sound class and outputs the best matches within the class assigned to the query sound. The right part of Figure 3.24 shows the sound similarity results according to the best match using the state-path histogram. The most similar sounds should be at the top of the list and the most dissimilar ones at the bottom.

3.7.5 Results for Speaker Recognition

Speaker recognition attempts to recognize a person from a spoken phrase, useful for radio and TV broadcast indexing. This section focuses on the performance of NASE, PCA, ICA and MFCC methods for speaker recognition.

We performed experiments where 30 speakers (14 male and 16 female) were used. Each speaker was instructed to read 20 different sentences. After recording the sentences spoken by each speaker, we cut the recordings into smaller clips: 31 training clips (about 5 minutes long) and 20 test clips (2 minutes) per speaker. Left–right HMM classifiers with seven states were used to model each speaker. For each feature space (NASE, PCA, ICA, MFCC), a set of 30 HMMs (30 speakers) was trained using a classical expectation and maximization (EM) algorithm.

In the case of NASE, the matching process was easy because there were no bases. We simply matched each test clip against each of the 25 HMMs (trained with NASE features) via the Viterbi algorithm. The HMM yielding the best acoustic score (along the most probable state path) determined the recognized speaker.

In the case of the PCA and ICA methods, each HMM had been trained with data projected onto a basis. Every time we tested a sound clip on an HMM, the sound clip's NASE was projected onto the basis (ASB) first. This process caused testing to take considerably longer, as each test clip had to be projected onto 30 different bases, before it could be tested on the 30 HMMs to determine what it should be recognized as. On the other hand, the performance due to the projection onto the well-chosen bases increased recognition performance considerably. The recognition rates for a smaller training set are depicted in Figure 3.25.

The best value E for both methods was 23. However, this was not always the case and was dependent on the training/test data sets. Results for speaker recognition among six male speakers revealed that the optimal dimension for E should be 16.

The results for using the different feature extraction methods are shown in Table 3.6. Total recognition rates are obtained by the maximum likelihood score among the 30 competing speaker models.

For PCA and ICA the recognition rate corresponding to $E = 23$ was chosen, even though in one case the recognition rate was 1.5% higher for $E = 28$

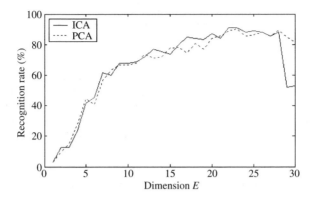

Figure 3.25   Effect of E on recognition rates obtained with PCA and ICA

Table 3.6   Total speaker recognition results of 30 speakers (%) and gender recognition rate between male and female speakers

Recognition mode	NASE	PCA	ICA	MFCC $+ \Delta + \Delta\Delta$
Speaker recognition (small set)	80.8	90.4	91.2	96.0
Speaker recognition (larger set)	80.0	85.6	93.6	98.4
Gender recognition (small set)	98.4	100.0	100.0	100.0

(PCA, with larger training set). For the recognition of 30 speakers, ICA yields better performance than PCA and NASE features, but significantly worse than MFCC $+ \Delta + \Delta\Delta$ based on 39 coefficients. Dynamic features such as Δ and $\Delta\Delta$ provide estimates of a gross shape (linear and second-order curvature) of a short segment of feature trajectory. It appears that MFCC, which is not an MPEG-7 feature, outperforms MPEG-7. To test gender recognition, we used the smaller set. Two HMMs were trained: one with the training clips from female speakers, the other with the training clips from male speakers. Because there were only two possible answers to the recognition question, male or female, this experiment was naturally much easier to carry out and resulted in excellent recognition rates, as depicted in Table 3.6; 100% indicates that no mistakes were made out of 125 test sound clips.

The ASP features based on three basis decomposition algorithms were further applied to speaker recognition including 30 speakers. For NMF of the audio signal we did not use *NMF method 2* using the spectrogram image patches, but computed the NMF basis from the NASE matrix according to *NMF method 1*. ASP projected onto the NMF basis (without further basis selection) was applied directly to the sound classifier. The results of speaker recognition for the direct approach are shown in Table 3.7.

Overall, MFCC achieves the best recognition rates. The recognition rate using the ASP projected onto NMF derived from the absolute NASE matrix is very

Table 3.7 Total speaker recognition accuracies of 30 speakers (%)

Feature extraction methods	Feature dimension		
	7	13	23
PCA-ASP	62.1	83.6	90.2
ICA-ASP	65.95	84.9	92.9
NMF-ASP	45.4	48.3	53.2
MFCC	72.80	92.7	96.25

poor. The reason is that the NMF basis matrix, which was produced without spectrogram image patches and basis ordering, reduced the data too much, and the HMM did not receive enough information.

3.7.6 Results of Musical Instrument Classification

Automatic musical instrument classification is a fascinating and essential sub-problem in music indexing, retrieval and automatic transcription. It is closely related to computational auditory scene analysis.

Our validation database consisted of 960 solo tones of 10 orchestral instruments, such as flute, horn, violin, cello, guitar, piano, oboe, bassoon, saxophone and trumpet, with several articulation styles. All tones were from the Iowa University samples collection (Iowa: http://theremin.MUSIC.viowa.edu/MIS.html). The database for training is partitioned into a testing set of 40 minutes/10 minutes. The classification accuracy for individual instruments is presented in Table 3.8.

The recognition accuracy depends on the recording circumstances, as might be expected. The best classification accuracy was 62% for individual instruments and was obtained with MPEG-7 ASP features on a PCA basis of feature dimension 30. MFCC performs slightly worse at dimension 23 and significantly worse at dimension 30. The experimental results illustrate that both the MPEG-7 ASP and the MFCC features are not very efficient for the classification of musical instruments.

Table 3.8 Total classification accuracies (%) of 10 musical instruments

Feature dimension	Feature extraction methods		
	PCA-ASP	ICA-ASP	MFCC
23	61.5	60.5	60.05
30	62.0	54.0	58.5

3.7.7   Audio Retrieval Results

Once an input sound a has been recognized as a sound of class Cl, the state paths of the sounds b in the MPEG-7 database, which belong to class Cl, can be compared with the state path of a using the Euclidean distance $\delta(a, b)$ as described in Section 3.7.4. These sounds can then be sorted so that those corresponding to the smallest distances are at the top of the list. That is, the items which are most similar to the query should be at the top of the list and the most dissimilar ones at the bottom. This system would basically be a search engine for similar sounds within a given sound class. In Table 3.9, telephone_37 was input as a test sound a and recognized as $Cl = telephone$. The list of the retrieved items indexed with *telephone*, sorted by similarity with query telephone_37, are presented.

The maximum likelihood scores used for classification are also included in Table 3.9, so that the reader can see that calculating the similarity by comparing the state paths and by comparing the maximum likelihood scores produce different results. Note that the similarity is calculated based on "objective" measures.

To compare lists of similar items, we used our own measure called *consistency*. A list is consistent when the elements next to each other belong to the same class, and a list is inconsistent when any two adjacent elements always belong to different classes. We used the following method to calculate the consistency C of a retrieval method.

M sound clips are tested to produce M lists l_m of similar sounds, such that $1 \leq m \leq M$. Let L_m be the length of the list l_m, and let N_m be the number of

Table 3.9   Results of sound similarity

Similar sound	Maximum likelihood score	Euclidean distance
Telephone 37	37.8924	0.111 033
Telephone 34	38.5650	0.111 627
Telephone 58	38.4153	0.116 466
Telephone 35	25.3898	0.135 812
Telephone 55	39.2438	0.150 099
Telephone 60	36.1829	0.158 053

Similar sound	Maximum likelihood score	Euclidean distance
Gunshot 27	27.8624	0.111 023
Gunshot 31	28.5342	0.111 532
Gunshot 46	28.4523	0.115 978
Gunshot 33	16.5835	0.138 513
Gunshot 41	29.5342	0.162 056
Gunshot 50	26.3256	0.167 023

Table 3.10   Consistencies

Method	With the state paths	With maximum likelihood scores
NASE	0.69	0.50
PCA	0.72	0.57
FastICA	0.73	0.58

times that two adjacent entries in the list l_m belong to the same class. Compute the consistency C according to:

$$C_m = \frac{N_m}{L_m - 1} \tag{3.43}$$

$$C = E\{C_M\} \cong \frac{1}{M} \sum_{m=1}^{M} C_m. \tag{3.44}$$

Thus, the consistency is a real number between 0 and 1, with 0 being as inconsistent as possible and 1 as consistent as possible.

Using the same library of test sounds, we then measured the inconsistency for retrieval methods using NASE, PCA projections and FastICA projections as inputs to the HMMs. As it was also possible to measure the similarity using just the maximum likelihood scores, we also list those results in Table 3.10.

The results indicate that the lists of similar sounds are more consistent, if the state paths instead of the maximum likelihood scores are used for comparison. We attribute this result to the fact that the state paths contain more information because they are multi-dimensional, whereas the maximum likelihood scores are one dimensional. Thus, our best technique for retrieving similar sounds is the FastICA method using the state paths for comparison.

3.8   CONCLUSIONS

In this chapter we reviewed various techniques frequently used for sound classification and similarity. Several methods for dimensionality reduction and classification were introduced. The MPEG-7 standard was discussed in this context. To provide the reader with an overview of the performance of MPEG-7, we compared the performance of MPEG-7 audio spectrum projection (ASP) features obtained with three different basis decomposition algorithms vs. mel-frequency cepstrum coefficients (MFCCs). These techniques were applied for sound classification, musical instrument identification, speaker recognition and speaker-based segmentation. For basis decomposition of the MPEG-7 ASP, principal component analysis (PCA), FastICA as independent component analysis (ICA) or non-negative matrix factorization (NMF) were used. Audio features are computed from these decorrelated vectors and fed into a continuous hidden Markov model (HMM) classifier.

Our average recognition/classification results show that the MFCC features yield better performance compared with MPEG-7 ASP in speaker recognition, general sound classification and audio segmentation except musical instrument identification, and classification of speech, music and environmental sounds. In the case of MFCC, the process of recognition, classification and segmentation is simple and fast because there are no bases used. On the other hand, the extraction of MPEG-7 ASP is more time and memory consuming compared with MFCC.

REFERENCES

Casey M. A. (2001) "MPEG-7 Sound Recognition Tools", *IEEE Transactions on Circuits and Systems for Video Technology*, vol. 11, no. 6, pp. 737–747.

Cho Y.-C., Choi S. and Bang S.-Y. (2003) "Non-Negative Component Parts of Sound for Classification", *IEEE International Symposium on Signal Processing and Information Technology*, Darmstadt, Germany, December.

Cortes C. and Vapnik V. (1995) "Support Vector Networks", *Machine Learning*, vol. 20, pp. 273–297.

Golub G. H. and Van Loan C. F. (1993) *Matrix Computations*, Johns Hopkins University Press, Baltimore, MD.

Haykins S. (1998) *Neural Networks*, 2nd Edition, Prentice Hall, Englewood Cliffs, NJ.

Hyvärinen A., (1999) "Fast and Robust Fixed-Point algorithms for Independent Component Analysis", *IEEE Transactions on Neural Networks*, vol. 10, no. 3, pp. 626–634.

Hyvärinen A., Karhunen J. and Oja E. (2001) *Independent Component Analysis*, John Wiley & Sons, Inc., New York.

Jollife I. T. (1986) *Principal Component Analysis*, Springer-Verlag, Berlin.

Kim H.-G. and Sikora T. (2004a) "Comparison of MPEG-7 Audio Spectrum Projection Features and MFCC applied to Speaker Recognition, Sound Classification and Audio Segmentation", *Proceedings IEEE ICASSP 2004*, Montreal, Canada, May.

Kim H.-G. and Sikora T. (2004b) "Audio Spectrum Projection Based on Several Basis Decomposition Algorithms Applied to General Sound Recognition and Audio Segmentation", *Proceedings of EURASIP-EUSIPCO 2004*, Vienna, Austria, September.

Kim H.-G. and Sikora T. (2004c) "How Efficient Is MPEG-7 Audio for Sound Classification, Musical Instrument Identification, Speaker Recognition, and Speaker-Based Segmentation?", *IEEE Transactions on Speech and Audio Processing*, submitted.

Kim H.-G., Berdahl E., Moreau N. and Sikora T. (2003) "Speaker Recognition Using MPEG-7 Descriptors", *Proceedings EUROSPEECH 2003*, Geneva, Switzerland, September.

Kim H.-G., Burred J. J. and Sikora T. (2004a) "How Efficient is MPEG-7 for General Sound Recognition?", *25th International AES Conference "Metadata for Audio"*, London, UK, June.

Kim H.-G., Moreau N. and Sikora T. (2004b) "Audio Classification Based on MPEG-7 Spectral Basis Representations", *IEEE Transactions on Circuits and Systems for Video Technology*, vol. 141, no. 5, pp. 716–725.

Lee D. D. and Seung H. S. (1999) "Learning the Parts of Objects by Non-Negative Matrix Factorization", *Nature*, vol. 401, pp. 788–791.

Lee D. D. and Seung H. S. (2001) "Algorithms for Non-Negative Matrix Factorization", *NIPS 2001 Conference*, Vancouver, Canada.

Manjunath B. S., Salembier P. and Sikora T. (2001) *Introduction to MPEG-7*, John Wiley & Sons, Ltd, Chichester.

Rabiner L. R. and Jung B. (1993) *Fundamentals of Speech Recognition*, Prentice Hall, Englewood Cliffs, NJ.

Reynolds D. A. (1995) Speaker Identification and Verification Using Gaussian Mixture Speaker Models, *Speech Communication*, pp. 91–108.

Smaragdis P. and Brown J. C. (2003) "Non-Negative Matrix Factorization for Polyphonic Music Transcription", *IEEE Workshop on Applications of Signal Processing to Audio and Acoustics*, New Paltz, NY, USA, October.

4

Spoken Content

4.1 INTRODUCTION

Audio streams of multimedia documents often contain spoken parts that enclose a lot of semantic information. This information, called *spoken content*, consists of the actual words spoken in the speech segments of an audio stream. As speech represents the primary means of human communication, a significant amount of the usable information enclosed in audiovisual documents may reside in the spoken content. In the past decade, the extraction of spoken content metadata has therefore become a key challenge for the development of efficient methods to index and retrieve audiovisual documents.

One method for exploiting the spoken information is to have a human being listen and transcribe it into textual information (full transcription or manual annotation with a series of spoken keywords). A classical text retrieval system could then exploit this information. In real-world applications, however, hand indexing of spoken audio material is generally impracticable because of the huge volume of data to process. An alternative is the automatization of the transcription process by means of an automatic speech recognition (ASR) system.

Research in ASR dates back several decades. Only in the last few years has ASR become a viable technology for commercial application. Due to the progress of computation power, speech recognition technologies have matured to the point where speech can be used to interact with automatic phone systems and control computer programs (Coden *et al.*, 2001). ASR algorithms have now reached sufficient levels of performance to make the processing of natural, continuous speech possible, e.g. in commercial dictation programs. In the near future, ASR will have the potential to change dramatically the way we create, store and manage knowledge. Combined with ever decreasing storage costs and ever more powerful processors, progress in the ASR field promises new applications able to treat speech as easily and efficiently as we currently treat text.

MPEG-7 Audio and Beyond: Audio Content Indexing and Retrieval   H.-G. Kim, N. Moreau and T. Sikora
© 2005 John Wiley & Sons, Ltd

In this chapter we use the well defined MPEG-7 Spoken Content description standard as an example to illustrate challenges in this domain. The audio part of MPEG-7 contains a *SpokenContent* high-level tool targeted at spoken data management applications. The MPEG-7 *SpokenContent* tool provides a standardized representation of an ASR output, i.e. of the semantic information (the *spoken content*) extracted by an ASR system from a spoken signal. The *SpokenContent* description attempts to be memory efficient and flexible enough to make currently unforeseen applications possible in the future. It consists of a compact representation of multiple word and/or sub-word hypotheses produced by an ASR engine. It also includes a header that contains information about the recognizer itself and the speaker's identity.

How the *SpokenContent* description should be extracted and used is not part of the standard. However, this chapter begins with a short introduction to ASR systems. The structure of the MPEG-7 *SpokenContent* description itself is presented in detail in the second section. The third section deals with the main field of application of the *SpokenContent* tool, called *spoken document retrieval* (SDR), which aims at retrieving information in speech signals based on their extracted contents. The contribution of the MPEG-7 *SpokenContent* tool to the standardization and development of future SDR applications is discussed at the end of the chapter.

4.2 AUTOMATIC SPEECH RECOGNITION

The MPEG-7 *SpokenContent* description is a normalized representation of the output of an ASR system. A detailed presentation of the ASR field is beyond the scope of this book. This section provides a basic overview of the main speech recognition principles. A large amount of literature has been published on the subject in the past decades. An excellent overview on ASR is given in (Rabiner and Juang, 1993).

Although the extraction of the MPEG-7 *SpokenContent* description is non-normative, this introduction is restrained to the case of ASR based on hidden Markov models, which is by far the most commonly used approach.

4.2.1 Basic Principles

Figure 4.1 gives a schematic description of an ASR process. Basically, it consists in two main steps:

1. *Acoustic analysis.* Speech recognition does not directly process the speech waveforms. A parametric representation X (called *acoustic observation*) of speech acoustic properties is extracted from the input signal A.
2. *Decoding.* The acoustic observation X is matched against a set of predefined acoustic models. Each model represents one of the symbols used by the system

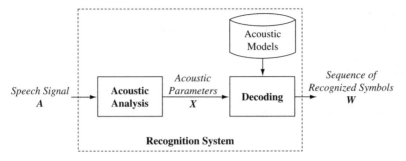

Figure 4.1 Schema of an ASR system

for describing the spoken language of the application (e.g. words, syllables or phonemes). The best scoring models determine the output sequence of symbols.

The main principles and definitions related to the acoustic analysis and decoding modules are briefly introduced in the following.

4.2.1.1 Acoustic Analysis

The acoustic observation X results from a time–frequency analysis of the input speech signal A. The main steps of this process are:

1. The analogue signal is first digitized. The sampling rate depends on the particular application requirements. The most common sampling rate is 16 kHz (one sample every 62.5 μs).
2. A high-pass, also called *pre-emphasis*, filter is often used to emphasize the high frequencies.
3. The digital signal is segmented into successive, regularly spaced time intervals called *acoustic frames*. Time frames overlap each other. Typically, a frame duration is between 20 and 40 ms, with an overlap of 50%.
4. Each frame is multiplied by a windowing function (e.g. Hanning).
5. The frequency spectrum of each single frame is obtained through a Fourier transform.
6. A vector of coefficients x, called an *observation vector*, is extracted from the spectrum. It is a compact representation of the spectral properties of the frame.

Many different types of coefficient vectors have been proposed. The most currently used ones are based on the frame cepstrum: namely, linear prediction cepstrum coefficients (LPCCs) and more especially mel-frequency cepstral coefficients (MFCCs) (Angelini *et al.* 1998; Rabiner and Juang, 1993). Finally, the acoustic analysis module delivers a sequence X of observation vectors, $X = (x_1, x_2, \ldots, x_T)$, which is input into the decoding process.

4.2.1.2 Decoding

In a probabilistic ASR system, the decoding algorithm aims at determining the most probable sequence of symbols W knowing the acoustic observation X:

$$\hat{W} = \underset{W}{\operatorname{argmax}} P(W|X). \tag{4.1}$$

Bayes' rule gives:

$$\hat{W} = \underset{W}{\operatorname{argmax}} \frac{P(X|W)P(W)}{P(X)}. \tag{4.2}$$

This formula makes two important terms appear in the numerator: $P(X|W)$ and $P(W)$. The estimation of these probabilities is the core of the ASR problem. The denominator $P(X)$ is usually discarded since it does not depend on W.

The $P(X|W)$ term is estimated through the *acoustic models* of the symbols contained in W. The hidden Markov model (HMM) approach is one of the most powerful statistical methods for modelling speech signals (Rabiner, 1989). Nowadays most ASR systems are based on this approach.

A basic example of an HMM topology frequently used to model speech is depicted in Figure 4.2. This left–right topology consists of different elements:

- A fixed number of states S_i.
- Probability density functions b_i, associated to each state S_i. These functions are defined in the same space of acoustic parameters as the observation vectors comprising X.
- Probabilities of transition a_{ij} between states S_i and S_j. Only transitions with non-null probabilities are represented in Figure 4.2. When modelling speech, no backward HMM transitions are allowed in general (*left–right* models).

These kinds of models allow us to account for the temporal and spectral variability of speech. A large variety of HMM topologies can be defined, depending on the nature of the speech unit to be modelled (words, phones, etc.).

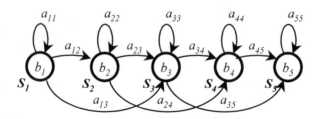

Figure 4.2 Example of a left–right HMM

When designing a speech recognition system, an HMM topology is defined a priori for each of the spoken content symbols in the recognizer's vocabulary. The training of model parameters (transition probabilities and probability density functions) is usually made through a Baum–Welch algorithm (Rabiner and Juang, 1993). It requires a large training corpus of labelled speech material with many occurrences of each speech unit to be modelled.

Once the recognizer's HMMs have been trained, acoustic observations can be matched against them using the Viterbi algorithm, which is based on the dynamic programming (DP) principle (Rabiner and Juang, 1993).

The result of a Viterbi decoding algorithm is depicted in Figure 4.3. In this example, we suppose that sequence W just consists of one symbol (e.g. one word) and that the five-state HMM λ_W depicted in Figure 4.2 models that word. An acoustic observation X consisting of six acoustic vectors is matched against λ_W. The Viterbi algorithm aims at determining the sequence of HMM states that best matches the sequence of acoustic vectors, called the best *alignment*. This is done by computing sequentially a likelihood score along every authorized paths in the DP grid depicted in Figure 4.3. The authorized trajectories within the grid are determined by the set of HMM transitions. An example of an authorized path is represented in Figure 4.3 and the corresponding likelihood score is indicated. Finally, the path with the higher score gives the best Viterbi alignment.

The likelihood score of the best Viterbi alignment is generally used to approximate $P(X|W)$ in the decision rule of Equation (4.2). The value corresponding to the best recognition hypothesis – that is, the estimation of $P(X|\widehat{W})$ – is called the *acoustic score* of X.

The second term in the numerator of Equation (4.2) is the probability $P(W)$ of a particular sequence of symbols W. It is estimated by means of a stochastic *language model* (LM). An LM models the syntactic rules (in the case of words)

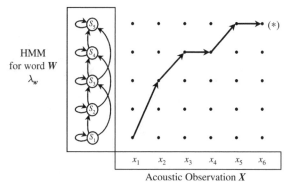

(*) Likelihood Score $= b_1(x_1).a_{13}.b_3(x_2).a_{34}.b_4(x_3).a_{44}.b_4(x_4).a_{45}.b_5(x_5).a_{55}.b_5(x_6)$

Figure 4.3 Result of a Viterbi decoding

or phonotactic rules (in the case of phonetic symbols) of a given language, i.e. the rules giving the permitted sequences of symbols for that language.

The acoustic scores and LM scores are not computed separately. Both are integrated in the same process: the LM is used to constrain the possible sequences of HMM units during the global Viterbi decoding. At the end of the decoding process, the sequence of models yielding the best accumulated LM and likelihood score gives the output transcription of the input signal. Each symbol comprising the transcription corresponds to an alignment with a sub-sequence of the input acoustic observation X and is attributed an acoustic score.

4.2.2 Types of Speech Recognition Systems

The HMM framework can model any kind of speech units (words, phones, etc.) allowing us to design systems with diverse degrees of complexity (Rabiner, 1993). The main types of ASR systems are listed below.

4.2.2.1 Connected Word Recognition

Connected word recognition systems are based on a fixed syntactic network, which strongly restrains the authorized sequences of output symbols. No stochastic language model is required. This type of recognition system is only used for very simple applications based on a small lexicon (e.g. digit sequence recognition for vocal dialling interfaces, telephone directory, etc.) and is generally not adequate for more complex transcription tasks.

An example of a syntactic network is depicted in Figure 4.4, which represents the basic grammar of a connected digit recognition system (with a backward transition to permit the repetition of digits).

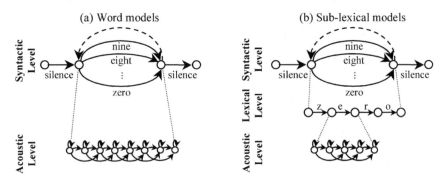

Figure 4.4 Connected digit recognition with (a) word modelling and (b) flexible modelling

Figure 4.4 also illustrates two modelling approaches. The first one (a) consists of modelling each vocabulary word with a dedicated HMM. The second (b) is a sub-lexical approach where each word model is formed from the concatenation of sub-lexical HMMs, according to the word's canonical transcription (a phonetic transcription in the example of Figure 4.4). This last method, called *flexible modelling*, has several advantages:

- Only a few models have to be trained. The lexicon of symbols necessary to describe words has a fixed and limited size (e.g. around 40 phonetic units to describe a given language).
- As a consequence, the required storage capacity is also limited.
- Any word with its different pronunciation variants can be easily modelled.
- New words can be added to the vocabulary of a given application without requiring any additional training effort.

Word modelling is only appropriate with the simplest recognition systems, such as the one depicted in Figure 4.4 for instance. When the vocabulary gets too large, as in the case of large-vocabulary continuous recognition addressed in the next section, word modelling becomes clearly impracticable and the flexible approach is mandatory.

4.2.2.2 Large-Vocabulary Continuous Speech Recognition

Large-vocabulary continuous speech recognition (LVCSR) is a speech-to-text approach, targeted at the automatic word transcription of the input speech signal. This requires a huge word lexicon. As mentioned in the previous section, words are modelled by the concatenation of sub-lexical HMMs in that case. This means that a complete pronunciation dictionary is available to provide the sub-lexical transcription of every vocabulary word.

Recognizing and understanding natural speech also requires the training of a complex language model which defines the rules that determine what sequences of words are grammatically well formed and meaningful. These rules are introduced in the decoding process by applying stochastic constraints on the permitted sequences of words.

As mentioned before (see Equation 4.2), the goal of stochastic language models is the estimation of the probability $P(W)$ of a sequence of words W. This not only makes speech recognition more accurate, but also helps to constrain the search space for speech recognition by discarding the less probable word sequences.

There exist many different types of LMs (Jelinek, 1998). The most widely used are the so-called *n-gram* models, where $P(W)$ is estimated based on probabilities $P(w_i|w_{i-n+1}, w_{i-n+2}, \ldots, w_{i-1})$ that a word w_i occurs after a sub-sequence of $n-1$ words $(w_{i-n+1}, w_{i-n+2}, \ldots, w_{i-1})$. For instance, an LM where the probability of a word only depends on the previous one $(P(w_i|w_{i-1}))$ is called a *bigram*. Similarly, a *trigram* takes the two previous words into account $(P(w_i | w_{i-2}, w_{i-1}))$.

Whatever the type of LM, its training requires large amounts of texts or spoken document transcriptions so that most of the possible word successions are observed (e.g. possible word pairs for a bigram LM). Smoothing methods are usually applied to tackle the problem of data sparseness (Katz, 1987). A language model is dependent on the topics addressed in the training material. That means that processing spoken documents dealing with a completely different topic could lead to a lower word recognition accuracy.

The main problem of LVCSR is the occurrence of out-of-vocabulary (OOV) words, since it is not possible to define a recognition vocabulary comprising every possible word that can be spoken in a given language. Proper names are particularly problematic since new ones regularly appear in the course of time (e.g. in broadcast news). They often carry a lot of useful semantic information that is lost at the end of the decoding process. In the output transcription, an OOV word is usually substituted by a vocabulary word or a sequence of vocabulary words that is acoustically close to it.

4.2.2.3 Automatic Phonetic Transcription

The goal of phonetic recognition systems is to provide full phonetic transcriptions of spoken documents, independently of any lexical knowledge. The lexicon is restrained to the set of *phone* units necessary to describe the sounds of a given language (e.g. around 40 phones for English).

As before, a stochastic language model is needed to prevent the generation of less probable phone sequences (Ng *et al.*, 2000). Generally, the recognizer's grammar is defined by a *phone loop*, where all phone HMMs are connected with each other according to the phone transition probabilities specified in the phone LM. Most systems use a simple stochastic phone–bigram language model, defined by the set of probabilities $P(\varphi_j | \varphi_i)$ that phone φ_j follows phone φ_i (James, 1995; Ng and Zue, 2000b).

Other, more refined phonetic recognition systems have been proposed. The extraction of phones by means of the SUMMIT system (Glass *et al.*, 1996) developed at MIT,[1] adopts a probabilistic segment-based approach that differs from conventional frame-based HMM approaches. In segment-based approaches, the basic speech units are variable in length and much longer in comparison with frame-based methods. The SUMMIT system uses an "acoustic segmentation" algorithm (Glass and Zue, 1988) to produce the segmentation hypotheses. Segment boundaries are hypothesized at locations of large spectral change. The boundaries are then fully interconnected to form a network of possible segmentations on which the recognition search is performed.

---

[1] Massachusetts Institute of Technology.

Another approach to word-independent sub-lexical recognition is to train HMMs for other types of sub-lexical units, such as syllables (Larson and Eickeler, 2003). But in any case, the major problem of sub-lexical recognition is the high rate of recognition errors in the output sequences.

4.2.2.4 Keyword Spotting

Keyword spotting is a particular type of ASR. It consists of detecting the occurrences of isolated words, called keywords, within the speech stream (Wilpon *et al.*, 1990). The target words are taken from a restrained, predefined list of keywords (the keyword vocabulary).

The main problem with keyword spotting systems is the modeling of irrelevant speech between keywords by means of so-called *filler models*. Different sorts of filler models have been proposed. A first approach consists of training different specific HMMs for distinct "non-keyword" events: silence, environmental noise, OOV speech, etc. (Wilpon *et al.*, 1990). Another, more flexible solution is to model non-keyword speech by means of an unconstrained phone loop that recognizes, as in the case of a phonetic transcriber, phonetic sequences without any lexical constraint (Rose, 1995). Finally, a keyword spotting decoder consists of a set of keyword HMMs looped with one or several filler models.

During the decoding process, a predefined threshold is set on the acoustic score of each keyword candidate. Words with scores above the threshold are considered true hits, while those with scores below are considered false alarms and ignored. Choosing the appropriate threshold is a trade-off between the number of type I (missed words) and type II (false alarms) errors, with the usual problem that reducing one increases the other. The performance of keyword spotting systems is determined by the trade-offs it is able to achieve. Generally, the desired trade-off is chosen on a performance curve plotting the false alarm rate vs. the missed word rate. This curve is obtained by measuring both error rates on a test corpus when varying the decision threshold.

4.2.3 Recognition Results

This section presents the different output formats of most ASR systems and gives the definition of recognition error rates.

4.2.3.1 Output Format

As mentioned above, the decoding process yields the best scoring sequence of symbols. A speech recognizer can also output the recognized hypotheses in several other ways. A single recognition hypothesis is sufficient for the most basic systems (connected word recognition), but when the recognition task is more complex, particularly for systems using an LM, the most probable transcription usually contains many errors. In this case, it is necessary to deliver a series of alternative recognition hypotheses on which further post-processing operations can be performed. The recognition alternatives to the best hypothesis can be represented in two ways:

- An *N-best list*, where the *N* most probable transcriptions are ranked according to their respective scores.
- A *lattice*, i.e. a graph whose different paths represent different possible transcriptions.

Figure 4.5 depicts the two possible representations of the transcription alternatives delivered by a recognizer (A, B, C and D represent recognized symbols).

A lattice offers a more compact representation of the transcription alternatives. It consists of an oriented graph in which nodes represent time points between the beginning (T_{start}) and the end (T_{end}) of the speech signal. The edges correspond to recognition hypotheses (e.g. words or phones). Each one is assigned the label and the likelihood score of the hypothesis it represents along with a transition probability (derived from the LM score). Such a graph can be seen as a reduced representation of the initial search space. It can be easily post-processed with an A* algorithm (Paul, 1992), in order to extract a list of *N*-best transcriptions.

4.2.3.2 Performance Measurements

The efficiency of an ASR system is generally measured based on the 1-best transcriptions it delivers. The transcriptions extracted from an evaluation collection of spoken documents are compared with reference transcriptions. By comparing reference and hypothesized sequences, the occurrences of three types or errors are usually counted:

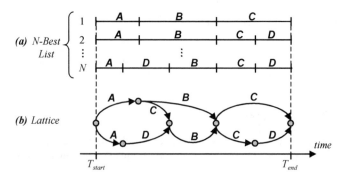

Figure 4.5 Two different representations of the output of a speech recognizer. Part (a) depicts a list of *N*-best transcriptions, and part (b) a word lattice

- *Substitution errors*, when a symbol in the reference transcription was substituted with a different one in the recognized transcription.
- *Deletion errors*, when a reference symbol has been omitted in the recognized transcription.
- *Insertion errors*, when the system recognized a symbol not contained in the reference transcription.

Two different measures of recognition performance are usually computed based on these error counts. The first is the recognition error rate:

$$Error\ Rate = \frac{\#Substitution + \#Insertion + \#Deletion}{\#Reference\ Symbols}, \qquad (4.3)$$

where *#Substitution*, *#Insertion* and *#Deletion* respectively denote the numbers of substitution, insertion and deletion occurrences observed when comparing the recognized transcriptions with the reference. *#Reference Symbols* is the number of symbols (e.g. words) in the reference transcriptions. The second measure is the recognition accuracy:

$$Accuracy = \frac{\#Correct - \#Insertion}{\#Reference\ Symbols}, \qquad (4.4)$$

where *#Correct* denotes the number of symbols correctly recognized. Only one performance measure is generally mentioned since:

$$Accuracy + Error\ Rate = 100\%. \qquad (4.5)$$

The best performing LVCSR systems can achieve word recognition accuracies greater than 90% under certain conditions (speech captured in a clean acoustic environment). Sub-lexical recognition is a more difficult task because it is syntactically less constrained than LVCSR. As far as phone recognition is concerned, a typical phone error rate is around 40% with clean speech.

4.3 MPEG-7 *SPOKENCONTENT* DESCRIPTION

There is a large variety of ASR systems. Each system is characterized by a large number of parameters: spoken language, word and phonetic lexicons, quality of the material used to train the acoustic models, parameters of the language models, etc. Consequently, the outputs of two different ASR systems may differ completely, making retrieval in heterogeneous spoken content databases difficult. The MPEG-7 *SpokenContent* high-level description aims at standardizing the representation of ASR outputs, in order to make interoperability possible. This is achieved independently of the peculiarities of the recognition engines used to extract spoken content.

4.3.1   General Structure

Basically, the MPEG-7 *SpokenContent* tool defines a standardized description
of the lattices delivered by a recognizer. Figure 4.6 is an illustration of what
an MPEG-7 *SpokenContent* description of the speech excerpt "film on Berlin"
could look like. Figure 4.6 shows a simple lattice structure where small circles
represent lattice nodes. Each link between nodes is associated with a recognition
hypothesis, a probability derived from the language model, and the acoustic score
delivered by the ASR system for the corresponding hypothesis. The standard
defines two types of lattice links: word type and phone type. An MPEG-7 lattice
can thus be a word-only graph, a phone-only graph or combine word and phone
hypotheses in the same graph as depicted in the example of Figure 4.6.

The MPEG-7 a *SpokenContent* description consists of two distinct elements:
a *SpokenContentHeader* and a *SpokenContentLattice*. The *SpokenContentLattice*
represents the actual decoding produced by an ASR engine (a lattice structure
such as the one depicted in Figure 4.6). The *SpokenContentHeader* contains
some metadata information that can be shared by different lattices, such as the
recognition lexicons of the ASR systems used for extraction or the speaker
identity. The *SpokenContentHeader* and *SpokenContentLattice* descriptions are
interrelated by means of specific MPEG-7 linking mechanisms that are beyond
the scope of this book (Lindsay *et al.*, 2000).

4.3.2   *SpokenContentHeader*

The *SpokenContentHeader* contains some header information that can be shared
by several *SpokenContentLattice* descriptions. It consists of five types of
metadata:

- *WordLexicon*: a list of words. A header may contain several word lexicons.
- *PhoneLexicon*: a list of phones. A header may contain several phone lexicons.

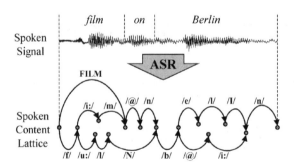

Figure 4.6   MPEG-7 *SpokenContent* description of an input spoken signal "film on
Berlin"

- *ConfusionInfo*: a data structure enclosing some phone confusion information. Although separate, the confusion information must map onto the phone lexicon with which it is associated via the *SpeakerInfo* descriptor.
- *DescriptionMetadata*: information about the extraction process used to generate the lattices. In particular, this data structure can store the name and settings of the speech recognition engine used for lattice extraction.
- *SpeakerInfo*: information about the persons speaking in the original audio signals, along with other information about their associated lattices.

These descriptors are mostly detailed in the following sections.

4.3.2.1 *WordLexicon*

A *WordLexicon* is a list of words, generally the vocabulary of a word-based recognizer. Each entry of the lexicon is an identifier (generally its orthographic representation) representing a word. A *WordLexicon* consists of the following elements:

- *phoneticAlphabet*: is the name of an encoding scheme for phonetic symbols. It is only needed if phonetic representations are used (see below). The possible values of this attribute are indicated in the *PhoneLexicon* section.
- *NumOfOriginalEntries*: is the original size of the lexicon. In the case of a word lexicon, this should be the number of words originally known to the ASR system.
- A series of *Token* elements: each one stores an entry of the lexicon.

Each *Token* entry is made up of the following elements:

- *Word*: a string that defines the label corresponding to the word entry. The *Word* string must not contain white-space characters.
- *representation*: an optional attribute that describes the type of representation of the lexicon entry. Two values are possible: *orthographic* (the word is represented by its normal orthographic spelling) or *nonorthographic* (the word is represented by another kind of identifier). A non-orthographic representation may be a phoneme string corresponding to the pronunciation of the entry, encoded according to the *phoneticAlphabet* attribute.
- *linguisticUnit*: an optional attribute that indicates the type of the linguistic unit corresponding to the entry.

The *WordLexicon* was originally designed to store an ASR word vocabulary. The *linguisticUnit* attribute was introduced also to allow the definition of other types of lexicons. The possible values for the *linguisticUnit* attribute are:

- *word*: the default value.
- *syllable*: a sub-word unit (generally comprising two or three phonetic units) derived from pronunciation considerations.
- *morpheme*: a sub-word unit bearing a semantic meaning in itself (e.g. the "psycho" part of word "psychology").
- *stem*: a prefix common to a family of words (e.g. "hous" for "house", "houses", "housing", etc.).
- *affix*: a word segment that needs to be added to a stem to form a word.
- *component*: a constituent part of a compound word that can be useful for compounding languages like German.
- *nonspeech*: a non-linguistic noise.
- *phrase*: a sequence of words, taken as a whole.
- *other*: another linguistic unit defined for a specific application.

The possibility to define non-word lexical entries is very useful. As will be later explained, some spoken content retrieval approaches exploit the above-mentioned linguistic units. The extraction of these units from speech can be done in two ways:

- A word-based ASR system extracts a word lattice. A post- processing of word labels (for instance, a word-to-syllable transcription algorithm based on pronunciation rules) extracts the desired units.
- The ASR system is based on a non-word lexicon. It extracts the desired linguistic information directly from speech. It could be, for instance, a syllable recognizer, based on a complete syllable vocabulary defined for a given language.

In the MPEG-7 *SpokenContent* standard, the case of phonetic units is handled separately with dedicated description tools.

4.3.2.2 *PhoneLexicon*

A *PhoneLexicon* is a list of phones representing the set of phonetic units (basic sounds) used to describe a given language. Each entry of the lexicon is an identifier representing a phonetic unit, according to a specific phonetic alphabet. A *WordLexicon* consists of the following elements:

- *phoneticAlphabet*: is the name of an encoding scheme for phonetic symbols (see below).
- *NumOfOriginalEntries*: is the size of the phonetic lexicon. It depends on the spoken language (generally around 40 units) and the chosen phonetic alphabet.
- A series of *Token* elements: each one stores a *Phone* string corresponding to an entry of the lexicon. The *Phone* strings must not contain white-space characters.

The *phoneticAlphabet* attribute has four possible values:

- *sampa*: use of the symbols from the SAMPA alphabet.[1]
- *ipaSymbol*: use of the symbols from the IPA alphabet.[2]
- *ipaNumber*: use of the three-digit IPA index.[3]
- *other*: use of another, application-specific alphabet.

A *PhoneLexicon* may be associated to one or several *ConfusionCount* descriptions.

4.3.2.3 *ConfusionInfo*

In the *SpokenContentHeader* description, the *ConfusionInfo* field actually refer to a description called *ConfusionCount*. The *ConfusionCount* description contains confusion statistics computed on a given evaluation collection, with a particular ASR system. Given a spoken document in the collection, these statistics are calculated by comparing the two following phonetic transcriptions:

- The reference transcription REF of the document. This results either from manual annotation or from automatic alignment of the canonical phonetic transcription of the speech signal. It is supposed to reflect exactly the phonetic pronunciation of what is spoken in the document.
- The recognized transcription REC of the document. This results from the decoding of the speech signal by the ASR engine. Unlike the reference transcription REF, it is corrupted by substitution, insertion and deletion errors.

The confusion statistics are obtained by string alignment of the two transcriptions, usually by means of a dynamic programming algorithm.

Structure

A *ConfusionCount* description consists of the following elements:

- *numOfDimensions*: the dimensionality of the vectors and matrix in the *ConfusionCount* description. This number must correspond to the size of the *PhoneLexicon* to which the data applies.
- *Insertion*: a vector (of length *numOfDimensions*) of counts, being the number of times a phone was inserted in sequence REC, which is not in REF.
- *Deletion*: a vector (of length *numOfDimensions*) of counts, being the number of times a phone present in sequence REF was deleted in REC.

---

[1] Speech Assessment Methods Phonetic Alphabet (SAMPA): www.phon.ucl.ac.uk/home/sampa.
[2] International Phonetic Association (IPA) Alphabet: http://www2.arts.gla.ac.uk/IPA.
[3] IPA Numbers: http://www2.arts.gla.ac.uk/IPA/IPANumberChart96.pdf.

- *Substitution*: a square matrix (dimension *numOfDimensions*) of counts, reporting for each phone r in row (REF) the number of times that phone has been substituted with the phones h in column (REC). The matrix diagonal gives the number of correct decodings for each phone.

Confusion statistics must be associated to a *PhoneLexicon*, also provided in the descriptor's header. The confusion counts in the above matrix and vectors are ranked according to the order of appearance of the corresponding phones in the lexicon.

Usage
We define the substitution count matrix *Sub*, the insertion and deletion count vectors *Ins* and *Del* respectively and denote the counts in *ConfusionCount* as follows:

- Each element $Sub(r, h)$ of the substitution matrix corresponds to the number of times that a reference phone r of transcription REF was confused with a hypothesized phone h in the recognized sequence REC. The diagonal elements $Sub(r, r)$ give the number of times a phone r was correctly recognized.
- Each element $Ins(h)$ of the insertion vector is the number of times that phone h was inserted in sequence REC when there was nothing in sequence REF at that point.
- Each element $Del(r)$ of the deletion vector is the number of times that phone r in sequence REF was deleted in sequence REC.

The MPEG-7 confusion statistics are stored as pure counts. To be usable in most applications, they must be converted into probabilities. The simplest method is based on the maximum likelihood criterion. According to this method, an estimation of the probability of confusing phone r as phone h (substitution error) is obtained by normalizing the confusion count $Sub(r, h)$ as follows (Ng and Zue, 2000):

$$P_C(r, h) = \frac{Sub(r, h)}{Del(r) + \sum_k Sub(r, k)} \approx P(h|r). \tag{4.6}$$

The denominator of this ratio represents the total number of occurrences of phone r in the whole collection of reference transcriptions.

The P_C matrix that results from the normalization of the confusion count matrix *Sub* is usually called the phone confusion matrix (PCM) of the ASR system. There are many other different ways to calculate such PCMs using Bayesian or maximum entropy techniques. However, the maximum likelihood approach is most straightforward and hence the most commonly used.

The deletion and insertion count vectors *Del* and *Ins* can be normalized in the same way. An estimation of the probability of a phone r being deleted is given by:

$$P_D(r) = \frac{Del(r)}{Del(r) + \sum_k Sub(r, k)} \approx P(\varnothing|r), \tag{4.7}$$

where $\varnothing$ is the null symbol, indicating a phone absence.

Similarly, an estimation of the probabilities of a phone h being inserted, given an insertion took place, is derived from the insertion count vector *Ins*:

$$P_I(h) = \frac{Ins(h)}{\sum_k Ins(k)} \approx P(h|\varnothing). \tag{4.8}$$

The denominator of this ratio represents the total number of insertions in the whole collection; that is, the number of times any phone appeared in a REC sequence where there was nothing in the corresponding REF sequence at that point.

Figure 4.7 gives an example of a phone confusion matrix, along with phone insertion and deletion vectors. This matrix was obtained with a German phone recognizer and a collection of German spoken documents.

The estimated probability values P in the matrix and vectors are represented by grey squares. We used a linear grey scale spanning from white $(P = 0)$ to black $(P = 1)$: the darker the square, the higher the P value.

The phone lexicon consists of 41 German phone symbols derived from the SAMPA phonetic alphabet (Wells, 1997). The blocks along the diagonal group together phones that belong to the same broad phonetic category. The following observations can be made from the results in Figure 4.7:

- The diagonal elements $P_C(r, r)$ correspond to the higher probability values. These are estimations of probabilities $P(r|r)$ that phones r are correctly recognized.
- Phone confusions are not symmetric. Given two phones i and j, we have $P_C(j, i) \neq P_C(i, j)$.
- Most of the phonetic substitution errors occur between phones that are within the same broad phonetic class (Halberstadt, 1998).

The phone confusion information can be used in phone-based retrieval systems, as will be explained later in this chapter.

4.3.2.4 *SpeakerInfo*

The *SpeakerInfo* description contains information about a speaker, which may be shared by several lattices. It effectively contains a *Person* element representing

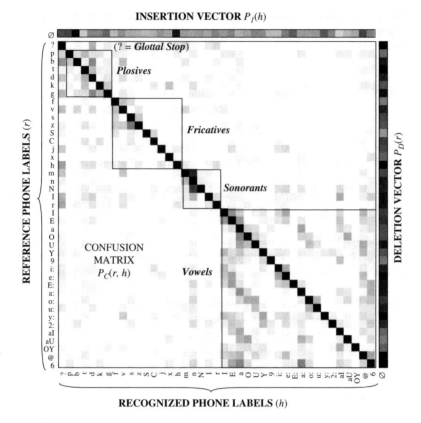

Figure 4.7   Phone confusion matrix of German phones with main phonetic classes

the person who is speaking, but also contains much more information about lattices, such as indexes and references to confusion information and lexicons. A *SpeakerInfo* consists of these elements:

- *Person*: is the name (or any other identifier) of the individual person who is speaking. If this field is not present, the identity of the speaker is unknown.
- *SpokenLanguage*: is the language that is spoken by the speaker. This is distinct from the language in which the corresponding lattices are written, but it is generally assumed that the word and/or phone lexicons of these lattices describe the same spoken language.
- *WordIndex*: consists of a list of words or word *n-grams* (sequences of *n* consecutive words), together with pointers to where each word or word *n*-gram occurs in the lattices concerned. Each speaker has a single word index.
- *PhoneIndex*: consists of a list of phones or phone *n-grams* (sequences of *n* consecutive phones), together with pointers to where each phone or phone

n-gram occurs in the corresponding lattices. Each speaker has a single phone index.

- *defaultLattice*: is the default lattice for the lattice entries in both the word and phone indexes.
- *wordLexiconRef*: is a reference to the word lexicon used by this speaker.
- *phoneLexiconRef*: is a reference to the phone lexicon used by this speaker. Several speakers may share the same word and phone lexicons.
- *confusionInfoRef*: is a reference to a *ConfusionInfo* description that can be used with the phone lexicon referred to by *phoneLexiconRef*.
- *DescriptionMetadata*: contains information about the extraction process.
- *provenance*: indicates the provenance of this decoding.

Five values are possible for the *provenance* attribute:

- *unknown*: the provenance of the lattice is unknown.
- *ASR*: the decoding is the output of an ASR system.
- *manual*: the lattice is manually derived rather than automatic.
- *keyword*: the lattice consists only of keywords rather than full text. This results either from an automatic keyword spotting system, or from manual annotation with a selected set of words. Each keyword should appear as it was spoken in the data.
- *parsing*: the lattice is the result of a higher-level parse, e.g. summary extraction. In this case, a word in the lattice might not correspond directly to words spoken in the data.

4.3.3 *SpokenContentLattice*

The *SpokenContentLattice* contains the complete description of a decoded lattice. It basically consists of a series of nodes and links. Each node contains timing information and each link contains a word or phone. The nodes are partitioned into blocks to allow fast access. A lattice is described by a series of blocks, each block containing a series of nodes and each node a series of links. The block, node and link levels are detailed below.

4.3.3.1 Blocks

A block is defined as a lattice with an upper limit on the number of nodes that it can contain. The decomposition of the lattice into successive blocks introduces some granularity in the spoken content representation of an input speech signal. A block contains the following elements:

- *Node*: is the series of lattice nodes within the block.
- *MediaTime*: indicates the start time and, optionally, the duration of the block.

- *defaultSpeakerInfoRef*: is a reference to a *SpeakerInfo* description. This reference is used where the speaker entry on a node in this lattice is blank. A typical use would be where there is only one speaker represented in the lattice, in which case it would be wasteful to put the same information on each node. In the extreme case that every node has a speaker reference, the *defaultSpeakerRef* is not used, but must contain a valid reference.
- *num*: represents the number of this block. Block numbers range from 0 to 65 535.
- *audio*: is a measure of the audio quality within this block.

The possible values of the *audio* attribute are:

- *unknown*: no information is available.
- *speech*: the signal is known to be clean speech, suggesting a high likelihood of a good transcription.
- *noise*: the signal is known to be non-speech. This might arise when segmentation would have been appropriate but inconvenient.
- *noisySpeech*: the signal is known to be speech, but with facets making recognition difficult. For instance, there could be music in the background.

4.3.3.2 Nodes

Each *Node* element in the lattice blocks encloses the following information:

- *num*: is the number of this node in the current block. Node numbers can range from 0 to 65 535 (the maximum size of a block, in terms of nodes).
- *timeOffset*: is the time offset of this node, measured in one-hundredths of a second, measured from the beginning of the current block. The absolute time is obtained by adding the node offset to the block starting time (given by the *MediaTime* attribute of the current *Block* element).
- *speakerInfoRef*: is an optional reference to the *SpeakerInfo* corresponding to this node. If this attribute is not present, the *DefaultSpeakerInfoRef* attribute of the current block is taken into account. A speaker reference placed on every node may lead to a very large description.
- *WordLink*: a series of *WordLink* descriptions (see the section below) all the links starting from this node and carrying a word hypothesis.
- *PhoneLink*: a series of *PhoneLink* descriptions (see the section below) all the links starting from this node and carrying a phone hypothesis.

4.3.3.3 Links

As mentioned in the node description, there are two kinds of lattice links: *WordLink*, which represents a recognized word; and *PhoneLink*, which represents a recognized phone. Both types can be combined in the same *SpokenContent-Lattice* description (see the example of Figure 4.6). Both word and phone link descriptors inherit from the *SpokenContentLink* descriptor, which contains the following three attributes:

- *probability*: is the probability of the link in the lattice. When several links start from the same node, this indicates which links are the more likely. This information is generally derived from the decoding process. It results from the scores yielded by the recognizer's language model. The *probability* values can be used to extract the most likely path (i.e. the most likely transcription) from the lattice. They may also be used to derive confidence measures on the recognition hypotheses stored in the lattice.
- *nodeOffset*: indicates the node to which this link leads, specified as a relative offset. When not specified, a default offset of 1 is used. A node offset leading out of the current block refers to the next block.
- *acousticScore*: is the score assigned to the link's recognition hypothesis by the acoustic models of the ASR engine. It is given in a logarithmic scale (base e) and indicates the quality of the match between the acoustic models and the corresponding signal segment. It may be used to derive a confidence measure on the link's hypothesis.

The *WordLink* and *PhoneLink* links must be respectively associated to a *WordLexicon* and a *PhoneLexicon* in the descriptor's header. Each phone or word is assigned an index according to its order of appearance in the corresponding phone or word lexicon. The first phone or word appearing in the lexicon is assigned an index value of 0. These indices are used to label word and phone links.

4.4 APPLICATION: SPOKEN DOCUMENT RETRIEVAL

The most common way of exploiting a database of spoken documents indexed by MPEG-7 *SpokenContent* descriptions is to use information retrieval (IR) techniques, adapted to the specifics of spoken content information (Coden *et al.*, 2001).

Traditional IR techniques were initially developed for collections of textual documents (Salton and McGill, 1983). They are still widely used in text databases to identify documents that are likely to be relevant to a free-text query. But the growing amount of data stored and accessible to the general population no longer consists of text-only documents. It includes an increasing part of other media like speech, video and images, requiring other IR techniques. In the past decade, a new IR field has emerged for speech media, which is called spoken document retrieval (SDR).

SDR is the task of retrieving information from a large collection of recorded speech messages (radio broadcasts, spoken segments in audio streams, spoken annotations of pictures, etc.) in response to a user-specified natural language text or spoken query. The relevant items are retrieved based on the spoken content metadata extracted from the spoken documents by means of an ASR system. In this case, ASR technologies are applied not to the traditional task of generating an orthographically correct transcript, but rather to the generation of metadata optimized to provide search and browsing capacity for large spoken word collections.

Compared with the traditional IR field (i.e. text retrieval), a series of questions arises when addressing the particular case of SDR:

- How far can the traditional IR methods and text analysis technologies be applied in the new application domains enabled by ASR?
- More precisely, to what extent are IR methods that work on perfect text applicable to imperfect speech transcripts? As speech recognition will never be perfect, SDR methods must be robust in the face of recognition errors.
- To what extent is the performance of an SDR system dependent on the ASR accuracy?
- What additional data resulting from the speech recognition process may be exploited by SDR applications?
- How can sub-word indexing units be used efficiently in the context of SDR?

This chapter aims at giving an insight into these different questions, and at providing an overview of what techniques have been proposed so far to address them.

4.4.1 Basic Principles of IR and SDR

This section is a general presentation of the IR and SDR fields. It introduces a series of terms and concept definitions.

4.4.1.1 IR Definitions

In an IR system a user has an information need, which is expressed as a text (or spoken) request. The system's task is to return a ranked list of documents (drawn from an archive) that are best matched to that information need. We recall the structure of a typical indexing and retrieval system in Figure 4.8. It mainly consists of the following steps:

1. Let us consider a given collection of documents, a *document* denoting here any object carrying information (a piece of text, an image, a sound or a video). Each new document added to the database is processed to obtain a *document representation D*, also called *document description*. It is this form

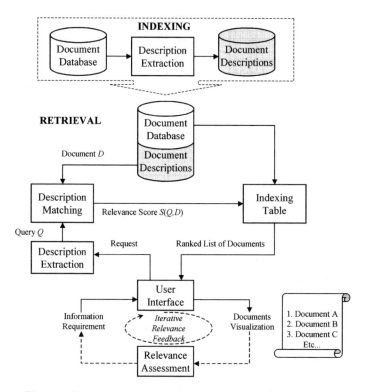

Figure 4.8 General structure of an indexing and retrieval system

of the document that represents it in the IR process. *Indexing* is the process of producing such document representations.

2. The *request*, i.e. the expression of the user's information need, is input to the system through an interface.

3. This request is processed to produce a *query Q* (the request description).

4. The query is matched against each document description in the database. In general, the matching process yields a relevance score for each document, where relevance means the extent to which a document satisfies the underlying user's information requirement. The relevance score is also called the retrieval status value (RSV).

5. A ranked list of documents is formed, according to their respective relevance scores.

6. The corresponding documents are extracted from the database and displayed by means of an interface.

7. Optionally, the initial request may be subsequently refined by means of an *iterative relevance feedback* strategy. After each retrieval pass, a relevance assessment made on the best-ranked documents allows a new request to be formed.

An indexing and retrieval strategy relies on the choice of an appropriate *retrieval model*. Basically, such a model is defined by the choice of two elements:

- The nature of the indexing information extracted from the documents and requests, and the way it is represented to form adequate queries and document descriptions.
- The retrieval function, which maps the set of possible query–document pairs onto a set of retrieval status values $RSV(Q, D)$, resulting from the matching between a query Q and a document representation D.

There are several ways of defining the relevance score: that is, a value that reflects how much a given document satisfies the user's information requirement. The different approaches can be classified according to two main types of retrieval models: similarity-based IR models and probabilistic IR models (Crestani *et al.*, 1998).

In the first case, the RSV is defined as a *measure of similarity*, reflecting the degree of resemblance between the query and the document descriptions. The most popular similarity-based models are based on the vector space model (VSM), which will be further detailed in the next section.

In the case of probabilistic retrieval models, the relevance status value is evaluated as the probability of relevance to the user's information need. In most probabilistic models, relevance is considered as a dichotomous event: a document is either relevant to a query or not. Then, according to the probability ranking principle (Robertson, 1977), optimal retrieval performance can be achieved by the retrieval system when documents D are ranked in decreasing order of their evaluated probabilities $P(\text{``}D\ relevant\text{''}|Q, D)$ of being judged relevant to a query Q.

In the following sections, different retrieval models are presented, in the particular context of SDR. A sound theoretical formalization of IR models is beyond the scope of this chapter. The following approaches will be described from the point of view of similarity-based models only, although some of them integrate some information in a probabilistic way, in particular the probabilistic string matching approaches introduced in Section 4.4.5.2. Hence, the retrieval status value (RSV) will be regarded in the following as a measure of similarity between a document description and a query.

4.4.1.2 SDR Definitions

The schema depicted in Figure 4.9 describes the structure of an SDR system. Compared with the general schema depicted in Figure 4.8, a spoken retrieval system presents the following peculiarities:

- Documents are speech recordings, either individually recorded or resulting from the segmentation of the audio streams of larger audiovisual (AV)

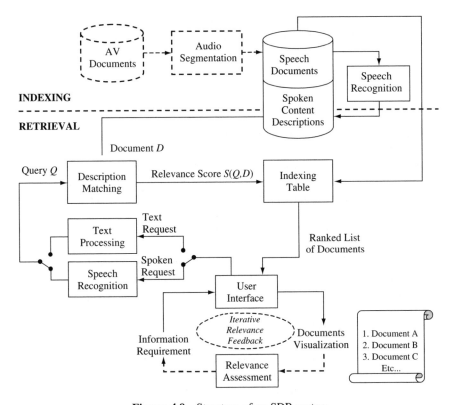

Figure 4.9 Structure of an SDR system

documents. If necessary, a segmentation step may be applied to identify spoken parts and discard non-speech signals (or non-exploitable speech signals, e.g. if too noisy), and/or to divide large spoken segments into shorter and semantically more relevant fragments, e.g. through speaker segmentation.

- A document representation D is the spoken content description extracted through ASR from the corresponding speech recording. To make the SDR system conform to the MPEG-7 standard, this representation must be encapsulated in an MPEG-7 *SpokenContent* description.
- The request is either a text or spoken input to the system. Depending on the retrieval scenario, whole sentences or single word requests may be used.
- The query is the text or spoken content description extracted from the request. A spoken request requires the use of an ASR system in order to extract a spoken content description. A text request may be submitted to a text processing module.

The relevance score results this time from the comparison between two spoken content descriptions. In case of a spoken request, the ASR system used to form the query must be compatible with the one used for indexing the database; that is, both systems must be working with the same set of phonetic symbols and/or similar word lexicons. In the same way, it may be necessary to process text requests in order to form queries using the same set of description terms as in the one used to describe the documents.

4.4.1.3 SDR Approaches

Indexing is the process of generating spoken content descriptions of the documents. The units that make up these descriptions are called *indexing features* or *indexing terms*. Given a particular IR application scenario, the choice of a retrieval strategy and, hence, of a calculation method of the relevance score depends on the nature of the indexing terms. These can be of two types in SDR: words or sub-word units. Therefore, researchers have addressed the problem of SDR in mainly two different ways: word-based SDR and sub-word-based SDR (Clements *et al.*, 2001; Logan *et al.*, 2002).

The most straightforward way consists in coupling a word-based ASR engine to a traditional IR system. An LVCSR system is used to convert the speech into text, to which well-established text retrieval methods can be applied (James, 1995).

However, ASR always implies a certain rate of recognition errors, which makes the SDR task different from the traditional text retrieval issue. Recognition errors usually degrade the effectiveness of an SDR system. A first way to address this problem is to improve the speech recognition accuracy, which requires a huge amount of training data and time. Another strategy is to develop retrieval methods that are more error tolerant, out of the traditional text retrieval field. Furthermore, there are two major drawbacks for the word-based approach of SDR.

The first one is the static nature and limited size of the recognition vocabulary, i.e. the set of words that the speech recognition engine uses to translate speech into text. The recognizer's decoding process matches the acoustics extracted from the speech input to words in the vocabulary. Therefore, only words in the vocabulary are capable of being recognized. Any other spoken term is considered OOV. This notion of in-vocabulary and OOV words is an important and well-known issue in SDR (Srinivasan and Petkovic, 2000).

The fact that the indexing vocabulary of a word-based SDR system has to be known beforehand precludes the handling of OOV words. This implies direct restrictions on indexing descriptions and queries:

- Words that are out of the vocabulary of the recognizer are lost in the indexing descriptions, replaced by one or several in-vocabulary words.
- The query vocabulary is implicitly defined by the recognition vocabulary. It is therefore also limited in size and has to be specified beforehand.

A related issue is the growth of the message collections. New words are continually encountered as more data is added. Many of these are out of the initial indexing vocabulary, in particular new proper names, which can be very important for IR purposes. Therefore, the recognizer vocabulary may need to be regularly updated and increased to handle these new words. It is then a difficult practical problem to determine when, how and what new words need to be added and whether the entire message collection needs to be reindexed when the recognizer vocabulary changes. Moreover, it should be kept in mind that there is a practical limit, with current ASR technologies, as far as the size of the recognition vocabulary is concerned.

A second major drawback of word-based SDR is the derivation of stochastic language models, which are necessary for reasonable-quality LVCSR systems. This requires huge amounts of training data containing a sufficient number of occurrences of each recognition–vocabulary word. Furthermore, the training of efficient LVCSR language models often relies on domain-specific data (economical news, medical reports, etc.). If new documents, whose content is not semantically consistent with the LM training data are added to the collection, then the indexing ASR system may perform poorly on them.

With regard to the previous considerations, an alternative way is to perform retrieval on sub-word-level transcriptions provided by a phoneme recognizer. In recent years, a lot of works have considered the indexing of spoken documents with sub-lexical units instead of word hypotheses (Ferrieux and Peillon, 1999; Larson and Eickeler, 2003; Ng, 2000; Ng and Zue, 2000; Wechsler, 1998). In this case, a limited amount of sub-word models is necessary, allowing any speech recording to be indexed (for a given language) with sub-lexical indexing terms, such as phones (Ng, 2000; Ng and Zue, 2000), phonemes (Ferrieux and Peillon, 1999; Wechsler, 1998) or syllables (Larson and Eickeler, 2003). Sub-word-based SDR has the advantages that:

- The use of sub-word indexing terms restrains the size of the indexing lexicon (to a few dozens of units in a given language in the case of phonemes). The memory needs are far smaller than in the case of word-based SDR, which requires the storage of several thousands of vocabulary words.
- The recognizer is less expensive with respect to the training effort. It does not require the training of complex language models, as LVCSR systems do.
- Open-vocabulary retrieval is possible, because the recognition component is not bound to any set of vocabulary words defined a priori.

However, sub-word recognition systems have a major drawback. They have to cope with high error rates, much higher than the word error rates of state-of-the-art LVCSR systems. The error rate of a phone recognition system, for instance, is typically between 30% and 40%. The challenge of sub-word-based SDR is to propose techniques that take into account the presence of these numerous recognition errors in the indexing transcriptions. The information provided by the indexing ASR system, e.g. the ones encapsulated into the header of MPEG-7

SpokenContent descriptions (PCM, acoustic scores, etc.), may be exploited to compensate for the indexing inaccuracy.

In the TREC SDR experiments (Voorhees and Harman, 1998), word-based approaches have consistently outperformed phoneme approaches. However, there are several reasons for using phonemes. Indeed, the successful use of LVCSR word-based recognition implies three assumptions about the recognition process:

- The recognizer uses a large vocabulary.
- The semantic content of spoken documents is consistent with the recognizer's vocabulary and language model.
- Enough computational resources are available.

If these prerequisites are not fulfilled, then a sub-word SDR approach may perform better than word-based SDR. Thus, limited computational resources, in the case of small hand-held speech recognition devices for example, may hinder the management of very large vocabularies. In the same way, the huge data resources required to build an efficient language model may not be available. Besides, as reported earlier, some retrieval systems may have to deal with steadily growing data collections, continuously enriched with new words, in particular new proper names (e.g. broadcast news).

Finally, both word and phoneme recognition-based SDR have also been investigated in combination. First results indicate that combined methods outperform either single approach; however, they require larger recognition effort. All these different approaches are detailed in the following sections.

4.4.2 Vector Space Models

The most basic IR strategy is the *Boolean matching searching*, which simply consists of looking for the documents containing at least one of the query terms, and outputting the results without ranking them. However, this method is only relevant for the most basic retrieval applications. More accurate retrieval results are obtained with *best-matching search* approaches, in which the comparison of the query with a document description returns a retrieval status value (RSV) reflecting their degree of similarity. In the traditional text retrieval field, the most widely used RSV calculation methods are based on the vector space model (VSM) (Salton and McGill, 1983).

A VSM creates an indexing term space T, formed by the set of all possible indexing terms, in which both document representations and queries are described by vectors. Given a query Q and a document representation D, two N_T-dimensional vectors q and d are generated, where N_T is the predefined number of indexing terms (i.e. the cardinality of set T, $N_T = |T|$). Each component of q and d represents a weight associated to a particular indexing term. We will denote by $q(t)$ and $d(t)$ the components of description vectors q and d corresponding to a particular indexing term t.

4.4.2.1 Weighting Methods

Different weighting schemes can be used (James, 1995; Salton and Buckley, 1988). The most straightforward is to use binary-valued vectors, in which each component is simply set to "1", if the corresponding indexing term is present in the description, or "0" otherwise. For a given term t, the binary weighting of q and d can be written as:

$$q(t) = \begin{cases} 1 & \text{if } t \in Q \\ 0 & \text{otherwise} \end{cases} \quad \text{and} \quad d(t) = \begin{cases} 1 & \text{if } t \in D \\ 0 & \text{otherwise.} \end{cases} \tag{4.9}$$

More complex weighting methods make use of real-valued vectors, allowing us to give a higher weight (not restricted to 0 and 1 values) to terms of higher importance.

A classical IR approach is to take account of indexing term statistics within individual document representations, as well as in the whole document collection. The weight of term t is expressed as:

$$d(t) = \log(1 + f_d(t)) \tag{4.10}$$

in the document vector d, and as:

$$q(t) = \log(1 + f_q(t)) \log\left(\frac{N_c}{n_c(t)}\right) \tag{4.11}$$

in the query vector q. In the two expressions above, $f_d(t)$ is the frequency (i.e. the number of occurrences) of term t in document description D, $f_q(t)$ is the frequency of term t in query Q, N_c is the total number of documents in the collection and $n_c(t)$ the number of documents containing term t. A term that does not occur in a representation (either D or Q) is given a null weight.

The $N_c/n_c(t)$ ratio is called the inverse document frequency (IDF) of term t. Terms that occur in a small number of documents have a higher IDF weight than terms occurring in many documents. It is supposed here that infrequent terms may carry more information in terms of relevancy. Given a document collection, the IDF can be computed beforehand, for every element of the indexing term set. It is taken into account into query term weights rather than document term weights for reasons of computational efficiency.

4.4.2.2 Retrieval Functions

After a weighting method has assigned weights to indexing terms occurring in the document and the query, these weights are combined by the retrieval function to calculate the RSV. As stated above, the RSV will be considered here as a similarity measure reflecting how relevant a document is for a given query. It allows us to create a list of documents, ordered according to the RSVs, which is returned to the user.

The most straightforward way of measuring the degree of similarity between a query Q and a document description D is to count the number of terms they have in common. Taking the binary weighting of Equation (4.9), the binary query–document similarity measure (also called *coordination level* or *quorum* matching function) is then expressed as:

$$RSV_{bin}(Q, D) = \sum_{t \in Q} q(t).d(t) = |Q \cap D|. \tag{4.12}$$

It should be noted that the Boolean matching searching mentioned at the beginning of the section can be formalized in the VSM framework, by considering $q(t)$ and $d(t)$ as Boolean variables (with a Boolean weighting scheme) and combining q and d as in Equation (4.12) with addition and multiplication operators representing the logical *AND* and *OR* operators. All relevant documents yield an RSV of 1, all the others a null value.

From a more general point of view, classical IR models evaluate the RSV of a document D with regard to a query Q using some variant of the following basic formula, which is the inner product of vectors d and q:

$$RSV_c(Q, D) = \sum_{t \in T} q(t).d(t), \tag{4.13}$$

where T is the global set of indexing terms, $d(t)$ is the indexing weight assigned to term t in the context of document D, and $q(t)$ is the indexing weight assigned to term t in the context of query Q.

Another formulation, which has proved to be effective for word-based retrieval (Salton and Buckley, 1988), is to normalize the inner product of Equation (4.13) by the product of the norms of vectors q and d. This formulation is called the cosine similarity measure:

$$RSV_{norm}(Q, D) = \frac{\sum_{t \in T} q(t).d(t)}{\sqrt{\sum_{t \in T} q(t)^2 . \sum_{t \in T} d(t)^2}} = \frac{1}{\|q\|.\|d\|} \sum_{t \in T} q(t).d(t). \tag{4.14}$$

Originally developed for use on text document collections, these models have some limitations when applied to SDR, in particular because there is no mechanism for an approximate matching of indexing terms. The next section addresses this issue.

4.4.2.3 Indexing Term Similarities

A fundamental and well-known problem of classical text retrieval systems is the *term mismatch* problem (Crestani, 2002). It has been observed that the requests of a given user and the corresponding relevant documents in the collection frequently use different terms to refer to the same concepts. Therefore, matching functions that look for exact occurrences of query terms in the documents often produce an incorrect relevance ranking. Naturally, this problem also concerns

SDR systems, which consist of an LVCSR system coupled with a text retrieval system.

Moreover, SDR has to cope with another more specific problem, when terms misrecognized by the ASR system (or simply out of the recognizer's vocabulary) are found not to match within query and document representations. This hinders the effectiveness of the IR system in a way similar to the term mismatch problem. By analogy to the term mismatch problem, this was called the *term misrecognition* problem by (Crestani, 2002).

By taking into account only the matching terms in query and document representations (i.e. terms t belonging to $Q \cap D$), the classical IR functions of the previous section are inappropriate to tackle the term mismatch and term misrecognition problems. However, supposing that some information about the degree of similarity between terms t in the term space T is available, it could be used in the evaluation of the RSV to account for the term mismatch problem.

This concept of term similarity is defined here as a measure that evaluates, for a given pair of index terms, how close the terms are according to a metric based on some properties of the space that we want to observe. For a given indexing space T, term similarity is a function s that we will define as follows:

$$T \times T \to R$$

$$(t_i, t_j) \to s(t_i, t_j). \tag{4.15}$$

Some works have proposed retrieval models that exploit the knowledge of term similarity in the term space (Crestani, 2002). Term similarity is used at retrieval time to estimate the relevance of a document in response to a query. The retrieval system looks not only at matching terms, but also at non-matching terms, which are considered similar according to the term similarity function.

There are two possible ways of exploiting the term similarity in the evaluation of relevance scores, each method being associated to one of the following types of IR models:

- The $Q \to D$ models examine each term in the query Q. In this case, the retrieval function measures how much of the query content is specified in the document (the *specificity* of the document to the query is measured).
- The $D \to Q$ models examine each term in the document D. In that case, the retrieval function measures how much of the document content is required by the query (the *exhaustivity* of the document to the query is measured).

The $Q \to D$ models consider the IR problem from the point of view of the query. If a matching document term cannot be found for a given query term t_i, we look for similar document terms t_j, based on the similarity term function $s(t_i, t_j)$.

The general formula of the RSV is then derived from Equation (4.13) in the following manner:

$$RSV_{Q \to D}(Q, D) = \sum_{t_i \in Q} q(t_i).\phi\left(s(t_i, t_j), d(t_j)\right)_{|t_j \in D} \qquad (4.16)$$

where t_i is a query term, t_j is a document term and ϕ is a function which determines the use that is made of the similarities between terms t_i and t_j.

This model can be seen as a generalization of the classical IR approach mentioned in Equation (4.13). The inner product of q and d is obtained by taking:

$$s(t_i, t_j) = \begin{cases} 1 & \text{if } t_i = t_j \\ 0 & \text{otherwise} \end{cases} \quad \text{and} \quad \phi(s(t_i, t_j), d(t_j))_{|t_j \in D} = d(t_i). \qquad (4.17)$$

A natural approach to the definition of function ϕ is to take into account for each query term t_i the contribution of all matching and non-matching document terms t_j:

$$\phi_{tot}(s(t_i, t_j), d(t_j))_{|t_j \in D} = \sum_{t_j \in D} s(t_i, t_j).d(t_j). \qquad (4.18)$$

The RSV is then expressed as:

$$RSV^{tot}_{Q \to D}(Q, D) = \sum_{t_i \in Q} \left[\sum_{t_j \in D} s(t_i, t_j).d(t_j) \right].q(t_i). \qquad (4.19)$$

A simpler approach consists of retaining for each query term the most similar document term only, by taking the following combination function:

$$\phi_{max}(s(t_i, t_j), d(t_j))_{|t_j \in D} = \max_{t_j \in D} \lfloor s(t_i, t_j).d(t_j) \rfloor, \qquad (4.20)$$

and then:

$$RSV^{max}_{Q \to D}(Q, D) = \sum_{t \in Q} s(t, t^*).d(t^*).q(t) \quad \text{with} \quad t^* = \underset{t' \in D}{\operatorname{argmax}}(s(t, t')). \quad (4.21)$$

Considering each query term $t(t \in Q)$ one by one, the RSV_{max} approach consists of the following procedure:

- If there is a matching term in the document ($t \in D$), the $q(t).d(t)$ term of the inner product of q and d is weighted by $s(t, t)$.
- In the case of non-matching ($t \notin D$), the closest term to t in D (denoted by t^*) is looked for, and a new term is introduced into the normal inner product. Within the document representation D, the absent indexing term t is approximated by t^*. It can be thus interpreted as an expansion of the document representation (Moreau *et al.*, 2004b, 2004c).

Compared with a classical IR approach, such as the binary approach of Equation (4.12), non-matching terms are taken into account.

In a symmetrical way, the $D \to Q$ *model considers* the IR problem from the point of view of the document. If a matching query term cannot be found for a given query term t_j, we look for similar query terms t_i, based on the similarity term function $s(t_i, t_j)$. The general formula of the RSV is then:

$$RSV_{D \to Q}(Q, D) = \sum_{t_j \in D} d(t_j) . \varphi(s(t_i, t_j), q(t_i))_{|t_i \in Q} \qquad (4.22)$$

where φ is a function which determines the use that is made of the similarities between a given document term t_j and the query terms t_i.

It is straightforward to apply to the $D \to Q$ case the RSV expressions given in Equation (4.19):

$$RSV_{D \to Q}^{tot}(Q, D) = \sum_{t_j \in D} \left[\sum_{t_i \in Q} s(t_i, t_j) . q(t_i) \right] . d(t_j) \qquad (4.23)$$

and Equation (4.21):

$$RSV_{D \to Q}^{max}(Q, D) = \sum_{t \in D} s(t^*, t) . d(t) . q(t^*) \quad \text{with} \quad t^* = \underset{t' \in Q}{\text{argmax}}(s(t', t)). \qquad (4.24)$$

According to the nature of the SDR indexing terms, different forms of term similarity functions can be defined.

In the same way that we have made a distinction in Section 4.4.1.3 between word-based and sub-word- based SDR approaches, we will distinguish two forms of term similarities:

- *Semantic term similarity*, when indexing terms are words. In this case, each individual indexing term carries some semantic information.
- *Acoustic similarity*, when indexing terms are sub-word units. In the case of phonetic indexing units, we will talk about *phonetic similarity*. The indexing terms have no semantic meaning in themselves and essentially carry some acoustic information.

The corresponding similarity functions and the way they can be used for computing retrieval scores will be presented in the next sections.

4.4.3 Word-Based SDR

Word-based SDR is quite similar to text-based IR. Most word-based SDR systems simply process text transcriptions delivered by an ASR system with text retrieval methods. Thus, we will mainly review approaches initially developed in the framework of text retrieval.

4.4.3.1 LVCSR and Text Retrieval

With state-of-the-art LVCSR systems it is possible to generate reasonably accurate word transcriptions. These can be used for indexing spoken document collections. The combination of word recognition and text retrieval allows the employment of text retrieval techniques that have been developed and optimized over decades.

Classical text-based approaches use the VSM described in Section 4.4.2. Most of them are based on the weighting schemes and retrieval functions given by Equations (4.10), (4.11) and (4.14).

Other retrieval functions have been proposed, notably the Okapi function, which is considered to work better than the cosine similarity measure with text retrieval. The relevance score is given by the Okapi formula (Srinivasan and Petkovic, 2000):

$$RSV_{Okapi}(Q, D) = \sum_{t \in Q} \frac{f_q(t) f_d(t) \log(IDF'(t))}{\alpha_1 + (\alpha_2 l_d / L_c) + f_d(t)} \qquad (4.25)$$

where l_d is the length of the document transcription in number of words and L_c is the mean document transcription length across the collection. The parameters α_1 and α_2 are positive real constants, set to $\alpha_1 = 0.5$ and $\alpha_2 = 1.5$ in (Srinivasan and Petkovic, 2000). The inverse document frequency $IDF'(t)$ of term t is defined here in a slightly different way compared with Equation (4.11):

$$IDF'(t) = \frac{N_c - n_c(t) + 0.5}{n_c(t) + 0.5} \qquad (4.26)$$

where N_c is the total number of documents in the collection, and $n_c(t)$ is the number of documents containing t.

However, as mentioned above, these classical text retrieval models fall into the term mismatch problem, since they do not take into account that the same concept could be expressed using different terms within documents and within queries. In word-based SDR, two main approaches are possible to tackle this problem:

- Text processing of the text transcriptions of documents, in order to map the initial indexing term space into a reduced term space, more suitable for retrieval purposes.
- Definition of a word similarity measure (also called semantic term similarity measure).

In most text retrieval systems, two standard IR text pre-processing steps are applied (Salton and McGill, 1983). The first one simply consists of removing *stop words* – usually consisting of high-frequency function words such as conjugations, prepositions and pronouns – which are considered uninteresting in terms of relevancy. This process, called *word stopping*, relies on a predefined list of stop words, such as the one used for English in the Cornell SMART system (Buckley, 1985).

Further text pre-processing usually aims at reducing the dimension of the indexing term space using a word mapping technique. The idea is to map words into a set of semantic clusters. Different dimensionality reduction methods can be used (Browne *et al.*, 2002; Gauvain *et al.*, 2000; Johnson *et al.*, 2000):

- Conflation of word variants using a word *stemming* (or *suffix stripping*) method: each indexing word is reduced to a *stem*, which is the common prefix – sometimes the common root – of a family of words. This is done according to a rule- based removal of the derivational and inflection suffixes of words (e.g. "house", "houses" and "housing" could be mapped to the stem "hous"). The most largely used stemming method is Porter's algorithm (Porter, 1980).
- Conflation based on the *n*-gram matching technique: words are clustered according to the count of common *n-grams* (sequences of three characters, or three phonetic units) within pairs of indexing words.
- Use of automatic or manual thesauri.

The application of these text normalization methods results in a new, more compact set of indexing terms. Using this reduced set in place of the initial indexing vocabulary makes the retrieval process less liable to term mismatch problems.

The second method to reduce the effects of the term mismatch problem relies on the notion of term similarity introduced in Section 4.4.2.3. It consists of deriving semantic similarity measures between words from the document collection, based on a statistical analysis of the different contexts in which terms occur in documents. The idea is to define a quantity which measures how semantically close two indexing terms are.

One of the most often used measures of semantic similarity is the expected mutual information measure (EMIM) (Crestani, 2002):

$$s_{word}(t_i, t_j) = EMIM(t_i, t_j) = \sum_{t_i, t_j} P(t_i \in D, t_j \in D) \log \frac{P(t_i \in D, t_j \in D)}{P(t_i \in D)P(t_j \in D)} \quad (4.27)$$

where t_i and t_j are two elements of the indexing term set. The EMIM between two terms can be interpreted as a measure of the statistical information contained in one term about the other. Two terms are considered semantically closed if they both tend to occur in the same documents. One EMIM estimation technique is proposed in (van Rijsbergen, 1979). Once a semantic similarity measure has been defined, it can be taken into account in the computation of the RSV as described in Section 4.4.2.3.

As mentioned above, SDR has also to cope with word recognition errors (term misrecognition problem). It is possible to recover some errors when alternative word hypotheses are generated by the recognizer through an *n*-best list of word transcriptions or a lattice of words. However, for most LVCSR-based SDR systems, the key point remains the quality of the ASR transcription machine itself, i.e. its ability to operate efficiently and accurately in a large and diverse domain.

4.4.3.2 Keyword Spotting

A simplified version of the word-based approach consists of using a keyword spotting system in place of a complete continuous recognizer (Morris *et al.*, 2004). In this case, only keywords (and not complete word transcriptions) are extracted from the input speech stream and used to index the requests and the spoken documents. The indexing term set is reduced to a small set of keywords.

As mentioned earlier, classical keyword spotting applies a threshold on the acoustic score of keyword candidates to decide validating or rejecting them. Retrieval performance varies with the choice of the decision threshold. At low threshold values, performance is impaired by a high proportion of false alarms. Conversely, higher thresholds remove a significant number of true hits, also degrading retrieval performance. Finding an acceptable trade-off point is not an easy problem to solve.

Speech retrieval using word spotting is limited by the small number of practical search terms (Jones *et al.*, 1996). Moreover, the set of keywords has to be chosen a priori, which requires advanced knowledge about the content of the speech documents or what the possible user queries may be.

4.4.3.3 Query Processing and Expansion Techniques

Different forms of user requests are possible for word-based SDR systems, depending on the indexing and retrieval scenario:

- Text requests: this is a natural form of request for LVCSR-based SDR systems. Written sentences usually have to be pre-processed (e.g. word stopping).
- Continuous spoken requests: these have to be processed by an LVCSR system. There is a risk in introducing new misrecognized terms in the retrieval process.
- Isolated query terms: this kind of query does not require any pre-processing. It fits the simple keyword-based indexing and retrieval systems.

Whatever the request is, the resulting query has to be processed with the same word stopping and conflation methods as the ones applied in the indexing step (Browne *et al.*, 2002). Before being matched with one another, the queries and document representations have to be formed from the same set of indexing terms.

From the query point of view, two approaches can be employed to tackle the term mismatch problem:

- Automatic expansion of queries;
- Relevance feedback techniques.

In fact, both approaches are different ways of *expanding* the query, i.e. of increasing the initial set of query terms in such a way that the new query corresponds better to the user's information need (Crestani, 1999). We give below a brief overview of these two techniques.

Automatic query expansion consists of automatically adding terms to the query by selecting those that are most similar to the ones used originally by the user. A semantic similarity measure such as the one given in Equation (4.27) is required. According to this measure, a list of similar terms is then generated for each query term. However, setting a threshold on similarity measures in order to form similar term lists is a difficult problem. If the threshold is too selective, not enough terms may be added to improve the retrieval performance significantly. On the contrary, the addition of too many terms may result in a sensible drop in retrieval efficiency.

Relevance feedback is another strategy for improving the retrieval efficiency. At the end of a retrieval pass, the user selects manually from the list of retrieved documents the ones he or she considers relevant. This process is called *relevance assessment* (see Figure 4.8). The query is then reformulated to make it more representative of the documents assessed as "relevant" (and hence less representative of the "irrelevant" ones). Finally, a new retrieval process is started, where documents are matched against the modified query. The initial query can be thus refined iteratively through consecutive retrieval and relevance assessment passes.

Several relevance feedback methods have been proposed (James, 1995, pp. 35–37). In the context of classical VSM approaches, they are generally based on a re-weighting method of the query vector q (Equation 4.11). For instance, a commonly used query reformulation strategy, the Rocchio algorithm (Ng and Zue, 2000), forms a new query vector q' from a query vector q by adding terms found in the documents assessed as relevant and removing terms found in the retrieved non-relevant documents in the following way:

$$q' = \alpha q + \beta \left(\frac{1}{N_r} \sum_{d \in D_r} d \right) - \gamma \left(\frac{1}{N_n} \sum_{d \in D_n} d \right) \tag{4.28}$$

where D_r is the set of N_r relevant documents, D_n is the set of N_n non-relevant documents, and α, β and γ are tuneable parameters controlling the relative contribution of the original, added and removed terms, respectively. The original terms are scaled by α, the added terms (resp. subtracted terms) are weighted proportionally to their average weight across the set of N_r relevant (resp. N_n non-relevant) documents. A threshold can be placed on the number of new terms that are added to the query.

Classical relevance feedback is an interactive and subjective process, where the user has to select a set of relevant documents at the end of a retrieval pass. In order to avoid human relevance assessment, a simple automatic relevance feedback procedure is also possible by assuming that the top N_r retrieved documents are relevant and the bottom N_n retrieved documents are non-relevant (Ng and Zue, 2000).

The basic principle of query expansion and relevance feedback techniques is rather simple. But practically, a major difficulty lies in finding the best terms to add and in weighting their importance in a correct way. Terms added to the query must be weighted in such a way that their importance in the context of the query will not modify the original concept expressed by the user.

4.4.4 Sub-Word-Based Vector Space Models

Word-based retrieval approaches face the problem of either having to know a priori the keywords to search for (keyword spotting), or requiring a very large recognition vocabulary in order to cover the growing and diverse message collections (LVCSR). The use of sub-words as indexing terms is a way of avoiding these difficulties. First, it dramatically restrains the set of indexing terms needed to cover the language. Furthermore, it makes the indexing and retrieval process independent of any word vocabulary, virtually allowing for the detection of any user query terms during retrieval.

Several works have investigated the feasibility of using sub-word unit representations for SDR as an alternative to words generated by either keyword spotting or continuous speech recognition. The next sections will review the most significant ones.

4.4.4.1 Sub-Word Indexing Units

This section provides a non-exhaustive list of different sub-lexical units that have been used in recent years for indexing spoken documents.

Phones and Phonemes

The most encountered sub-lexical indexing terms are phonetic units, among which one makes the distinction between the two notions of *phone* and *phoneme* (Gold and Morgan, 1999). The phones of a given language are defined as the base set of all individual sounds used to describe this language. Phones are usually written in square brackets (e.g. [m a t]). Phonemes form the set of unique sound categories used by a given language. A phoneme represents a class of phones. It is generally defined by the fact that within a given word, replacing a phone with another of the same phoneme class does not change the word's meaning. Phonemes are usually written between slashes (e.g. /m a t/). Whereas phonemes are defined by human perception, phones are generally derived from data and used as a basic speech unit by most speech recognition systems.

Examples of phone–phoneme mapping are given in (Ng *et al.*, 2000) for the English language (an initial phone set of 42 phones is mapped to a set of 32 phonemes), and in (Wechsler, 1998) for the German language (an initial phone set of 41 phones is mapped to a set of 35 phonemes). As phoneme classes generally group phonetically similar phones that are easily confusable by an ASR system, the phoneme error rate is lower than the phone error rate.

The MPEG-7 *SpokenContent* description allows for the storing of the recognizer's phone dictionary (SAMPA is recommended (Wells, 1997)). In order to work with phonemes, the stored phone-based descriptions have to be post-processed by operating the desired phone–phoneme mapping. Another possibility is to store phoneme-based descriptions directly along with the corresponding set of phonemes.

Broad Phonetic Classes

Phonetic classes other than phonemes have been used in the context of IR. These classes can be formed by grouping acoustically similar phones based on some acoustic measurements and data-driven clustering methods, such as the standard hierarchical clustering algorithm (Hartigan, 1975). Another approach consists of using a predefined set of linguistic rules to map the individual phones into broad phonetic classes such as back vowel, voiced fricative, nasal, etc. (Chomsky and Halle, 1968). Using such a reduced set of indexing symbols offers some advantages in terms of storage and computational efficiency. However, experiments have shown that using too coarse phonetic classes strongly degrades the retrieval efficiency in comparison with phones or phoneme classes (Ng, 2000).

Sequences of Phonetic Units

Instead of using phones or phonemes as the basic indexing unit, it was proposed to develop retrieval methods where sequences of phonetic units constitute the sub-word indexing term representation. A two-step procedure is used to generate the sub-word unit representations. First, a speech recognizer (based on a phone or phoneme lexicon) is used to create phonetic transcriptions of the speech messages. Then the recognized phonetic units are processed to produce the sub-word unit indexing terms.

The most widely used multi-phone units are *phonetic n-grams*. These sub-word units are produced by successively concatenating the appropriate number n of consecutive phones (or phonemes) from the phonetic transcriptions. Figure 4.10 shows the expansion of the English phonetic transcription of the word "*Retrieval*" to its corresponding set of 3-grams.

Aside from the one-best transcription, additional recognizer hypotheses can also be used, in particular the alternative transcriptions stored in an output lattice. The n-grams are extracted from phonetic lattices in the same way as before. Figure 4.11 shows the set of 3-grams extracted from a lattice of English phonetic hypotheses resulting from the ASR processing of the word "*Retrieval*" spoken in isolation.

Figure 4.10   Extraction of phone 3-grams from a phonetic transcription

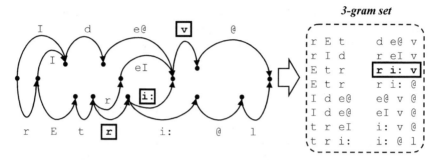

Figure 4.11 Extraction of phone 3-gram from a phone lattice decoding

As can be seen in the two examples above, the *n*-grams overlap with each other. Non-overlapping types of phonetic sequences have been explored. One of these is called *multigrams* (Ng and Zue, 2000). These are variable-length, phonetic sequences discovered automatically by applying an iterative unsupervised learning algorithm previously used in developing multigram language models for speech recognition (Deligne and Binbot, 1995). The multigram model assumes that a phone sequence is composed of a concatenation of independent, non-overlapping, variable-length phone sub-sequences (with some maximal length *m*). Another possible type of non-overlapping phonetic sequences is variable-length syllable units generated automatically from phonetic transcriptions by means of linguistic rules (Ng and Zue, 2000).

Experiments by (Ng and Zue, 1998) lead to the conclusion that overlapping sub-word units (*n*-grams) are better suited for SDR than non-overlapping units (multigrams, rule-based syllables). Units with overlap provide more chances for partial matches and, as a result, are more robust to variations in the phonetic realization of the words. Hence, the impact of phonetic variations is reduced for overlapping sub-word units.

Several sequence lengths *n* have been proposed for *n*-grams. There exists a trade-off between the number of phonetic classes and the sequence length required to achieve good performance. As the number of classes is reduced, the length of the sequence needs to increase to retain performance. Generally, the phone or phoneme 3-gram terms are chosen in the context of sub-word SDR. The choice of $n = 3$ as the optimal length of the phone sequences has been motivated in several studies either by the average length of syllables in most languages or by empirical studies (Moreau *et al.*, 2004a; Ng *et al.*, 2000; Ng, 2000; Srinivasan and Petkovic, 2000). In most cases, the use of individual phones as indexing terms, which is a particular case of *n*-gram (with $n = 1$), does not allow any acceptable level of retrieval performance.

All those different indexing terms are not directly accessible from MPEG-7 *SpokenContent* descriptors. They have to be extracted as depicted in Figure 4.11 in the case of 3-grams.

Syllables

Instead of generating syllable units from phonetic transcriptions as mentioned above, a predefined set of syllable models can be trained to design a syllable recognizer. In this case, each syllable is modelled with an HMM, and a specific LM, such as a syllable bigram, is trained (Larson and Eickeler, 2003). The sequence or graph of recognized syllables is then directly generated by the indexing recognition system.

An advantage of this approach is that the recognizer can be optimized specifically for the sub-word units of interest. In addition, the recognition units are larger and should be easier to recognize. The recognition accuracy of the syllable indexing terms is improved in comparison with the case of phone- or phoneme-based indexing. A disadvantage is that the vocabulary size is significantly increased, making the indexing a little less flexible and requiring more storage and computation capacities (both for model training and decoding). There is a trade-off in the selection of a satisfactory set of syllable units. It has both to be restricted in size and to describe accurately the linguistic content of large spoken document collections.

The MPEG-7 *SpokenContent* description offers the possibility to store the results of a syllable-based recognizer, along with the corresponding syllable lexicon. It is important to mention that, contrary to the previous case (e.g. *n*-grams), the indexing terms here are directly accessible from *SpokenContent* descriptors.

VCV Features

Another classical sub-word retrieval approach is the VCV (Vowel–Consonant–Vowel) method (Glavitsch and Schäuble, 1992; James, 1995). A VCV indexing term results from the concatenation of three consecutive phonetic sequences, the first and last ones consisting of vowels, the middle one of consonants: for example, the word "information" contains the three VCV features "info", "orma" and "atio" (Wechsler, 1998). The recognition system (used for indexing) is built by training an acoustic model for each predetermined VCV feature.

VCV features can be useful to describe common stems of equivalent word inflection and compounds (e.g. "descr" in "describe", "description", etc.). The weakness of this approach is that VCV features are selected from text, without taking acoustic and linguistic properties into account as in the case of syllables.

4.4.4.2 Query Processing

As seen in Section 4.4.3.3, different forms of user query strategies can be designed in the context of SDR. But the use of sub-word indexing terms implies some differences with the word-based case:

- *Text request.* A text request requires that user query words are transformed into sequences of sub-word units so that they can be matched against the sub-lexical representations of the documents. Single words are generally transcribed by means of a pronunciation dictionary.

- *Continuous spoken request.* If the request is processed by an LVCSR system (which means that a second recognizer, different from the one used for indexing, is required), a word transcription is generated and processed as above. The direct use of a sub-word recognizer to yield an adequate sub-lexical transcription of the query can lead to some difficulties, mainly because word boundaries are ignored. Therefore, no word stopping technique is possible. Moreover, sub-lexical units spanning across word boundaries may be generated. As a result, the query representation may consist of a large set of sub-lexical terms (including a lot of undesired ones), inadequate for IR.
- *Word spoken in isolation.* In that particular case, the indexing recognizer may be used to generate a sub-word transcription directly. This makes the system totally independent of any word vocabulary, but recognition errors are introduced in the query too.

In most SDR systems the lexical information (i.e. word boundaries) is taken into account in the query processing process. On the one hand, this makes the application of classical text pre-processing techniques possible (such as the word stopping process already described in Section 4.4.3.3). On the other hand, each query word can be processed independently. Figure 4.12 depicts how a text query can be processed by a phone-based retrieval system.

In the example of Figure 4.12, the query is processed on two levels:

- *Semantic level.* The initial query is a sequence of words. Word stopping is applied to discard words that do not carry any exploitable information. Other text pre-processing techniques such as word stemming can also be used.
- *Phonetic level.* Each query word is transcribed into a sequence of phonetic units and processed separately as an independent query by the retrieval algorithm.

Words can be phonetically transcribed via a pronunciation dictionary, such as the CMU dictionary[1] for English or the BOMP[2] dictionary for German. Another automatic word-to-phone transcription method consists of applying a rule-based text-to-phone algorithm.[3] Both transcription approaches can be combined, the rule-based phone transcription system being used for OOV words (Ng *et al.*, 2000; Wechsler *et al.*, 1998b).

Once a word has been transcribed, it is matched against sub-lexical document representations with one of the sub-word-based techniques that will be described in the following two sections. Finally, the RSV of a document is a combination

---

[1] CMU Pronunciation Dictionary (cmudict.0.4): www.speech.cs.cmu.edu/cgi-bin/cmudict.

[2] Bonn Machine-Readable Pronunciation Dictionary (BOMP): www.ikp.uni-bonn.de/dt/forsch/phonetik/bomp.

[3] Wasser, J. A. (1985). English to phoneme translation. Program in public domain.

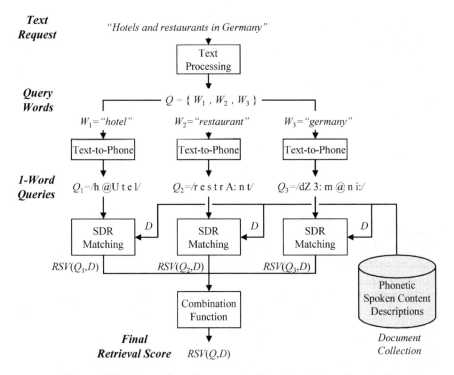

Figure 4.12 Processing of text queries for sub-word-based retrieval

of the retrieval scores obtained with each individual query word. Scores of query words can be simply averaged (Larson and Eickeler, 2003).

4.4.4.3 Adaptation of VSM to Sub-Word Indexing

In Section 4.4.3, we gave an overview of the application of the VSM approach (Section 4.4.2) in the context of word-based SDR. Classical VSM-based SDR approaches have already been experimented with sub-words, mostly n-grams of phones or phonemes (Ng and Zue, 2000). Other sub-lexical indexing features have been used in the VSM framework, such as syllables (Larson and Eickeler, 2003). In the rest of this section, however, we will mainly deal with approaches based on phone n-grams.

When applying the standard normalized cosine measure of Equation (4.14) to sub-word-based SDR, t represents a sub-lexical indexing term (e.g. a phonetic n-gram) extracted from a query or a document representation. Term weights similar or close to those given in Equations (4.10) and (4.11) are generally used. The term frequencies $f_q(t)$ and $f_d(t)$ are in that case the number of times n-gram t has been extracted from the request and document phonetic representations. In the example of Figure 4.11, the frequency of the phone 3-gram "[I d e@]" is $f([\text{I d e@}]) = 2$.

The Okapi similarity measure – already introduced in Equation (4.25) – can also be used in the context of sub-word-based retrieval. In (Ng *et al.*, 2000), the Okapi formula proposed by (Walker *et al.*, 1997) – differing slightly from the formula of Equation (4.25) – is applied to n-gram query and document representations:

$$RSV_{Okapi}(Q, D) = \sum_{t \in Q} \frac{(k_1 + 1)f_d(t)}{k_1\left((1 - b) + b\frac{l_d}{L_c}\right) + f_d(t)} \frac{(k_3 + 1)f_q(t)}{k_3 + f_q(t)} \log(IDF'(t))$$

(4.29)

where k_1, k_3 and b are constants (respectively set to 1.2, 1000 and 0.75 in (Ng *et al.*, 2000)), l_d is the length of the document transcription in number of phonetic units and L_c is the average document transcription length in number of phonetic units across the collection. The inverse document frequency $IDF'(t)$ is given in Equation (4.26).

Originally developed for text document collections, these classical IR methods turn out to be unsuitable when applied to sub-word-based SDR. Due to the high error rates of sub-word (especially phone) recognizer systems, the misrecognition problem here has even more disturbing effects than in the case of word-based indexing. Modifications of the above methods are required to propose new document–query retrieval measures that are less sensitive to speech recognition errors. This is generally done by making use of approximate term matching.

As before, taking non-matching terms into account requires the definition of a sub-lexical term similarity measure. Phonetic similarity measures are usually based on a phone confusion matrix (PCM) which will be called P_C henceforth. Each element $P_C(r, h)$ in the matrix represents the probability of confusion for a specific phone pair (r, h). As mentioned in Equation (4.6), it is an estimation of the probability $P(h|)$ that phone h is recognized given that the concerned acoustical segment actually belongs to phone class r. This value is a numerical measure of how confusable phone r is with phone h. A PCM can be derived from the phone error count matrix stored in the header of MPEG-7 *SpokenContent* descriptors as described in the section on usage in Section 4.3.2.3.

In a sub-word-based VSM approach, the phone confusion matrix P_C is used as a similarity matrix. The element $P_C(r, h)$ is seen as a measure of acoustic similarity between phones r and h. However, in the n-gram-based retrieval methods, individual phones are barely used as basic indexing terms ($n = 1$). With n values greater than 1, new similarity measures must be defined at the n-gram term level.

A natural approach would be to compute an n-gram confusion matrix in the same way as the PCM, by deriving n-gram confusion statistics from an evaluation database of spoken documents. However, building a confusion matrix at the term level would be too expensive, since the size of the term space can be very large. Moreover, such a matrix would be very sparse. Therefore, it is necessary to find a simple way of deriving similarity measures at the n-gram level from the phone-level similarities. Assuming that phones making up an n-gram term are independent, a straightforward approach is to evaluate n-gram similarity measures by combining individual phone confusion probabilities as follows (Moreau *et al.*, 2004c):

$$s(t_i, t_j) = \prod_{k=1}^{n} P_C(t_i[k], t_j[k]) \qquad (4.30)$$

where t_i and t_j are two phone n-grams comprising the following phones:

$$t_i = [t_i[1]t_i[2]\ldots t_i[n]] \quad \text{and} \quad t_j = \lfloor t_j[1]t_j[2]\ldots t_j[n] \rfloor \qquad (4.31)$$

Under the assumption of statistical independence between individual phones, this can be interpreted as an estimation of the probability of confusing n-gram terms t_i and t_j:

$$s(t_i, t_j) \approx P(t_j | t_i). \qquad (4.32)$$

Many other simple phonetic similarity measures can be derived from the PCM, or even directly from the integer confusion counts of matrix *Sub* described in Section 4.3.2.3, thus avoiding the computation and multiplication of real probability values. An example of this is the similarity measure between two n-gram terms t_i and t_j of size n proposed in (Ng and Zue, 2000):

$$s(t_i, t_j) = \frac{\sum_{k=1}^{n} Sub(t_i[k], t_j[k])}{\sum_{k=1}^{n} Sub(t_i[k], t_i[k])}, \qquad (4.33)$$

where $Sub(t_i[k], t_j[k])$ is the count of confusions between $t_i[k]$ and $t_j[k]$, the kth phones in sub-word units t_i and t_j respectively. The measure is normalized so that it is equal to 1 when $t_i = t_j$.

However, the n-gram similarity measures proposed in Equations (4.30) and (4.33) are rather coarse. Their main weakness is that they only consider substitution error probabilities and ignore the insertion and deletion errors. More complex methods, based on the dynamic programming (DP) principle, have been proposed to take the insertions and deletions into account. Making the simplifying assumption that the phones within n-gram terms t_i and t_j are independent, estimation of the $P(t_i|t_j)$ can be made via a DP procedure. In order to compare two phone n-grams t_i and t_j of length n defined as in Equation (4.31), we define an $(n+1) \times (n+1)$ DP matrix A. The elements of A can be recursively computed according to the procedure given in Figure 4.13 (Ng, 1998).

P_C, P_D and P_I are the PCM, the deletion and insertion probability vectors respectively. The corresponding probabilities can be estimated according to the maximum likelihood criteria, for instance as in Equations (4.6), (4.7) and (4.8).

BEGIN:

$$A(0,0) = 1 \qquad\qquad\qquad u = v = 0$$

$$A(u,0) = A(u-1,0).P_D(t_i[u]) \quad 0 < u \le n$$

$$A(0,v) = A(0,v-1).P_I(t_j[v]) \quad 0 < v \le n$$

ITERATIONS:

$$A(u,v) = \max \begin{cases} A(u-1,v).P_D(t_i[u]) & \text{(Deletion)} \\ A(u-1,v-1).P_C(t_i[u],t_j[v]) & \text{(Substitution)} \\ A(u,v-1).P_I(t_j[v]) & \text{(Insertion)} \end{cases} \quad \begin{aligned} (0 < u \le m) \\ (0 < v \le n) \end{aligned}$$

END:

$$A(n,n) = s(t_i,t_j) \approx P(t_j|t_i).$$

Figure 4.13   Example of a DP procedure for the computation of n- gram similarity measures

This DP procedure represents a significant increase of the computation need compared with the simpler product of Equation (4.30). However, provided that enough memory resources are available, the computation of the similarity measures $s(t_i, t_j)$ for all pairs of phones t_i and t_j can be done once off-line and stored in a table for future use during retrieval.

A first way to exploit these similarity measures is the automatic expansion of the query set of n-gram terms (Ng and Zue, 2000; Srinivasan and Petkovic, 2000). The query expansion techniques address the corruption of indexing terms in the document representation by augmenting the query representation with similar or confusable terms that could erroneously match recognized speech. These "approximate match" terms are determined using information from the phonetic error confusion matrix as described above. For instance, a thresholded, fixed-length list of near-miss terms t_j can be generated for each query term t_i, according to the phonetic similarity measures $s(t_i, t_j)$ (Ng and Zue, 2000).

However, it is difficult to select automatically the similarity threshold above which additional "closed" terms should be taken into account. There is a risk that too many additional terms are included in the query representation, thus impeding the retrieval efficiency.

A more efficient use of phonetic similarity measures is to integrate them in the computation of the RSV as described in Section 4.4.2.3. The approximate matching approach of Equation (4.19) implicitly considers all possible matches between the "clean" query n-gram terms and the "noisy" document n-gram terms (Ng and Zue, 2000). As proposed in Equation (4.21), a less expensive RSV in terms of computation is to consider, for each query n-gram, the "closest" document n-gram term (Moreau et al., 2004b, 2004c). These different VSM-based approximate matching approaches have proven to make sub-word SDR robust enough to recognition errors to allow reasonable retrieval performance.

Robust sub-word SDR can even be improved by indexing documents (and queries, if spoken) with multiple recognition candidates rather than just the single best phonetic transcriptions. The expanded document representation may be a list of N-best phonetic transcriptions delivered by the ASR system or a phone lattice, as described in the MPEG-7 standard. Both increase the chance of capturing the correct hypotheses. More competing n-gram terms can be extracted from these enriched representations, as depicted in Figure 4.11. Moreover, if a term appears many times in the top N hypotheses or in the different lattice paths, it is more likely to have actually occurred than if it appears in only a few. This information can be taken into account in the VSM weighting of the indexing terms.

For instance, a simple estimate of the frequency of term t in a document D was obtained in (Ng and Zue, 2000) by considering the number of times n_t it appears in the top N recognition hypotheses and normalizing it by N:

$$f_d(t) = \frac{n_t}{N}.$$ (4.34)

This normalized term frequency can then be used in the classical VSM document term weighting formula of Equation (4.10).

As in the case of automatic query expansion, however, one danger of document expansion is to include too many additional phones in the representation. Numerous erroneous n-gram terms may result from low scoring recognition hypotheses. This can lead to spurious matches with query terms resulting in a decrease in retrieval precision.

All the techniques presented above handle one type of sub-word indexing term (e.g. n-grams with a fixed length n). A further refinement can consist in combining different types of sub-word units, the underlying idea being that each one may capture some different kinds of information. The different sets of indexing terms are first processed separately. The scores obtained with each one are then combined to get a final document–query retrieval score, e.g. via a linear combination function such as (Ng and Zue, 2000):

$$RSV_C(Q, D) = \sum_k w_k RSV_k(Q, D),$$ (4.35)

where RSV_k is the document–query score obtained using sub-words of type k and w_k the corresponding weight parameter.

In particular, this approach allows us to use phone n-grams of different lengths in combination. Short and long phone sequences have opposite properties: the shorter units are more robust to errors and word variants compared with the longer units, but the latest capture more discrimination information and are less susceptible to false matches. The combined use of short and long n-grams is supposed to take advantage of both properties. In that case, the retrieval system handles distinct sets of n-gram indexing terms, each one corresponding to a different length n. The retrieval scores resulting from each set are then merged. For instance, it has been proposed to combine monograms ($n = 1$), bigrams

($n = 2$) and trigrams ($n = 3$) by means of the following retrieval function (Moreau *et al.*, 2004a, 2004b):

$$RSV_{\{1;2;3\}}(Q, D) = \sum_{n=1}^{3} nRSV_n(Q, D), \qquad (4.36)$$

where RSV_n represents the relevance score obtained with the set of n-gram terms of size n. This combination function gives more weight to the longer units, which are more sensitive to recognition errors (a single erroneous phone modifies the whole indexing term) but carry more information.

However, a few experimental studies have shown that the fusion of different sub-word units results in marginal gains in terms of retrieval efficiency (Moreau *et al.*, 2004a; Ng and Zue, 2000).

4.4.4.4 Example Experiment with Sub-Word VSM

This section presents an example of an SDR evaluation experiment. The evaluation was performed on a very simple retrieval task, using a phone-based VSM approach.

A phone-only recognizer was used for extracting MPEG-7 phone lattices from spoken documents. It is based on 43 speaker-independent phone HMMs describing the German language. These acoustic models are looped, according to a bigram phone language model. Experiments have been conducted with data from the PhonDat corpus.[1] The spoken document set consists of 19 306 short sentences read by more than 200 German speakers. The average document length is 4 seconds and 37.7 phones (average number of phones in the best transcriptions delivered by the recognizer). A phone-only *SpokenContentLattice* containing several alternative phonetic transcriptions is extracted from each document and stored in a separate database.

The set of evaluation queries consists of 10 city names: *Augsburg, Dortmund, Frankfurt, Hamburg, Koeln, Muenchen, Oldenburg, Regensburg, Ulm* and *Wuerzburg*. Their phonetic transcriptions were used as single word queries. In a word-only-based indexing approach, one can imagine that such proper names might be OOV words and thus impossible to retrieve.

The phone recognizer was run on a separate evaluation corpus to provide the phone confusion counts stored, along with the phone lexicon, in an MPEG-7 *SpokenContentHeader* shared by all extracted lattices.

The retrieval system evaluated here is independent of any a priori word vocabulary (as in keyword- or LVCSR-based systems). This leads to the notion of *open-vocabulary* retrieval because in principle the query vocabulary is unrestricted (Wechsler, 1998). The only practical restriction is given by the pronunciation

---

[1] BAS (Bavarian Archive for Speech Signals) Corpora: http://www.phonetik.uni-muenchen.de/Bas/.

dictionary for the case that the text queries are transcribed automatically. The use of phonetic retrieval also makes "sound-like" retrieval applications possible.

However, as mentioned earlier, this phone-based retrieval has to cope with high error rates. The phone error rate of the ASR system used for this experiment is 43.0% (it was measured on a separate development corpus). Besides, the use of phonetic-only indexing might lose discrimination power between relevant and irrelevant documents when compared with word indexing, because of the exclusion of lexical knowledge. In the TREC SDR experiments (Voorhees and Harman, 1998), word-based approaches have consistently outperformed phoneme approaches.

However, this particular retrieval experiment is straightforward due to the relatively small number and concise nature of the speech messages, and the use of single word queries. One could imagine the scenario of a database of photos annotated with short spoken descriptions. In that case, the use of a simple vocabulary-independent phone recognizer is a reasonable indexing approach.

Evaluation Method

The classical evaluation measures for retrieval effectiveness are *Recall* and *Precision*. Given a set of retrieved documents, the recall rate is the fraction of relevant documents in the whole database that have been retrieved:

$$Recall = \frac{Number\ of\ Relevant\ Retrieved\ Documents}{Number\ of\ Relevant\ Documents\ in\ the\ Database}. \tag{4.37}$$

The precision rate is the fraction of retrieved documents that are relevant:

$$Precision = \frac{Number\ of\ Relevant\ Retrieved\ Documents}{Number\ of\ Retrieved\ Documents}. \tag{4.38}$$

The precision and recall rates depend on how many documents are kept to form the N-best retrieved document set. *Precision* and *Recall* vary with N, generally inversely with each other. To evaluate the ranked list, a common approach is to plot *Precision* vs. *Recall* after each retrieved document. To facilitate the evaluation of the SDR performance across different queries (each corresponding to a different set of relevant documents), it is convenient to use the plot normalization proposed by TREC (TREC, 2001): the precision values are interpolated according to 11 standard recall levels $(0.0, 0.1, \ldots, 1.0)$ as represented in Figure 4.14. These values can be averaged over all queries.

Finally, a single performance measure can be derived from a series of *Precision–Recall* measures by computing the *mean average precision* (mAP). It is the average of precision values across all recall points. It can be interpreted as the area under the *Precision–Recall* curve. A perfect retrieval system would result in a mean average precision of 100% (mAP $= 1$).

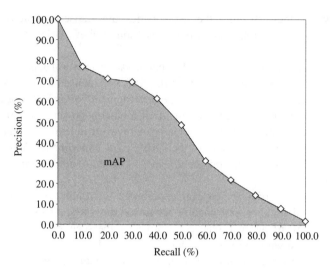

Figure 4.14   *Precision–Recall* plot, with mAP measure

Results

The indexing terms used in this experiment are the phone *n*-grams introduced in Section 4.4.4.1. In that case, a set of indexing *n*-gram terms is extracted from each MPEG-7 lattice in the database and each query. These terms are used in the VSM weighting schemes and retrieval functions introduced earlier. The best *n*-gram length was determined by the results in Figure 4.15 (Moreau *et al.*, 2004a). These are average values of the mAP obtained with each of the 10 queries, and four different *n*-gram lengths ($n = 1$, 2, 3 and 4). The simple binary weighting of Equation (4.9) and the cosine retrieval function of Equation (4.14) were used.

The trigrams ($n = 3$) represent the best trade-off. The combination of trigrams with bigrams ($n = 2$) and individual phones ($n = 1$), according to the retrieval

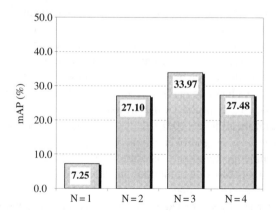

Figure 4.15   mAP values for different *n*-gram lengths

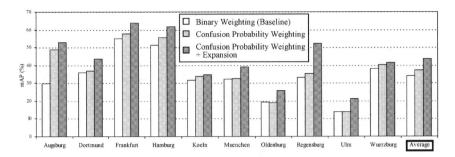

Figure 4.16   mAP for 10 different queries and three weighting strategies

function of Equation (4.36), resulted in marginal mAP gains (Moreau *et al.*, 2004a).

Figure 4.16 depicts the mAP values obtained with each of the 10 city name queries and different weighting strategies. The rightmost part of the figure represents the average values of the 10 previous measures.

The first measure (□) was obtained from the baseline system, i.e. using the binary weighting and the cosine retrieval function. The second one (▨) results from the use of the inner product retrieval function where each query n-gram term t is weighted by its recognition probability (i.e. $q(t) = P(t|t)$). The last mAP measure (■) is obtained with the retrieval function of Equation (4.21).

We observe in Figure 4.16 that not every query benefits from the introduction of confusion probabilities (▨ compared with □). For some of them, this weighting factor yielded no improvement in comparison with the performance of the baseline system (*Muenchen, Oldenburg, Ulm*). For the other queries, the retrieval effectiveness is clearly increased. A query such as *Augsburg* might contain one or more 3-grams for which the ASR system has produced high recognition probabilities. On average (right part of Figure 4.16), this technique improves the overall retrieval performance. In comparison with the baseline average performance (mAP = 33.97%), the mAP increases by 9.8% (mAP = 37.29%).

The retrieval function of Equation (4.21) further improves the retrieval effectiveness. As reported in Figure 4.16 (■), the average performance is improved by 28.3% (from mAP = 33.97% to 43.59%) in comparison with the baseline system (□), and by 16.9% in comparison with the use of confusion weighting with no expansion (▨). Even in the case of poorly performing queries (in particular *Oldenburg* and *Ulm*), this approach significantly improves the retrieval performance. In the case of the short, three-phone long *Ulm* query, we obtain one of the best relative mAP improvements in comparison with the baseline value (+54.0%). Queries that are poorly retrieved indicate that the recognition of the corresponding targets within the indexed documents contains a lot of recognition errors. This is particularly problematic when the query is short. In that case, the corresponding targets may not contain any correctly recognized 3-grams that can compensate for the badly recognized ones. The use of the expansion strategy can recover some of the missed targets by taking into account some document indexing 3-grams that, although different from the ones contained in the query, are "close" to them in terms of confusion probability.

Compared with a simple 1-best phonetic transcription, a multi-hypothesis phone lattice is an expanded representation of a document. To verify if the use of lattice expansion is not redundant with the confusion-based expansion of Equation (4.21), "1-best" transcriptions (i.e. the best path in the lattice) were also used to index the documents. The results are reported in Figure 4.17 (mAP values averaged over all queries). As expected in the baseline case (binary weighting, cosine function), the use of lattices yields an improvement compared with the use of simple transcriptions: from mAP $= 28.89\%$ with 1-best to mAP $= 33.97\%$ with lattices ($+17.6\%$). It is interesting to observe the same phenomenon when applying the confusion-based expansion technique; lattices perform significantly better than transcriptions in that case too: from mAP $= 38.01\%$ with 1-best to mAP $= 43.59\%$ with lattices ($+14.7\%$). The combination of confusion-based expansion with multi-hypothesis lattices seems to be relevant.

These experiments show that sub-word units are able to capture enough information to perform effective retrieval, provided that adequate expansion techniques are applied in order to compensate for the high phone error rate of the indexing engine.

4.4.5   Sub-Word String Matching

The techniques reviewed in the previous section are all based on the VSM. There exists a second, radically different approach to sub-word-based SDR, where the

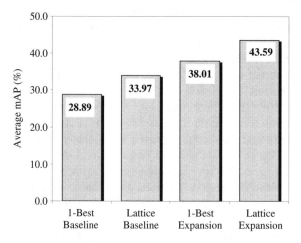

Figure 4.17   Average mAP obtained when indexing with 1-best transcriptions or lattices

sub-lexical transcriptions of queries and documents are considered as a whole and not as a set of individual terms or sub-sequence units as before.

This approach relies on approximate string matching techniques whose goal is to search for approximate occurrences (i.e. taking into account symbol mismatches, insertions and deletions) of a query string in a document string. A method of this type, also called fuzzy matching search, works in the following way:

- Each query keyword is broken down into a string of sub-lexical units (either by means of a pronunciation dictionary, in the case of text queries, or through automatic recognition, in the case of query words spoken in isolation). The query string will be called the *source* string.
- The document transcription (i.e. a string of sub-lexical units in this case) is scanned to find the sub-string that best corresponds to a possible occurrence of the source string. This sub-string will be called the *target* string.
- A similarity measure between the source string and the target string constitutes the RSV of the document for the corresponding query word.

It is actually a subword-based word spotting technique, performed on sub-lexical representations of the spoken documents. Contrary to the traditional keyword spotting approach (Section 4.4.3.2), which relies on a fixed, predefined set of keyword models, the fuzzy sub-lexical matching techniques allow flexibility in the presence of recognition errors, and OOV query words can potentially find matches.

4.4.5.1   Edit Distance

A prerequisite for any fuzzy matching search algorithm is the definition of a distance or a similarity measure between two given fixed-length sequences of symbols. A well-known and simple string distance is called the *Levenshtein distance* (Levenshtein, 1966), also known as the *edit distance*. In information theory, the Levenshtein distance between two strings is given by the minimum number of operations (insertions, deletions and substitutions) needed to transform one string (source string) into another (target string).

Let us consider a source string α and a target string β, with respective sizes m and n, comprising the following symbols:

$$\alpha = \alpha[1]\alpha[2]\dots\alpha[m] \quad \text{and} \quad \beta = \beta[1]\beta[2]\dots\beta[n]. \quad (4.39)$$

The edit distance $LD(\alpha, \beta)$ between α and β can be automatically derived from a DP procedure by defining an $(m+1) \times (n+1)$ matrix A and applying the algorithm given in Figure 4.18.

BEGIN:

$$A(0,0) = 0 \quad u = v = 0$$
$$A(u,0) = u \quad 0 < u \leqslant m$$
$$A(0,v) = v \quad 0 < v \leqslant n$$

ITERATIONS:

$$A(u,v) = \min \begin{cases} A(u-1,v) + 1 & \text{(Deletion)} \\ A(u-1,v-1) + [1 - \delta(\alpha[u], \beta[v])] & \text{(Substitution)} \\ A(u,v-1) + 1 & \text{(Insertion)} \end{cases} \quad \begin{matrix} (0 < u \leqslant m) \\ (0 < v \leqslant n) \end{matrix}$$

$$\text{with } \delta(\alpha[u], \beta[v]) = \begin{cases} 1 & \text{if } \alpha[u] = \beta[v] \\ 0 & \text{if } \alpha[u] \neq \beta[v] \end{cases}$$

END:

$$A(m,n) = LD(\alpha, \beta)$$

Figure 4.18   Algorithm to compute the Levenshtein distance between two strings

Two identical strings have a null distance, and the greater the Levenshtein distance is, the more different the strings are. Finally, the edit distance $LD(\alpha, \beta)$ between two strings α and β can be converted into a similarity measure called the *inverse normalized edit distance* (Wechsler *et al.*, 1998b):

$$INED(\alpha, \beta) = 1 - \frac{LD(\alpha, \beta)}{\max(m, n)}. \tag{4.40}$$

The measure of similarity $INED(\alpha, \beta)$ between a query string α and a sub-string β forms the relevance score of the document containing β for the query word corresponding to α.

In the example of Figure 4.19 two strings of phonetic symbols are compared using this procedure. The source string α is the canonical transcription of "*Muenchen*" using the German phone set. The target string β represents an errorful transcription of the same word, provided by a speech decoder. The edit distance between α and β is $LD(\alpha, \beta) = 5$, which means that a minimum of five operations is required to transform α and β. The alignment path indicated in bold in Figure 4.19 corresponds to one deletion (phone /C/) followed by four substitutions. Other possible optimal alignment paths are also represented with dashed lines. Each one yields an edit distance of 5.

This example illustrates the weakness of this approach where all phones have an equal acoustic distance of 1 between each other. It does not take into account the strong acoustic similarities between some phones in α and β: for instance, between /@/ in α and /E/ in β or between /n/ in α and /m/ in β. The alignment depicted in Figure 4.19 is clearly not optimal in terms of acoustic similarity.

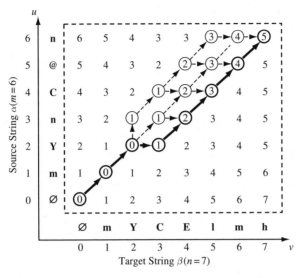

Final Alignment: $\alpha = \mathbf{m\ Y\ \varnothing\ n\ C\ @\ n}$ Levenshtein Distance:
$\beta = \mathbf{m\ Y\ C\ E\ l\ m\ h}$ $LD(\alpha,\ \beta) = 5$

Figure 4.19   Computation of a Levenshtein distance

4.4.5.2 Probabilistic String Matching

The main drawback of the edit distance approach is that it relies very much on the precision of the best phonetic transcription. In that case, some of the misrecognized phones cannot be recovered through a multi-hypotheses lattice. The only way to cope with the recognition inaccuracy is to develop fuzzy matching techniques – also called *probabilistic string matching* (PSM) techniques (Wechsler, 1998) – which integrate phone (or syllable) confusion probabilities into the string matching process itself. The principle of PSM was introduced in Section 4.4.4.3, where it was used for measuring *n*-gram similarities. Thus, the algorithm described in Figure 4.13 also offers a way of estimating a measure of similarity between the source and the target strings.

This algorithm uses the same DP transitions (horizontal, vertical, diagonal) as in the edit distance case. But instead of applying the same uniform cost ($= 1$) to every transition, it defines a transition probability that depends on both the end node and the direction of the transition. Suppose that the end node is $(\alpha[u], \beta[v])$, where $\alpha[u]$ is the uth phone in the source string α (query), and $\beta[v]$ is the vth phone in the target sub-string β (document):

- A vertical move corresponds to the deletion of $\alpha[u]$, and the transition probability is $P_D(\alpha[u])$.
- A horizontal move corresponds to the insertion of $\beta[v]$, and the transition probability is $P_I(\beta[v])$.

- A diagonal move corresponds to the substitution of $\alpha[u]$ by $\beta[v]$, and the transition probability is $P_C(\alpha[u], \beta[v])$ (see Figure 4.22).

If strings α and β respectively comprise m and n phones, an $(m+1) \times (n+1)$ DP matrix A is processed by the algorithm of Figure 4.13. The final similarity score is given by $A(m, n)$, which can be interpreted as an estimation of the probability $P(\beta|\alpha)$.

In Figure 4.20, the two strings whose edit distance was depicted in Figure 4.19 are compared once again using the above PSM procedure. The intersections (u, v) of the DP matrix are represented by circles whose sizes are proportional to the probability of substitution of the corresponding phone pairs $(\alpha[u], \beta[v])$. The grey circles represent probabilities of correct recognition (i.e. when $\alpha[u] = \beta[v]$) and are depicted at a reduced scale compared with the others.

Contrary to the case of edit distance (Figure 4.19), the high probabilities of confusion $P_C(@, E)$ and $P_C(n, m)$, used here as a measure of acoustic similarity, are taken into account. The final decoding path aligns $\alpha[5] = /@/$ on $\beta[4] = /E/$ and $\alpha[6] = /n/$ on $\beta[6] = /m/$.

Many other PSM algorithm structures can be designed to compute a stochastic similarity measure between two phone strings. An interesting one is proposed in (Wechsler, 1998) and outlined in Figure 4.21.

The previous PSM procedure (Figure 4.13), as well as the edit distance procedure (Figure 4.18), did not restrict the number of vertical (i.e. deletion) and

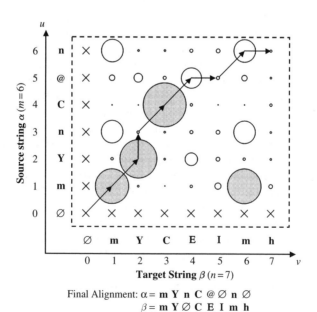

Final Alignment: $\alpha = $ **m Y n C @ $\varnothing$ n $\varnothing$**
$\beta = $ **m Y $\varnothing$ C E I m h**

Figure 4.20 Computation of a string similarity score using a PSM procedure

BEGIN:

$A(0,0) = 1$ $u = v = 0$

$A(u, 0) = A(u-1, 0).P_D(\alpha[u])$ $0 < u \leq m$

$A(0, v) = A(0, v-1).P_I(\beta[v])$ $0 < v \leq n$

ITERATIONS:

$$A(u, v) = \max \begin{cases} A(u-2, v-1).P_D(\alpha[u-1]).P_C(\alpha[u], \beta[v]) & \text{(1 Del.} + \text{1 Sub.)} \\ A(u-1, v-1).P_C(\alpha[u], \beta[v]) & \text{(1 Sub.)} \\ A(u-1, v-2).P_I(\beta[v-1]).P_C(\alpha[u], \beta[v]) & \text{(1 Ins.} + \text{1 Sub.)} \end{cases} \quad \begin{matrix} (0 < u \leq m) \\ (0 < v \leq n) \end{matrix}$$

END:

$A(m, n) = s(\alpha, \beta) \approx P(\beta | \alpha)$

Figure 4.21 PSM algorithm with restrictions on deletions and insertions

horizontal (i.e. insertion) moves. This can be a problem, notably if too many phones are inserted in the target string before and/or after the actual sub-string of interest. Here, a maximum of only one insertion or one deletion is allowed between two phone matching (or mismatching) pairs. Figure 4.22 illustrates this, by showing the DP transition schemes of the edit distance and the two PSM algorithms described above.

Another original way of measuring the similarity between two strings consists of modelling the source string with a discrete HMM which allows variations of the correct pronunciation of the corresponding word (Ferrieux and Peillon, 1999; Kupiec *et al.*, 1994). The target string is aligned on the model by means of a DP algorithm similar to the ones described above.

Finally, the measure of similarity between the query string and the target sub-string within a given document forms the RSV of that document for the corresponding query word.

4.4.5.3 Slot Detection

After a relevance score has been defined by one of the above string matching techniques, there remains the question of the detection of target sub-strings within a document transcription for a given query word. As the sub-word sequences provided by the indexing recognizer do not contain word boundaries, the retrieval system must be able to locate automatically possible occurrences of the query word.

The most straightforward way is to scan dynamically the document transcription for each query keyword. The fuzzy matching search returns an identified keyword whenever the distance between the query keyword string and a sub-string in the document is less than an empirically determined threshold (Larson and Eickeler, 2003).

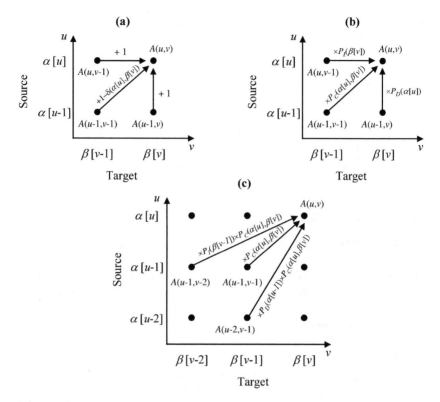

Figure 4.22 Transition schemes for different string matching algorithms: (a) edit distance (see Figure 4.18), (b) first PSM algorithm (see Figure 4.13) and (c) second PSM algorithm (see Figure 4.21)

A more refined approach consists of applying a *slot detection* step prior to the string fuzzy matching procedure. Wechsler proposed an error-tolerant detection algorithm to spot efficiently several possible occurrences of a query string in a document (Wechsler, 1998, p. 20). A sub-sequence of the document in which an occurrence of the query string is hypothesized is called a slot. Only slots that do not overlap a previously selected one and contain a sufficient number of query phonemes (a threshold is applied) are retained. Finally, slot probabilities are estimated by means of a fuzzy matching technique such as the PSM algorithms mentioned above (the edit distance approach being too coarse when strings are corrupted by numerous recognition errors).

Whatever the target location method is, the probability of the best document sub-string candidate for the occurrence of a query word forms the document relevance score for that query word. The final document RSV is the combination of the relevance scores obtained with the different query words. In a comparative study made by (Wechsler, 1998), the string matching SDR method (with slot detection) proved significantly more effective than retrieval based on phoneme

n-grams. But a major weakness of the string matching SDR approaches in general remains the computational cost of the fuzzy matching algorithms.

4.4.6 Combining Word and Sub-Word Indexing

The previous sections have reviewed different SDR approaches based on two distinct indexing levels: words and sub-lexical terms. As mentioned above, each indexing level has particular advantages and drawbacks. A further refinement in the SDR field consists of combining word and sub-word indexing terms for optimal retrieval performance.

4.4.6.1 Word-to-Phone Conversion

Sub-word-based retrieval is not specific to SDR. In particular, the extraction of phoneme n-grams and their use as indexing features is a well-established text retrieval technique. Document and query words are first transformed in phonetic sequences by means of pronunciation dictionaries or rule-based text-to-phone algorithms. Then, a phonetic-based approach can be used for retrieval.

The main difference from the case where documents are directly indexed by a phone recognizer is the absence of phonetic transcription errors in the documents. Another important difference lies in the fact that word boundaries are available (Ng *et al.*, 2000). It is therefore possible, for instance, to forbid phone n-grams to form across neighbouring words. Phonetic string matching methods can also be used for mapping a query phone sequence to the most probable corresponding words in a text (Kupiec *et al.*, 1994).

These methods can be applied to word transcription resulting from LVCSR, transcribed into phone sequences just after the ASR extraction step. The problem of word substitution errors in the document transcriptions can be alleviated by phone-based SDR because the substituted words are generally phonetically close to the ones actually spoken, and hence may have close phonetic transcriptions (Srinivasan and Petkovic, 2000). In the same way, OOV query words can potentially find matches. An OOV word will often be erroneously recognized as an in-vocabulary word that is phonetically similar. The use of sub-word-based retrieval may allow detection of some of its occurrences in the LVCSR-transcribed documents by making "sound-like" retrieval possible.

4.4.6.2 Combination of Multiple Index Sources

The approach mentioned above relies on a single LVCSR-based spoken content extraction system. The derivation of sub-lexical transcriptions from the recognized words requires some additional information (pronunciation dictionaries or transcription rules), which may not always be available.

An alternative is the extraction of sub-word indexing terms via a second recognition pass, by means of a sub-word-based ASR system. The underlying motivation is that independent sub-lexical indexing systems can be useful for complementing word indexing when word recognition has failed, especially in situations where names and unknown words are misrecognized. This leads to the idea of integrating different indexing descriptions, resulting from distinct recognition systems, into the SDR process.

There are different approaches to the exploitation of multiple recognition outputs for indexing and retrieval purposes. The first one is to use the extracted sub-lexical information in the case of OOV query words only. In that case, the word index is used for in-vocabulary query words and the sub-word index is used to spot OOV query words (James, 1995; Logan *et al.*, 2002).

Other approaches consist of combining the different sources of information in a global retrieval framework. Multiple recognition outputs can be integrated into an SDR system in two ways (Wechsler, 1998):

- *Data merging*: multiple recognition outputs of a document are merged and then treated as a single document representation for indexing.
- *Data fusion*: a separate retrieval sub-system is applied for each type of recognition output. Then, the retrieval scores resulting from each sub-system are combined to form a final composite score.

Generally, an LVCSR-based word indexing system is fused with a phonetic indexing system (Jones *et al.*, 1996; Witbrock and Hauptmann, 1997). The fusion function often consists of a simple addition (Jones *et al.*, 1996) or linear combination of the retrieval scores obtained independently from each information source:

$$RSV_{mixed}(q, d) = \alpha RSV_{word}(q, d) + \beta RSV_{phone}(q, d), \qquad (4.41)$$

where RSV_{word} (resp. RSV_{phone}) is a retrieval score obtained with one of the word-based (phone-based) retrieval methods mentioned in the previous sections, and α and β weight the contribution of each information source.

Another simple approach to multi-indexing fusion is the combined use of term similarities computed at the semantic and phonetic levels (Crestani, 2002). Semantic term similarity and phonetic similarity are linearly combined to form a relevance score. These are very simplistic linear combinations of semantic and phonetic similarities, and other more complex combinations can be devised.

The combination of word-based retrieval and phonetic sub-string matching techniques experimented in the Informedia project (Witbrock and Hauptmann, 1997) has shown that increased relative retrieval effectiveness is observed with data fusion, when compared with either the word-based approach or the phone-based approach alone. These experiments verified that phonetic sub-string retrieval has the capacity to correct some of the transcription errors occurring in the word-based document descriptions.

4.5 CONCLUSIONS

Given that increasingly large portions of the available data contain spoken language information (such as recorded speech messages, radio broadcasts and TV broadcasts), the development of automatic methods to index and retrieve spoken documents will become even more important in the future. In that context, the standardization effort of MPEG with the definition of the MPEG-7 *SpokenContent* tool could play a key role in the development of next-generation multimedia indexing and retrieval tools.

The MPEG-7 *SpokenContent* description allows interoperability across databases indexed by different ASR systems. The description is flexible enough to be used by various kinds of spoken content indexing and retrieval systems.

4.5.1 MPEG-7 Interoperability

It is not possible to standardize the ASR process itself, due to the huge variety and complexity of existing ASR technologies, and to economical considerations. Therefore, multimedia content management applications will continue to cope with heterogeneous databases of spoken content metadata, extracted with different ASR engines.

These recognizers may have different error rates, and result in recognition outputs with diverse levels of *reliability*. Moreover, the same recognition engine may produce outputs with different levels of reliability if inputs themselves differ in quality (different speech quality, different recording environments, etc.). It is therefore difficult to rank efficiently this heterogeneous metadata based on the same retrieval parameters. At some level, the degree of reliability of spoken content metadata should be assessed and used to weight its ranking in the retrieval list. The *SpokenContent* description offers different ways of assessing the reliability of a recognition output:

- Two scores are attached to both word and phone links in a *SpokenContent-Lattice* (Section 4.3.3.3): the *probability* attached to the link (derived from the language model) and the *acousticScore* of the corresponding recognition hypothesis (derived from the acoustic models). These attributes give indications of the reliability of the recognition hypothesis they refer to. This information may be used to weight different outputs provided by the same ASR system, helping retrieval to cope with input heterogeneity (i.e. different input speech qualities, resulting in more or less reliable decodings).
- In the case of word-based indexing, another important parameter is the size of the word lexicon used in the decoding. The outputs of a recognizer based on a small lexicon should be considered less reliable than those yielded by a large-vocabulary ASR system. With a restrained set of possible words, a recognizer is very likely to encounter OOV inputs and produce recognition

errors. The word lexicon size may be used to weight outputs from different ASR systems, helping retrieval to cope with the heterogeneity of indexing sources.

- In the case of phone-based indexing, it is possible to measure a complete set of phone confusion statistics due to the retrained size of the indexing vocabulary. This information is stored in the *ConfusionInfo* metadata (Section 4.3.2.3) of a *SpokenContentHeader*. Integrating phone confusion probabilities directly in the computation of the RSVs (as explained in Sections 4.4.4.3 and 4.4.5.2) ensures that *SpokenContentLattices* produced by different phone recognizers (i.e. with different phone error rates) are treated equally.

- Another feature of potentially useful MPEG-7 metadata is the *audio* attribute enclosed in the *Block* description of a *SpokenContentLattice* (Section 4.3.3.1). It is a coarse category of audio quality, indicating if a lattice *Block* was extracted from noise, noisy speech or clean speech. Given in this order, each of these labels may indicate an increasing level of recognition reliability. This discrete parameter can help retrieval coping with speech input heterogeneity.

The integration of these various parameters in the computation of retrieval scores is a major issue for robust SDR. Another possibility is to use this information for selecting documents in a database, according to the reliability of their spoken content descriptions.

4.5.2 MPEG-7 Flexibility

The *SpokenContent* description has been designed to fit the output formats of most up-to-date ASR systems. Thus, a *SpokenContentLattice* may enclose one of the following ASR outputs:

- Many recognizers deliver a single transcription hypothesis of the input speech. This can be stored as a *SpokenContentLattice* enclosing a single path.
- Some commercial recognizers also provide word alternatives for each recognized word, or a list of *n*-best transcriptions. These outputs can also be encoded in MPEG-7 lattices. Word alternatives may be attached to parallel links, starting and ending at the same start and end nodes. The *n*-best transcriptions may be stored in parallel single paths, starting and ending at the start and end nodes of the global lattice.
- Finally, some more refined ASR systems are capable of outputting multi-hypotheses lattices directly. An encoding operation may be necessary to convert the ASR specific lattice format into a valid MPEG-7 *SpokenContent* description.

The level of detail in the lattice depends on the particular application. As mentioned in Sections 4.3.2.1 and 4.3.2.2, the MPEG-7 *SpokenContent* standard allows for multiple indexing levels: phones, syllables, words, sequence of words, etc. All this makes the *SpokenContent* description compatible with the different SDR approaches detailed in Section 4.4:

- Classical word-based retrieval techniques (Section 4.4.3) may be applied to word lattices generated by an LVCSR system. In that case, only the *WordLinks* are activated in the *SpokenContentLattice* descriptions. The lattices must refer to a *SpokenContentHeader* enclosing the *WordLexicon* of the LVCSR system. However, it should be noted that *SpokenContent* descriptions have no field to store word similarity measures, such as the EMIM distance given in Equation (4.27).
- Some classical text pre-processing may be applied to reduce the dimension of the indexing term space using a word mapping technique (Section 4.4.3.1). The result can be stored in a *SpokenContent* word lattice by setting the *linguisticUnit* attribute of the *WordLexicon* (set to *word* by default) to the appropriate value, e.g. *linguisticUnit=stem* to store the output of a word stemming algorithm.
- Some intermediate level between words and phones may be chosen. For example, the output of a syllable recognizer (Larson and Eickeler, 2003) can be stored in a word lattice. The complete set of syllables is stored in a *WordLexicon* descriptor with *linguisticUnit=syllable*.
- Phone-based VSM retrieval techniques (Section 4.4.4) may be applied to phonetic lattices. In that case, only the *PhoneLinks* are activated in the *SpokenContentLattice* descriptions. The lattices must refer to a *SpokenContentHeader* enclosing the *PhoneLexicon* of the phone recognizer and the corresponding *ConfusionInfo* metadata. It should be noted that the *PhoneIndex* descriptions can be activated in the *SpeakerInfo* header metadata. The index can be used to store the lists of phone *n-* gram terms extracted from the lattices.
- Phonetic string matching techniques (Section 4.4.5) may be applied to 1-best phonetic transcriptions directly stored in single-path *SpokenContent* lattices or extracted from multi-hypotheses *SpokenContent* lattices. *ConfusionInfo* metadata is required to apply PSM techniques (Section 4.4.5.2).
- The combination of word and phone indexing methods (Section 4.4.6), allowing retrieval at different semantic levels, is possible. A *SpokenContent* description can store different types of recognition hypotheses in the same *SpokenContentLattice* (mixing *WordLinks* and *PhoneLinks*), as depicted in Figure 4.6.

It is even possible to make classical text retrieval applications conform to the MPEG-7 standard, since hand-annotated metadata can be stored in the same scheme as the ASR output. The *provenance* attribute enclosed in the *SpeakerInfo* metadata can be used to distinguish between data sources (e.g. *manual* for a written text or *ASR* for automatic word annotation).

The flexibility of the MPEG-7 *SpokenContent* description makes it usable in many different application contexts. The main possible types of applications are:

- *Spoken document retrieval.* This is the most obvious application of spoken content metadata, already detailed in this chapter. The goal is to retrieve information in a database of spoken documents. The result of the query may be the top-ranked relevant documents. As *SpokenContent* descriptions include the time locations of recognition hypotheses, the position of the retrieved query word(s) in the most relevant documents may also be returned to the user. Mixed *SpokenContent* lattices (i.e. combining words and phones) could be an efficient approach in most cases.
- *Indexing of audiovisual data.* The spoken segments in the audio stream can be annotated with *SpokenContent* descriptions (e.g. word lattices yielded by an LVCSR system). A preliminary audio segmentation of the audio stream is necessary to spot the spoken parts. The spoken content metadata can be used to search particular events in a film or a video (e.g. the occurrence of a query word or sequence of words in the audio stream).
- *Spoken annotation of databases.* Each item in a database is annotated with a short spoken description. This annotation is processed by an ASR system and attached to the item as a *SpokenContent* description. This metadata can then be used to search items in the database, by processing the *SpokenContent* annotations with an SDR engine. A typical example of such applications, already on the market, is the spoken annotation of photographs. In that case, speech decoding is performed on a mobile device (integrated in the camera itself) with limited storage and computational capacities. The use of a simple phone recognizer may be appropriate.

4.5.3 Perspectives

One of the most promising perspectives for the development of efficient spoken content retrieval methods is the combination of multiple independent index sources. A *SpokenContent* description can represent the same spoken information at different levels of granularity in the same lattice by merging words and sub-lexical terms.

These multi-level descriptions lead to retrieval approaches that combine the discriminative power of large-vocabulary word-based indexing with the open-vocabulary property of sub-word-based indexing, by which the problem of OOV words is greatly alleviated. As outlined in Section 4.4.6.2, some steps have already been made in this direction. However, hybrid word/sub-word-based SDR strategies have to be further investigated, with new fusion methods (Yu and Seide, 2004) or new combinations of index sources, e.g. combined use of distinct types of sub-lexical units (Lee *et al.*, 2004) or distinct LVCSR systems (Matsushita *et al.*, 2004).

Another important perspective is the combination of spoken content with other metadata derived from speech (Begeja *et al.*, 2004; Hu *et al.*, 2004). In general, the information contained in a spoken message consists of more than just words. In the query, users could be given the possibility to search for words, phrases, speakers, words and speakers together, non-verbal speech characteristics (male/female), non-speech events (like coughing or other human noises), etc. In particular, the speakers' identities may be of great interest for retrieving information in audio. If a speaker segmentation and identification algorithm is applied to annotate the lattices with some speaker identifiers (stored in *SpeakerInfo* metadata), this can help searching for particular events in a film or a video (e.g. sentences or words spoken by a given character in a film). The *SpokenContent* descriptions enclose other types of valuable indexing information, such as the spoken language.

REFERENCES

Angelini B., Falavigna D., Omologo M. and De Mori R. (1998) *"Basic Speech Sounds, their Analysis and Features"*, in *Spoken Dialogues with Computers*, pp. 69–121, R. De Mori (ed.), Academic Press, London.

Begeja L., Renger B., Saraclar M., Gibbon D., Liu Z. and Shahraray B. (2004) "A System for Searching and Browsing Spoken Communications", *HLT-NAACL 2004 Workshop on Interdisciplinary Approaches to Speech Indexing and Retrieval*, pp. 1–8, Boston, MA, USA, May.

Browne P., Czirjek C., Gurrin C., Jarina R., Lee H., Marlow S., McDonald K., Murphy N., O'Connor N. E., Smeaton A. F. and Ye J. (2002) "Dublin City University Video Track Experiments for TREC 2002", *NIST, 11th Text Retrieval Conference (TREC 2002)*, Gaithersburg, MD, USA, November.

Buckley C. (1985) "Implementation of the SMART Information Retrieval System", Computer Science Department, Cornell University, Report 85–686.

Chomsky N. and Halle M. (1968) *The Sound Pattern of English*, MIT Press, Cambridge, MA.

Clements M., Cardillo P. S. and Miller M. S. (2001) "Phonetic Searching vs. LVCSR: How to Find What You Really Want in Audio Archives", *AVIOS 2001*, San Jose, CA, USA, April.

Coden A. R., Brown E. and Srinivasan S. (2001) "Information Retrieval Techniques for Speech Applications", *ACM SIGIR 2001 Workshop "Information Retrieval Techniques for Speech Applications"*.

Crestani F. (1999) "A Model for Combining Semantic and Phonetic Term Similarity for Spoken Document and Spoken Query Retrieval", International Computer Science Institute, Berkeley, CA, tr-99-020, December.

Crestani F. (2002) "Using Semantic and Phonetic Term Similarity for Spoken Document Retrieval and Spoken Query Processing" in *Technologies for Constructing Intelligent Systems*, pp. 363–376, J. G.-R. B. Bouchon-Meunier and R. R. Yager (eds) Springer-Verlag, Heidelberg, Germany.

Crestani F., Lalmas M., van Rijsbergen C. J. and Campbell I. (1998) " "Is This Document Relevant? . . . Probably": A Survey of Probabilistic Models in Information Retrieval", *ACM Computing Surveys*, vol. 30, no. 4, pp. 528–552.

Deligne S. and Bimbot F. (1995) "Language Modelling by Variable Length Sequences: Theoretical Formulation and Evaluation of Multigrams", *ICASSP'95*, pp. 169–172, Detroit, USA.

Ferrieux A. and Peillon S. (1999) "Phoneme-Level Indexing for Fast and Vocabulary-Independent Voice/Voice Retrieval", *ESCA Tutorial and Research Workshop (ETRW)*, *"Accessing Information in Spoken Audio"*, Cambridge, UK, April.

Gauvain J.-L., Lamel L., Barras C., Adda G. and de Kercardio Y. (2000) "The LIMSI SDR System for TREC-9", *NIST, 9th Text Retrieval Conference (TREC 9)*, pp. 335–341, Gaithersburg, MD, USA, November.

Glass J. and Zue V. W. (1988) "Multi-Level Acoustic Segmentation of Continuous Speech", *ICASSP'88*, pp. 429–432, New York, USA, April.

Glass J., Chang J. and McCandless M. (1996) "A Probabilistic Framework for Feature-based Speech Recognition", *ICSLP'96*, vol. 4, pp. 2277–2280, Philadelphia, PA, USA, October.

Glavitsch U. and Schäuble P. (1992) "A System for Retrieving Speech Documents", *ACM, SIGIR*, pp. 168–176.

Gold B. and Morgan N. (1999) *Speech and Audio Signal Processing*, John Wiley & Sons, Inc., New York.

Halberstadt A. K. (1998) "Heterogeneous acoustic measurements and multiple classifiers for speech recognition", PhD Thesis, Massachusetts Institute of Technology (MIT), Cambridge, MA.

Hartigan J. (1975) *Clustering Algorithms*, John Wiley & Sons, Inc., New York.

Hu Q., Goodman F., Boykin S., Fish R. and Greiff W. (2004) "Audio Hot Spotting and Retrieval using Multiple Features", *HLT-NAACL 2004 Workshop on Interdisciplinary Approaches to Speech Indexing and Retrieval*, pp. 13–17, Boston, MA, USA, May.

James D. A. (1995) "The Application of Classical Information Retrieval Techniques to Spoken Documents", PhD Thesis, University of Cambridge, Speech, Vision and Robotic Group, Cambridge, UK.

Jelinek F. (1998) *Statistical Methods for Speech Recognition*, MIT Press, Cambridge, MA.

Johnson S. E., Jourlin P., Spärck Jones K. and Woodland P. C. (2000) "Spoken Document Retrieval for TREC-9 at Cambridge University", *NIST, 9th Text Retrieval Conference (TREC 9)*, pp. 117–126, Gaithersburg, MD, USA, November.

Jones G. J. F., Foote J. T., Spärk Jones K. and Young S. J. (1996) "Retrieving Spoken Documents by Combining Multiple Index Sources", *ACM SIGIR'96*, pp. 30–38, Zurich, Switzerland, August.

Katz S. M. (1987) "Estimation of Probabilities from Sparse Data for the Language Model Component of a Speech Recognizer", *IEEE Transactions on Acoustics, Speech and Signal Processing*, vol. 3, pp. 400–401.

Kupiec J., Kimber D. and Balasubramanian V. (1994) "Speech-based Retrieval using Semantic Co-Occurrence Filtering", *ARPA, Human Language Technologies (HLT) Conference*, pp. 373–377, Plainsboro, NJ, USA.

Larson M. and Eickeler S. (2003) "Using Syllable-based Indexing Features and Language Models to Improve German Spoken Document Retrieval", *ISCA, Eurospeech 2003*, pp. 1217–1220, Geneva, Switzerland, September.

Lee S. W., Tanaka K. and Itoh Y. (2004) "Multi-layer Subword Units for Open-Vocabulary Spoken Document Retrieval", *ICSLP'2004*, Jeju Island, Korea, October.

Levenshtein V. I. (1966) "Binary Codes Capable of Correcting Deletions, Insertions and Reversals", *Soviet Physics Doklady*, vol. 10, no. 8, pp. 707–710.

Lindsay A. T., Srinivasan S., Charlesworth J. P. A., Garner P. N. and Kriechbaum W. (2000) "Representation and linking mechanisms for audio in MPEG-7", *Signal Processing: Image Communication Journal, Special Issue on MPEG-7*, vol. 16, pp. 193–209.

Logan B., Moreno P. J. and Deshmukh O. (2002) "Word and Sub-word Indexing Approaches for Reducing the Effects of OOV Queries on Spoken Audio", *Human Language Technology Conference (HLT 2002)*, San Diego, CA, USA, March.

Matsushita M., Nishizaki H., Nakagawa S. and Utsuro T. (2004) "Keyword Recognition and Extraction by Multiple-LVCSRs with 60,000 Words in Speech-driven WEB Retrieval Task", *ICSLP'2004*, Jeju Island, Korea, October.

Moreau N., Kim H.-G. and Sikora T. (2004a) "Combination of Phone N-Grams for a MPEG-7-based Spoken Document Retrieval System", *EUSIPCO 2004*, Vienna, Austria, September.

Moreau N., Kim H.-G. and Sikora T. (2004b) "Phone-based Spoken Document Retrieval in Conformance with the MPEG-7 Standard", *25th International AES Conference "Metadata for Audio"*, London, UK, June.

Moreau N., Kim H.-G. and Sikora T. (2004c) "Phonetic Confusion Based Document Expansion for Spoken Document Retrieval", *ICSLP Interspeech 2004*, Jeju Island, Korea, October.

Morris R. W., Arrowood J. A., Cardillo P. S. and Clements M. A. (2004) "Scoring Algorithms for Wordspotting Systems", *HLT- NAACL 2004 Workshop on Interdisciplinary Approaches to Speech Indexing and Retrieval*, pp. 18–21, Boston, MA, USA, May.

Ng C., Wilkinson R. and Zobel J. (2000) "Experiments in Spoken Document Retrieval Using Phoneme N-grams", *Speech Communication*, vol. 32, no. 1, pp. 61–77.

Ng K. (1998) "Towards Robust Methods for Spoken Document Retrieval", *ICSLP'98*, vol. 3, pp. 939–342, Sydney, Australia, November.

Ng K. (2000) "Subword-based Approaches for Spoken Document Retrieval", PhD Thesis, Massachusetts Institute of Technology (MIT), Cambridge, MA.

Ng K. and Zue V. (1998) "Phonetic Recognition for Spoken Document Retrieval", *ICASSP'98*, pp. 325–328, Seattle, WA, USA.

Ng K. and Zue V. W. (2000) "Subword-based Approaches for Spoken Document Retrieval", *Speech Communication*, vol. 32, no. 3, pp. 157–186.

Paul D. B. (1992) "An Efficient A* Stack Decoder Algorithm for Continuous Speech Recognition with a Stochastic Language Model", *ICASSP'92*, pp. 25–28, San Francisco, USA.

Porter M. (1980) "An Algorithm for Suffix Stripping", *Program*, vol. 14, no. 3, pp. 130–137.

Rabiner L. (1989) "A Tutorial on Hidden Markov Models and Selected Applications in Speech Recognition", *Proceedings of the IEEE*, vol. 77, no. 2, pp. 257–286.

Rabiner L. and Juang B.-H. (1993) *Fundamentals of Speech Recognition*, Prentice Hall, Englewood Cliffs, NJ.

Robertson E. S. (1977) "The probability ranking principle in IR", *Journal of Documentation*, vol. 33, no. 4, pp. 294–304.

Rose R. C. (1995) "Keyword Detection in Conversational Speech Utterances Using Hidden Markov Model Based Continuous Speech Recognition", *Computer, Speech and Language*, vol. 9, no. 4, pp. 309–333.

Salton G. and Buckley C. (1988) "Term-Weighting Approaches in Automatic Text Retrieval", *Information Processing and Management*, vol. 24, no. 5, pp. 513–523.

Salton G. and McGill M. J. (1983) *Introduction to Modern Information Retrieval*, McGraw-Hill, New York.

Srinivasan S. and Petkovic D. (2000) "Phonetic Confusion Matrix Based Spoken Document Retrieval", *23rd Annual ACM Conference on Research and Development in Information Retrieval (SIGIR'00)*, pp. 81–87, Athens, Greece, July.

TREC (2001) "Common Evaluation Measures", *NIST, 10th Text Retrieval Conference (TREC 2001)*, pp. A–14, Gaithersburg, MD, USA, November.

van Rijsbergen C. J. (1979) *Information Retrieval*, Butterworths, London.

Voorhees E. and Harman D. K. (1998) "Overview of the Seventh Text REtrieval Conference", *NIST, 7th Text Retrieval Conference (TREC-7)*, pp. 1–24, Gaithersburg, MD, USA, November.

Walker S., Robertson S. E., Boughanem M., Jones G. J. F. and Spärck Jones K. (1997) "Okapi at TREC-6 Automatic Ad Hoc, VLC, Routing, Filtering and QSDR", *6th Text Retrieval Conference (TREC-6)*, pp. 125–136, Gaithersburg, MD, USA, November.

Wechsler M. (1998) "Spoken Document Retrieval Based on Phoneme Recognition", PhD Thesis, Swiss Federal Institute of Technology (ETH), Zurich.

Wechsler M., Munteanu E. and Schäuble P. (1998) "New Techniques for Open-Vocabulary Spoken Document Retrieval", *21st Annual ACM Conference on Research and Development in Information Retrieval (SIGIR'98)*, pp. 20–27, Melbourne, Australia, August.

Wells J. C. (1997) "SAMPA computer readable phonetic alphabet", in *Handbook of Standards and Resources for Spoken Language Systems*, D. Gibbon, R. Moore and R. Winski (eds), Mouton de Gruyter, Berlin and New York.

Wilpon J. G., Rabiner L. R. and Lee C.-H. (1990) "Automatic Recognition of Keywords in Unconstrained Speech Using Hidden Markov Models", *Transactions on Acoustics, Speech and Signal Processing*, vol. 38, no. 11, pp. 1870–1878.

Witbrock M. and Hauptmann A. G. (1997) "Speech Recognition and Information Retrieval: Experiments in Retrieving Spoken Documents", *DARPA Speech Recognition Workshop*, Chantilly, VA, USA, February.

Yu P. and Seide F. T. B. (2004) "A Hybrid Word/Phoneme-Based Approach for Improved Vocabulary-Independent Search in Spontaneous Speech", *ICSLP'2004*, Jeju Island, Korea, October.

5

Music Description Tools

The purpose of this chapter is to outline how music and musical signals can be described. Several MPEG-7 high-level tools were designed to describe the properties of musical signals. Our prime goal is to use these descriptors to compare music signals and to query for pieces of music.

The aim of the MPEG-7 *Timbre DS* is to describe some perceptual features of musical sounds with a reduced set of descriptors. These descriptors relate to notions such as "attack", "brightness" or "richness" of a sound. The *Melody DS* is a representation for melodic information which mainly aims at facilitating efficient melodic similarity matching. The musical *Tempo DS* is defined to characterize the underlying temporal structure of musical sounds. In this chapter we focus exclusively on MPEG-7 tools and applications. We outline how distance measures can be constructed that allow queries for music based on the MPEG-7 DS.

5.1 TIMBRE

5.1.1 Introduction

In music, timbre is the quality of a musical note which distinguishes different types of musical instrument, see (Wikipedia, 2001). The timbre is like a formant in speech; a certain timbre is typical for a musical instrument. This is why, with a little practice, it is possible for human beings to distinguish a saxophone from a trumpet in a jazz group or a flute from a violin in an orchestra, even if they are playing notes at the same pitch and amplitude. Timbre has been called the psycho-acoustician's waste-basket as it can include so many factors.

Though the phrase tone colour is often used as a synonym for timbre, colours of the optical spectrum are not generally explicitly associated with particular sounds. Rather, the sound of an instrument may be described with words like "warm" or

MPEG-7 Audio and Beyond: Audio Content Indexing and Retrieval   H.-G. Kim, N. Moreau and T. Sikora
© 2005 John Wiley & Sons, Ltd

"harsh" or other terms, perhaps suggesting that tone colour has more in common with the sense of touch than of sight. People who experience synaesthesia, however, may see certain colours when they hear particular instruments.

Two sounds with similar physical characteristics like pitch and loudness may have different timbres. The aim of the MPEG-7 *Timbre DS* is to describe perceptual features with a reduced set of descriptors.

MPEG-7 distinguishes four different families of sounds:

- Harmonic sounds
- Inharmonic sounds
- Percussive sounds
- Non-coherent sounds

These families are characterized using the following features of sounds:

- Harmony: related to the periodicity of a signal, distinguishes harmonic from inharmonic and noisy signals.
- Sustain: related to the duration of excitation of the sound source, distinguishes sustained from impulsive signals.
- Coherence: related to the temporal behaviour of the signal's spectral components, distinguishes spectra with prominent components from noisy spectra.

The four sound families correspond to these characteristics, see Table 5.1. Possible target applications are, following the standard (ISO, 2001a):

- Authoring tools for sound designers or musicians (music sample database management). Consider a musician using a sample player for music production, playing the drum sounds of in his or her musical recordings. Large libraries of sound files for use with sample players are already available. The MPEG-7 *Timbre DS* could be facilitated to find percussive sounds in such a library which matches best the musician's idea for his or her production.
- Retrieval tools for producers (query-by-example (QBE) search based on perceptual features). If a producer wants a certain type of sound and already has

Table 5.1 Sound families and sound characteristics (from ISO, 2001a)

Sound family	Harmonic	Inharmonic	Percussive	Non-coherent
Characteristics	Sustained Harmonic Coherent	Sustained Inharmonic Coherent	Impulsive	Sustained Non-coherent
Example Timbre	Violin, flute *Harmonic-Instrument-Timbre*	Bell, triangle	Snare, claves *Percussive-Instrument-Timbre*	Cymbals

a sample sound, the MPEG-7 *Timbre DS* provides the means to find the most similar sound in a sound file of a music database. Note that this problem is often referred to as audio fingerprinting.

All descriptors of the MPEG-7 *Timbre DS* use the *low-level* timbral descriptors already defined in Chapter 2 of this book. The following sections describe the high-level DS *InstrumentTimbre, HarmonicInstrumentTimbre* and *PercussiveInstrumentTimbre*.

5.1.2 *InstrumentTimbre*

The structure of the *InstrumentTimbre* is depicted in Figure 5.1. It is a set of timbre descriptors in order to describe timbres with harmonic and percussive aspects:

- *LogAttackTime* (LAT), the *LogAttackTime* descriptor, see Section 2.7.2.
- *HarmonicSpectralCentroid* (HSC), the *HarmonicSpectralCentroid* descriptor, see Section 2.7.5.
- *HarmonicSpectralDeviation* (HSD), the *HarmonicSpectralDeviation* descriptor, see Section 2.7.6.
- *HarmonicSpectralSpread* (HSS), the *HarmonicSpectralSpread* descriptor, see Section 2.7.7.

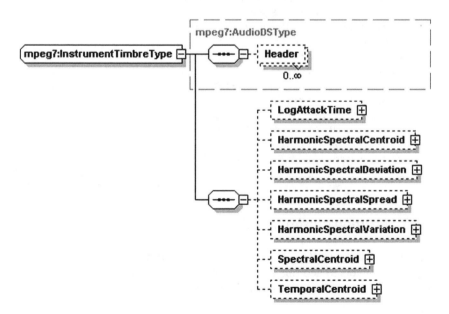

Figure 5.1 The *InstrumentTimbre*: + signs at the end of a field indicate further structured content; – signs mean unfold content; ··· indicate a sequence (from Manjunath *et al.*, 2002)

- *HarmonicSpectralVariation* (HSV), the *HarmonicSpectralVariation* descriptor, see Section 2.7.8.
- *SpectralCentroid* (SC), the *SpectralCentroid* descriptor, see Section 2.7.9.
- *TemporalCentroid* (TC), the *TemporalCentroid* descriptor, see Section 2.7.3.

Example As an example consider the sound of a harp which contains harmonic and percussive features. The following listing represents a harp using the *InstrumentTimbre*. It is written in MPEG-7 XML syntax, as mentioned in the introduction (Chapter 1).

```
<AudioDescriptionScheme xsi:type="InstrumentTimbreType">
 <LogAttackTime>
   <Scalar>-1.660812</Scalar>
 </LogAttackTime>
 <HarmonicSpectralCentroid>
   <Scalar>698.586713</Scalar>
 </HarmonicSpectralCentroid>
 <HarmonicSpectralDeviation>
   <Scalar>-0.014473</Scalar>
 </HarmonicSpectralDeviation>
 <HarmonicSpectralSpread>
   <Scalar>0.345456</Scalar>
 </HarmonicSpectralSpread>
 <HarmonicSpectralVariation>
   <Scalar>0.015437</Scalar>
 </HarmonicSpectralVariation>
 <SpectralCentroid>
   <Scalar>867.486074</Scalar>
 </SpectralCentroid>
 <TemporalCentroid>
   <Scalar>0.231309</Scalar>
 </TemporalCentroid>
</AudioDescriptionScheme>
```

5.1.3 *HarmonicInstrumentTimbre*

Figure 5.2 shows the *HarmonicInstrumentTimbre*. It holds the following set of timbre descriptors to describe the timbre perception among sounds belonging to the harmonic sound family, see (ISO, 2001a):

- *LogAttackTime* (LAT), the *LogAttackTime* descriptor, see Section 2.7.2.
- *HarmonicSpectralCentroid* (HSC), the *HarmonicSpectralCentroid* descriptor, see Section 2.7.5.

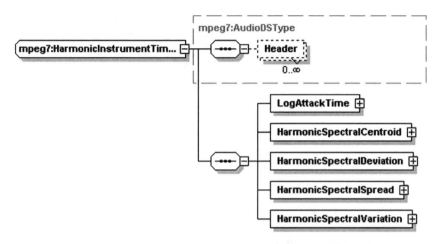

Figure 5.2 The *HarmonicInstrumentTimbre*. (from Manjunath *et al.*, 2002)

- *HarmonicSpectralDeviation* (HSD), the *HarmonicSpectralDeviation* descriptor, see Section 2.7.6.
- *HarmonicSpectralSpread* (HSS), the *HarmonicSpectralSpread* descriptor, see Section 2.7.7.
- *HarmonicSpectralVariation* (HSV), the *HarmonicSpectralVariation* descriptor, see Section 2.7.8.

Example The MPEG-7 description of a sound measured from a violin is depicted below.

```
<AudioDescriptionScheme
 xsi:type="HarmonicInstrumentTimbreType">
 <LogAttackTime>
  <Scalar>-0.150702</Scalar>
 </LogAttackTime>
<HarmonicSpectralCentroid>
  <Scalar>1586.892383</Scalar>
 </HarmonicSpectralCentroid>
<HarmonicSpectralDeviation>
  <Scalar>-0.027864</Scalar>
 </HarmonicSpectralDeviation>
<HarmonicSpectralSpread>
  <Scalar>0.550866</Scalar>
 </HarmonicSpectralSpread>
<HarmonicSpectralVariation>
  <Scalar>0.001877</Scalar>
 </HarmonicSpectralVariation>
</AudioDescriptionScheme>
```

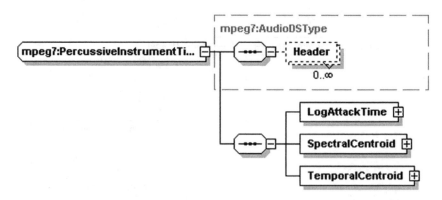

Figure 5.3   The *PercussiveInstrumentTimbre* (from Manjunath *et al.*, 2002)

5.1.4 *PercussiveInstrumentTimbre*

The *PercussiveInstrumentTimbre* depicted in Figure 5.3 can describe impulsive
sounds without any harmonic portions. To this end it includes:

- *LogAttackTime* (LAT), the *LogAttackTime* descriptor, see Section 2.7.2.
- *SpectralCentroid* (SC), the *SpectralCentroid* descriptor, see Section 2.7.9.
- *TemporalCentroid* (TC), the *TemporalCentroid* descriptor, see Section 2.7.3.

Example   A side drum is thus represented using only three scalar values in the
following example.

```
<AudioDescriptionScheme
 xsi:type="PercussiveInstrumentTimbreType">
 <LogAttackTime>
   <Scalar>-1.683017</Scalar>
 </LogAttackTime>
 <SpectralCentroid>
   <Scalar>1217.341518</Scalar>
 </SpectralCentroid>
 <TemporalCentroid>
   <Scalar>0.081574</Scalar>
 </TemporalCentroid>
</AudioDescriptionScheme>
```

5.1.5 Distance Measures

Timbre descriptors can be combined in order to allow a comparison of two
sounds according to perceptual features.

For comparing harmonic sounds this distance measure may be employed:

$$d = \sqrt{8(\Delta LAT)^2 + 3 \cdot 10^{-5}(\Delta HSC)^2 + 3 \cdot 10^{-4}(\Delta HSD)^2 + (10\Delta HSS - 60\Delta HSV)^2} \quad (5.1)$$

For percussive sounds this distance measure is useful:

$$d = \sqrt{(-0.3\Delta LAT - 0.6\Delta TC)^2 + (-10^{-4}\Delta SC)^2} \quad (5.2)$$

In both cases, Δ is the difference between the values of the same acoustical parameter for the two sounds considered, see (ISO, 2001a).

5.2 MELODY

The MPEG-7 *Melody DS* provides a rich representation for monophonic melodic information to facilitate efficient, robust and expressive melodic similarity matching.

The term melody denotes a series of notes or a succession, not a simultaneity as in a chord, see (Wikipedia, 2001). However, this succession must contain change of some kind and be perceived as a single entity (possibly gestalt) to be called a melody. More specifically, this includes patterns of changing pitches and durations, while more generally it includes any interacting patterns of changing events or quality.

What is called a "melody" depends greatly on the musical genre. Rock music and folk songs tend to concentrate on one or two melodies, verse and chorus. Much variety may occur in phrasing and lyrics. In western classical music, composers often introduce an initial melody, or theme, and then create variations. Classical music often has several melodic layers, called polyphony, such as those in a fugue, a type of counterpoint. Often melodies are constructed from motifs or short melodic fragments, such as the opening of Beethoven's Ninth Symphony. Richard Wagner popularized the concept of a leitmotif: a motif or melody associated with a certain idea, person or place.

For jazz music a melody is often understood as a sketch and widely changed by the musicians. It is more understood as a starting point for improvization. Indian classical music relies heavily on melody and rhythm, and not so much on harmony as the above forms. A special problem arises for styles like Hip Hop and Techno. This music often presents no clear melody and is more related to rhythmic issues. Moreover, rhythm alone is enough to picture a piece of music, e.g. a distinct percussion riff, as mentioned in (Manjunath *et al.*, 2002). Jobim's famous "One Note Samba" is an nice example where the melody switches between pure rhythmical and melodic features.

5.2.1 *Melody*

The structure of the MPEG-7 *Melody* is depicted in Figure 5.4. It contains information about meter, scale and key of the melody. The representation

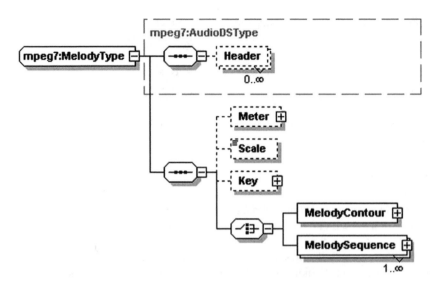

Figure 5.4 The MPEG-7 *Melody* (from Manjunath *et al.*, 2002)

of the melody itself resides inside either the fields *MelodyContour* or *MelodySequence*.

Besides the optional field *Header* there are the following entries:

- *Meter*: the time signature is held in the *Meter* (optional).
- *Scale*: in this array the intervals representing the scale steps are held (optional).
- *Key*: a container containing degree, alteration and mode (optional).
- *MelodyContour*: a structure of *MelodyContour* (choice).
- *MelodySequence*: a structure of *MelodySequence* (choice).

All these fields and necessary MPEG-7 types will be described in more detail in the following sections.

5.2.2 *Meter*

The field *Meter* contains the time signature. It specifies how many beats are in each bar and which note value constitutes one beat. This is done using a fraction: the numerator holds the number of beats in a bar, the denominator contains the length of one beat. For example, for the time signature 4/4 each beat contains three quarter notes. The most common time signatures in western music are 4/4, 3/4 and 2/4.

The time signature also gives information about the rhythmic subdivision of each bar, e.g. a 4/4 meter is stressed on the first and third bar by convention. For unusual rhythmical patterns in music complex signatures like $3 + 2 + 3/8$ are given. Note that this cannot be represented exactly by MPEG-7 (see example next page).

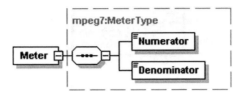

Figure 5.5   The MPEG-7 *Meter* (from Manjunath *et al.*, 2002)

The *Meter* is shown in Figure 5.5. It is defined by:

- *Numerator*: contains values from 1 to 128.
- *Denominator*: contains powers of 2: $2^0, \ldots, 2^7$, e.g. $1, 2, \ldots, 128$.

Example   Time signatures like 5/4, 3/2, 19/16 can be easily represented using MPEG-7. Complex signatures like $3 + 2 + 3/8$ have to be defined in a simplified manner like 8/8.

```
<Meter>
  <Numerator>8</Numerator>
  <Denominator>8</Denominator>
</Meter>
```

5.2.3 *Scale*

The *Scale* descriptor contains a list of intervals representing a sequence of intervals dividing the octave. The intervals result in a list of frequencies giving the pitches of the single notes of the scale. In traditional western music, scales consist of seven notes, made up of a root note and six other scale degrees whose pitches lie between the root and its first octave. Notes in the scale are separated by whole and half step intervals of tones and semitones, see (Wikipedia, 2001).

There are a number of different types of scales commonly used in western music, including *major, minor, chromatic, modal, whole tone* and *pentatonic* scales. There are also synthetic scales like the *diminished* scales (also known as *octatonic*), the *altered* scale, the *Spanish* and *Jewish* scales, or the *Arabic* scale.

The relative pitches of individual notes in a scale may be determined by one of a number of tuning systems. Nowadays, in most western music, the *equal temperament* is the most common tuning system. Starting with a pitch at F_0, the pitch of note n can be calculated using:

$$f(n) = F_0 \, 2^{n/12}. \tag{5.3}$$

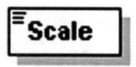

Figure 5.6 The MPEG-7 *Scale*. It is a simple vector of float values. From (Manjunath *et al.*, 2002)

Using $n = 1 \ldots 12$ results in all 12 pitches of the chromatic scale, related to a pitch at F_0 (e.g. 440 Hz). Note that $f(12)$ is the octave to F_0.

The *well temperaments* are another form of well-known tuning systems. They evolved in the baroque period and were made popular by Bach's *Well Tempered Clavier*. There are many well temperament schemes: *French Temperament Ordinaire, Kirnberger, Vallotti, Werckmeister* or *Young*. Some of them are given as an example below.

Also mentioned in the MPEG-7 standard is the *Bohlen–Pierce* (BP) scale, a non-traditional scale containing 13 notes. It was independently developed in 1972 by Heinz Bohlen, a microwave electronics and communications engineer, and later by John Robinson Pierce,[1] also a microwave electronics and communications engineer! See the examples for more details.

The information of the *Scale* descriptor may be helpful for reference purposes. The structure of the *Scale* is a simple vector of floats as shown in Figure 5.6:

- *Scale*: the vector contains the parameter n of Equation (5.3). Using the whole numbers 1–12 results in the equal tempered chromatic scale, which is also the default of the *Scale* vector. If a number of frequencies $f(n)$ of pitches building a scale are given, the values scale(n) of the *Scale* vector can be calculated using:

$$\text{scale}(n) = 12 \log_2 \left(\frac{f(n)}{F_0} \right). \tag{5.4}$$

Example The default of the *Scale* vector, the chromatic scale using the *equal temperature*, is simply represented as:

```
<Scale>
   1.0 2.0 3.0 4.0   5.0   6.0
   7.0 8.0 9.0 10.0 11.0 12.0
</Scale>
```

[1] Note that Pierce is also known as the "Father of the Communications Satellite".

An example of a well tempered tuning, the *Kirnberger III* temperature, is written as:

```
<Scale>
   1.098 2.068 3.059 4.137   5.020   6.098
   7.034 8.078 9.103 10.039 11.117 12.0
</Scale>
```

The *BP scale* represented by the *Scale* vector contains 13 values:

```
<Scale>
   1.3324   3.0185   4.3508   5.8251   7.3693 8.8436
   10.1760 11.6502 13.1944 14.6687 16.0011 17.6872
   19.0196
</Scale>
```

5.2.4 *Key*

In music theory, the *key* is the tonal centre of a piece, see (Wikipedia, 2001). It is designated by a note name (the tonic), such as "C", and is the base of the musical scale (see above) from which most of the notes of the piece are drawn. Most commonly, the mode of that scale can be either in major or minor mode. Other modes are also possible, e.g. dorian, phrygian, lydian, but most popular music uses either the major (ionian) and minor (aeolian) modes. Eighteenth- and nineteenth-century music also tends to focus on these modes.

The structure of the MPEG-7 *Key* is given in Figure 5.7. Besides the optional *Header* it contains only a field *KeyNote* which is a complex type using some attributes.

- *KeyNote* is a complex type that contains a *degreeNote* with possible strings *A, B, C, D, E, F, G*. An optional attribute field *Display* contains a string to be displayed instead of the note name, e.g. "do" instead of "C".

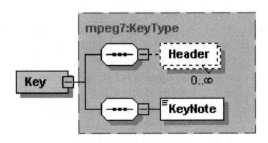

Figure 5.7 The structure of the MPEG-7 *Key* (from Manjunath *et al.*, 2002)

- Two attributes can be set for the *KeyNote*:

  - *accidental*: an enumeration of alterations for the alphabetic note name; possible values are natural (default), flat (♭), sharp (♯), double flat (♭♭), double sharp (♯♯).
  - *mode*: the mode is a controlled term by reference, e.g. major or minor.

A possible melody key is "B♭ major":

```
<Key>
 <KeyNote accidental="flat" mode="major">B</KeyNote>
</Key>
```

5.2.5 *MelodyContour*

Melody information is usually stored in formats allowing good musical reproduction or visual representation, e.g. as a score. A popular format for playback of melodies or generally music is MIDI (Music Instrument Digital Interface), which stores the melody as it is played on a musical instrument. GUIDO[1] in turn is one of many formats related to score representation of music, see (Hoos *et al.*, 2001). MPEG-7 provides melody representations specifically dedicated to multimedia systems. The *MelodyContour* described in this section and the *MelodySequence* described in Section 5.2.6 are standardized for this purpose.

MPEG-7 melody representations are particularly useful for "melody search", such as in query-by-humming (QBH) systems. QBH describes the application where a user sings or "hums" a melody into a query system. The system searches in a database for music entries with identical or similar melodies. For such purposes a reasonable representation of melodies is necessary. This representation is required on the one hand for melody description of the user and on the other hand as a database representation, which is searched for the user query. In many cases it is sufficient to describe only the contour of the melody instead of a detailed description given by MIDI or GUIDO. The simplest form is to use only three contour values describing the intervals from note to note: up (U), down (D) and repeat (R). Coding a melody using U, D and R is also known as Parsons code, see (Prechelt and Typke, 2001). An example is given in Figure 5.8. "As time goes by", written by Herman Hupfield, is encoded as UDDDUUUDDDUUUDDDU.

A more detailed contour representation is to represent the melody as a sequence of changes in pitch, see (Uitdenbogerd and Zobel, 1999). In this *relative pitch* or *interval method*, each note is represented as a change in pitch form the prior note,

---

[1] Guido of Arezzo or Guido Monaco (995–1050) is regarded as the inventor of modern musical notation, see (Wikipedia, 2001).

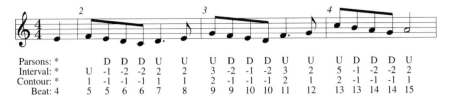

Parsons:	*		D	D	D	U		U		U	D	D	D	U		U		U	D	D	D	U
Interval:	*	U	-1	-2	-2	2		2		3	-2	-1	-2	3		2		5	-1	-2	-2	2
Contour:	*		1	-1	-1	-1	1		1		2	-1	-1	-1	2		1		2	-1	-1	-1	1
Beat:	4		5	5	6	6	7		8		9	9	10	10	11		12		13	13	14	14	15

Figure 5.8 Example score: "As time goes by – theme from *Casablanca*", written by Herman Hupfield. Three different codings are given: the *Parsons* code, the *interval method* and the *MPEG-7 MelodyContour*

e.g. providing the number of semitones up (positive value) or down (negative value). A variant of this technique is *modulo interval*, in which changes of more than an octave are reduced by 12. Figure 5.8 shows the relative pitches.

MPEG-7 *MelodyContour DS* is a compact contour representation using five steps as proposed by (Kim *et al.*, 2000). For all contour representations described so far, no rhythmical features are taken into account. However, rhythm can be an important feature of a melody. The *MelodyContour DS* also includes rhythmical information (ISO, 2001a) for this purpose.

The MPEG-7 *MelodyContour* is shown in Figure 5.9. It contains two vectors, *Contour* and *Beat*:

- *Contour*: this vector contains a five-level pitch contour representation of the melody using values as shown in Table 5.2. These values are declared in the MPEG-7 *Contour*.
- *Beat*: this vector contains the beat numbers where the contour changes take place, truncated to whole beats. The beat information is stored as a series of integers. The beats are enumerated continuously, disregarding the number of bars.

The contour values given in Table 5.2 are quantized by examining the change in the original interval value in cents. A cent is one-hundredth of a

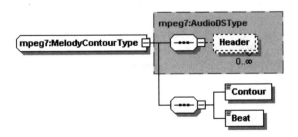

Figure 5.9 The MPEG-7 *MelodyContour*. *Contour*: holds interval steps of the melody contour; *Beat*: contains the beat numbers where the contour changes (from Manjunath *et al.*, 2002)

Table 5.2   Melodic contour intervals defined for five-step representation. The deviation of pitch is given in cents (1 cent is one-hundredth of a semitone)

Contour value	Change of $c(f)$ in cents	Musical interval
-2	$c \leq -250$	Minor third or more down
-1	$-50 \leq c < -250$	Major or minor second down
0	$-50 < c < 50$	Unison
1	$50 \leq c < 250$	Major or minor second up
2	$250 \leq c$	Minor third or more up

semitone following the equal temperature, e.g. the deviation of frequency F_1 from frequency F_0 in Hz is given by:

$$c = 1200 \log_2 \left(\frac{F_1}{F_0} \right). \tag{5.5}$$

In terms of the western tuning standard, a change of a minor third or more, i.e. three semitones, is denoted using ± 2. Three semitones mean 300 cents, thus the threshold of 250 cents also includes very flat minor thirds. A major second makes a 200-cent step in tune, therefore a 249-cent step is an extreme wide major second, denoted with ± 1. The same holds for the prime, 0.

The *Beat* information is given in whole beats only, e.g. the beat number is determined by truncation. If a melody starts on beat 1.5, the beat number is 1. The beat information is simply enumerated: beat 1.5 in the second bar counted meter 4/4 is $4 + 1.5 = 5$.

Example   The following example is used to illustrate this concept. In Figure 5.8 the values for the *MelodyContour DS* are denoted using *Contour* and *Beat*. *Contour* shows the gradient of the interval values. The melody starts going up one semitone, resulting in contour value 1. Then it goes down one semitone, yielding -1, then two semitones down, yielding -1 again. Larger intervals as ± 3 semitones are denoted with a contour value ± 2. The first note has no preceding note; a * denotes there is no interval.

The *Beat* vector in Figure 5.8 starts with 4, because the melody starts with an offbeat. The successive eight notes are counted 5, 5, 6, 6, because of the time signature 4/4. Note that there is one more beat value than contour values.

```
< !— MelodyContour description of "As time goes by" —>
<AudioDescriptionScheme xsi:type="MelodyType">
<Meter>
<Numerator>4</Numerator>
<Denominator>4</Denominator>
</Meter>
```

```
<MelodyContour>
<Contour>
 1 −1 −1 −1  1  1 <!—— bar 2 ——>
 2  1 −1 −1  2  1 <!—— bar 3 ——>
 2 −1 −1 −1  1    <!—— bar 4 ——>
</Contour>
<Beat>
 4                        <!—— bar 1 ——>
 5    5   6   6   7   8 <!—— bar 2 ——>
 9    9  10  10  11  12 <!—— bar 3 ——>
 13  13  14  14  15     <!—— bar 4 ——>
</Beat>
</MelodyContour>
</AudioDescriptionScheme>
```

5.2.6 *MelodySequence*

The *MelodyContour DS* is useful in many applications, but sometimes provides not enough information. One might wish to restore the precise notes of a melody for auditory display or know the pitch of a melody's starting note and want to search using that criterion. The contour representation is designed to be lossy, but is sometimes ambiguous among similar melodies. The MPEG-7 *MelodySequence DS* was defined for these purposes.

For melodic description it employs the interval method, which is restricted not only to pure intervals but also to exact frequency relations. Rhythmic properties are described in a similar manner using differences of note durations, instead of a beat vector. So, the note durations are treated in a analogous way to the pitches. Also lyrics, including a phonetic representation, are possible.

The structure of the *MelodySequence* is displayed in Figure 5.10. It contains:

- *StartingNote*: a container for the absolute pitch in the first note in a sequence, necessary for reconstruction of the original melody, or if absolute pitch is needed for comparison purposes (optional).
- *NoteArray*: the array of intervals, durations and optional lyrics; see description following below.

StartingNote
The *StartingNote*'s structure given in Figure 5.11 contains optional values for frequency or pitch information, using the following fields:

- *StartingFrequency*: the fundamental frequency of the first note in the represented sequence in units of Hz (optional).
- *StartingPitch*: a field containing a note name as described in Section 5.2.4 for the field *KeyNote*. There are two optional attributes:

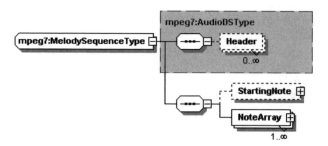

Figure 5.10 The structure of the MPEG-7 *MelodySequence* (from Manjunath *et al.*, 2002)

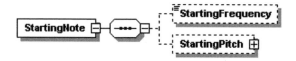

Figure 5.11 The structure of the *StartingNote* (from Manjunath *et al.*, 2002)

- *accidental*: an alteration sign as described in Section 5.2.4 for the same field.
- *Height*: the number of the octave of the *StartingPitch*, counting octaves upwards from a standard piano's lowest A as 0. In the case of a non-octave cycle in the scale (i.e. the last entry of the *Scale* vector shows a significant deviation from 12.0), it the number of repetitions of the base pitch of the scale over 27.5 Hz needed to reach the pitch height of the starting note.

NoteArray

The structure of the *NoteArray* is shown in Figure 5.12. It contains optional header information and a sequence of *Notes*. The handling of multiple *NoteArrays* is described in the MPEG-7 standard see (ISO, 2001a).

- *NoteArray*: the array of intervals, durations and optional lyrics. In the case of multiple *NoteArrays*, all of the *NoteArrays* following the first one listed are to be interpreted as secondary, alternative choices to the primary hypothesis. Use of the alternatives is application specific, and they are included here in simple recognition that neither segmentation nor pitch extraction are infallible in every case (N57, 2003).

  The *Note* contained in the *NoteArray* has the following entries (see Figure 5.13):
- *Interval*: a vector of interval values of the previous note and following note. The values are numbers of semitones, so the content of all interval fields of a *NoteArray* is a vector like the interval method. If this is not applicable, the

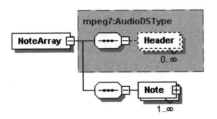

Figure 5.12 The MPEG-7 *NoteArray* (from Manjunath *et al.*, 2002)

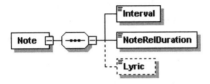

Figure 5.13 The MPEG-7 *Note* (from Manjunath *et al.*, 2002)

interval value $i(n)$ at time step n can be calculated using the fundamental
frequencies of the current note $f(n+1)$ and the previous note $f(n)$:

$$i(n) = 12 \log_2 \left(\frac{f(n+1)}{f(n)} \right). \tag{5.6}$$

As values $i(n)$ are float values, a more precise representation as the pure
interval method is possible. The use of float values is also important for
temperatures other than the equal temperature.

Note that for N notes in a sequence, there are $N-1$ intervals.

- *NoteRelDuration*: the log ratio of the differential onsets for the notes in the
series. This is a logarithmic "rhythm space" that is resilient to gradual changes
in tempo. An extraction algorithm for extracting this is:

$$d(n) = \begin{cases} \log_2 \frac{o(n+1)-o(n)}{0,5}, & n = 1 \\ \log_2 \frac{o(n+1)-o(n)}{o(n)-o(n-1)}, & n \geq 2, \end{cases} \tag{5.7}$$

where $o(n)$ is the time of onset of note n in seconds (measured from the onset
of the first note).

The first note duration is in relation to a quarter note at 120 beats per minute
(0.5 seconds), which gives an absolute reference point for the first note.

- *Lyric*: text information like syllables or words is assigned to the notes in the
Lyric field. It may include a phonetic representation, as allowed by *Textual*
from (ISO, 2001b).

Example An example is used to illustrate this description. The melody "As time goes by" shown in Figure 5.8 is now encoded as a melody sequence. To fill the field *Interval* of the *Note* structure, the interval values of the interval method can be taken. In opposition to this method, the interval is now assigned to the first of both notes building the interval. As a result, the last note of the melody sequence has no following note and an arbitrary interval value has to be chosen, e.g. 0.

For calculation of the *NoteRelDuration* values using Equation (5.7), preceding and following onsets of a note are taken into account. Therefore, the value for the last *NoteRelDuration* value has to be determined using a meaningful phantom note following the last note. Obviously, the onset of this imaginary note is the time point when the last note ends. A ballad tempo of 60 beats per minute was chosen. The resulting listing is shown here.

```
< !— MelodySequence description of "As time goes by" —>
<AudioDescriptionScheme xsi:type="MelodyType">
<MelodySequence>
<NoteArray>
<!— bar 1 —>
<Note>
<Interval> 1</Interval>
<NoteRelDuration> 1.0000</NoteRelDuration>
</Note>
<!— bar 2 —>
<Note>
<Interval>-1</Interval>
<NoteRelDuration>-1.0000</NoteRelDuration>
</Note>
<Note>
<Interval>-2</Interval>
<NoteRelDuration> 0</NoteRelDuration>
</Note>
<Note>
<Interval>-2</Interval>
<NoteRelDuration> 0</NoteRelDuration>
</Note>
<Note>
<Interval> 2</Interval>
<NoteRelDuration> 0</NoteRelDuration>
</Note>
<Note>
<Interval> 2</Interval>
<NoteRelDuration> 1.5850</NoteRelDuration>
</Note>
<!— bar 3 —>
```

```
<Note>
<Interval> 3</Interval>
<NoteRelDuration>-1.5850</NoteRelDuration>
</Note>
<!— Other notes elided —>
<NoteArray>
<MelodySequence>
</AudioDescriptionScheme>
```

An example of usage of the lyrics field within the *Note* of the *MelodySequence* is given in the following listing, from (ISO, 2001a). It describes "Moon River" by Henry Mancini as shown in Figure 5.14. Notice that in this example all fields of the *Melody DS* are used: *Meter*, *Scale* and *Key*. Moreover, the optional *StartingNote* is given.

```
< !— MelodySequence description of "Moon River" —>
<AudioDescriptionScheme xsi:type="MelodyType">
<Meter>
<Numerator>3</Numerator>
<Denominator>4</Denominator>
</Meter>
<Scale>1 2 3 4 5 6 7 8 9 10 11 12</Scale>
<Key> <KeyNote display="do">C</KeyNote> </Key>
<MelodySequence>
<StartingNote>
<StartingFrequency>391.995</StartingFrequency>
<StartingPitch height="4">
<PitchNote display="sol">G</PitchNote>
</StartingPitch>
</StartingNote>
<NoteArray>
<Note>
<Interval>7</Interval>
<NoteRelDuration>2.3219</NoteRelDuration>
<Lyric phoneticTranscription="m u: n">Moon</Lyric>
</Note>
<Note>
<Interval>-2</Interval>
<NoteRelDuration>-1.5850</NoteRelDuration>
<Lyric>Ri-</Lyric>
</Note>
<Note>
<Interval>-1</Interval>
```

(*Continued*)

```
<NoteRelDuration>1</NoteRelDuration>
<Lyric>ver</Lyric>
</Note>
<!-Other notes elided ->
</NoteArray>
</MelodySequence>
</AudioDescriptionScheme>
```

Figure 5.14 "Moon River" by Henry Mancini (from ISO, 2001a)

5.3 TEMPO

In musical terminology, tempo (Italian for time) is the speed or pace of a given piece, see (Wikipedia, 2001). The tempo will typically be written at the start of a piece of music, and is usually indicated in beats per minute (BPM). This means that a particular note value (e.g. a quarter note = crochet) is specified as the beat, and the marking indicates that a certain number of these beats must be played per minute. Mathematical tempo markings of this kind became increasingly popular during the first half of the nineteenth century, after the metronome had been invented by Johann Nepomuk Mälzel in 1816. Therefore the tempo indication shows for example 'M.M. = 120', where M.M. denotes Metronom Mälzel. MIDI files today also use the BPM system to denote tempo.

Whether a music piece has a mathematical time indication or not, in classical music it is customary to describe the tempo of a piece by one or more words. Most of these words are Italian, a result of the fact that many of the most important composers of the Renaissance were Italian, and this period was when tempo indications were used extensively for the first time.

Before the metronome, words were the only way to describe the tempo of a composition, see Table 5.3. Yet, after the metronome's invention, these words continued to be used, often additionally indicating the mood of the piece, thus blurring the traditional distinction between tempo and mood indicators. For example, presto and allegro both indicate a speedy execution (presto being faster), but allegro has more of a connotation of joy (seen in its original meaning in Italian), while presto rather indicates speed as such (with possibly an additional connotation of virtuosity).

Table 5.3 Tempo markings in different languages

Italian	Largo	Slowly and broadly
	Larghetto	A little less slow than largo
	Adagio	Slowly
	Andante	At a walking pace
	Moderato	Moderate tempo
	Allegretto	Not quite allegro
	Allegro	Quickly
	Presto	Fast
	Prestissimo	Very fast
	Larghissimo	As slow as possible
	Vivace	Lively
	Maestoso	Majestic or stately (generally a solemn slow movement)
French	Grave	Slowly and solemnly
	Lent	Slow
	Modéré	Moderate tempo
	Vif	Lively
	Vite	Fast
German	Langsam	Slowly
	Mäßig	Moderately
	Lebhaft	Lively
	Rasch	Quickly
	Schnell	Fast

Metronome manufacturers usually assign BPM values to the traditional terms, in an attempt, perhaps misguided, to be helpful. For instance, a Wittner model MT-50 electronic metronome manufactured in the early 1990s gives the values shown in Table 5.4.

Table 5.4 Usual tempo markings and related BPM values

Marking	BPM
Largo	40–60
Larghetto	60–66
Adagio	66–76
Andante	76–108
Moderato	106–120
Allegro	120–168
Presto	168–208

5.3.1 *AudioTempo*

The MPEG-7 *AudioTempo* is a structure describing musical tempo information.
It contains the fields:

- *BPM*: the BPM (Beats Per Minute) information of the audio signal of type
  AudioBPM.
- *Meter*: the information of the current unit of measurement of beats in *Meter*
  as described in Section 5.2.2 (optional).

The *AudioBPM* is described in the following section.

5.3.2 *AudioBPM*

The *AudioBPM* describes the frequency of beats of an audio signal representing a
musical item in units of beats per minute (BPM). It extends the *AudioLLDScalar*
with two attributes:

- *loLimit*: indicates the smallest valid BPM value for this description and defines
  the upper limit for an extraction mechanism calculating the BPM information
  (optional).
- *hiLimit*: indicates the biggest valid BPM value for this description and defines
  the lower limit for an extraction mechanism calculating the BPM information
  (optional).

A default hopSize of 2 seconds is assumed for the extraction of the BPM
value. This is meaningful for automatic tempo estimation where a block-wise
BPM estimation is performed. A well-established method for beat extraction is
described by (Scheirer, 1998).

Example   Let us assume that the tempo is already given. A piece constantly
played in moderate tempo M.M. = 106 with meter 2/4 is then described by:

```
<AudioTempo>
<BPM>
<SeriesOfScalar totalNumOfSamples="1">
<Raw>106</Raw>
<Weight>1</Weight>
</SeriesOfScalar></BPM>
<Meter>
<Numerator>2</Numerator>
<Denominator>4</Denominator>
</Meter>
</AudioTempo>
```

5.4 APPLICATION EXAMPLE: QUERY-BY-HUMMING

A QBH system enables a user to hum a melody into a microphone connected to a computer in order to retrieve a list of possible song titles that match the query melody. The system analyses the melodic and rhythmic information of the input signal. The extracted data set is used as a database query. The result is presented as a list of, for example, 10 best-matching results. A QBH system is a typical music information retrieval (MIR) system, which can make use of the MPEG-7 standard.

Different QBH systems are already available on the World Wide Web (WWW). *Musicline* is a commercial QBH system developed by Fraunhofer IDMT which can be found at (Musicline, n.d.). The database contains about 3500 melodies of mainly pop music. A Java interface allows a hummed query to be submitted.

The website (Musipedia, 2004) is inspired by (Wikipedia, 2001), and provides a searchable, editable and expandable collection of tunes, melodies and musical themes. It uses the QBH system *Melodyhound* by (Prechelt and Typke, 2001) and provides a database with tunes of about 17 000 folk songs, 11 000 classic tunes, 1500 rock/pop tunes and 100 national anthems. One or more of these categories can be chosen to narrow down the database and increase chances for correct answers. Melodyhound uses the Parsons code as melody representation. The query input can be submitted via the keyboard or as whistled input, using a Java application.

A typical architecture for a QBH system is depicted in Figure 5.15. The user input is taken using a microphone which converts the acoustic input to a pulse code modulated (PCM) signal, the necessary information is extracted and transcribed for comparison. The representation of the melody information can use MPEG-7 *MelodyContour* or *MelodySequence*, respectively. Also the content of the music database, which might be files containing PCM or MIDI information, must be converted into a symbolic representation. Thus, the crucial processing steps of a QBH system are transcription and comparison of melody information. They are discussed in the following sections.

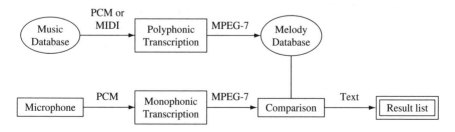

Figure 5.15 A generic architecture for a QBH system

5.4.1 Monophonic Melody Transcription

The transcription of the user query to a symbolic representation is a mandatory part of a QBH system. Many publications are related to this problem, e.g. (McNab *et al.*, 1996b; Haus and Pollastri, 2001; Clarisse *et al.*, 2002; Viitaniemi *et al.*, 2003) to mention a few. (Clarisse *et al.*, 2002) also give an overview of commercial systems used for the transcription of singing input.

Queryhammer is a development tool for a QBH system using MPEG-7 descriptors in all stages, which also addresses this problem, see (Batke *et al.*, 2004b). The transcription block is also referred to as the *acoustic front-end*, see (Clarisse *et al.*, 2002). In existing systems, this part is often implemented as a Java applet, e.g. (Musicline, n.d.), or (Musipedia, 2004). For illustration purposes we will now step through all the processing steps of the query transcription part of Queryhammer.

Figure 5.16 shows the score of a possible user query. This query results in a waveform as depicted in Figure 5.18 (top). The singer used the syllable /da/. Other syllables often used are /na/, /ta/, /du/ and so on. Lyrics are much more difficult to transcribe, therefore most QBH systems ask the user to use /na/ or /da/.

In Figure 5.17 the processing steps to transcribe this query are shown. After recording the signal with a computer sound card the signal is bandpass filtered to reduce environmental noise and distortion. In this system a sampling rate of 8000 Hz is used. The signal is band limited to 80 to 800 Hz, which is sufficient for sung input, see (McNab *et al.*, 1996a). This frequency range corresponds to a musical note range of $D\sharp_2 - G_5$.

MPEG-7 contour: *   −2   −1   0   1   2

Figure 5.16 Some notes a user might query. They should result in all possible contour values of the MPEG-7 *MelodyContour DS*

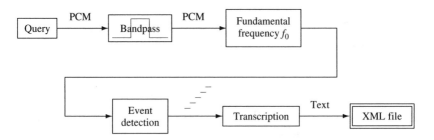

Figure 5.17 Processing steps for melody extraction

Following pre-processing, the signal is analysed by a pitch detection algorithm. Queryhammer uses the autocorrelation method as used in the well-known speech processing tool *Praat* by Paul Boersma (Boersma, 1993). This algorithm weights the autocorrelation function using a Hanning window, followed by a parabolic interpolation in the lag domain for higher precision. The result of the pitch detection is shown in Figure 5.18 (bottom).

The next task is to segment the input stream into single notes. This can be done using amplitude or pitch information, as shown in (McNab *et al.*, 1996a). The event detection stage extracts note events from the frequency information. A note event carries information about the onset time, the pitch and the duration of a single note. This task is difficult because no singer will sing in perfect tune, therefore a certain amount of unsteadiness is expected. A first frequency value is taken for determination of the musical pitch, e.g. a "D". The consecutive sequence of frequency values is evaluated for this pitch. If the frequency results in the same musical pitch with a deviation of ±50 cents, this "D" in our example, the frequency value belongs to the same note event. To adapt the tuning of the singer, frequency values of long-lasting events (about 250 ms) are passed through a median filter. The median frequency determines a new tuning note,

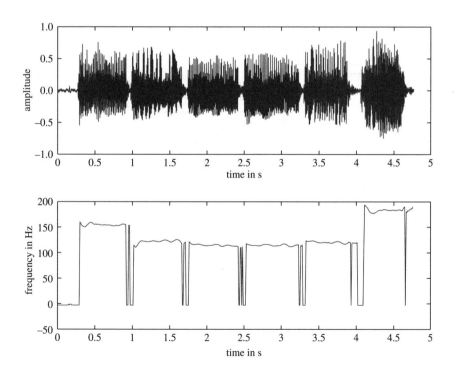

Figure 5.18 Top: the PCM signal of the user query; bottom: the fundamental frequency of the singing input

which is assumed to be 440 Hz at the beginning. The next event is then searched using the new tuning note, e.g. 438 Hz (most singers tend to fall in pitch).

Finally very short events less than 100 ms are discarded. Since no exact transcription of the singing signal is required, this is sufficient for building a melody contour. In Figure 5.19 (top) the events found from the frequencies of Figure 5.19 are shown. The selected events in Figure 5.19 (bottom) are passed to the transcription block.

The melodic information is now transcribed into a more general representation, the *MelodyContour*, as outlined in Section 5.2.5.

5.4.2 Polyphonic Melody Transcription

The "Polyphonic Transcription" block in Figure 5.15 is not a mandatory part of a QBH system itself, but necessary to build up the melody database. If the "Music Database" consists of MIDI files as a symbolic representation, melody information can be easily extracted.

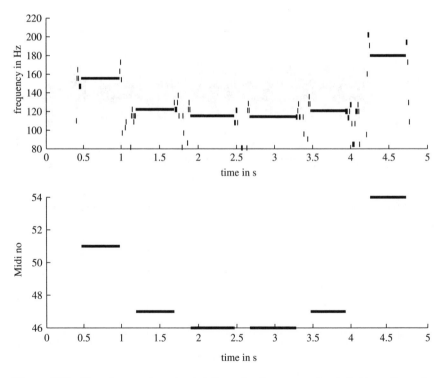

Figure 5.19 Top: the events extracted from the frequency signal; bottom: the note events extracted with minimum length

The extraction of symbolic information like a melody contour from music is strongly related to the music transcription problem, and an extremely difficult task. This is because of the fact that most music files contain polyphonic sounds, meaning that there are two or more concurrent sounds, harmonies accompanying a melody or melodies with several voices.

Technically speaking this task can be seen as the "multiple fundamental frequency estimation" (MFFE) problem, also known as "multi-pitch estimation". An overview of this research field can be found in (Klapuri, 2004). The work of (Goto, 2000, 2001) is especially interesting for QBH applications, because Goto uses real work CD recordings in his evaluations.

The methods used for MFFE can be divided into the following categories, see (Klapuri, 2004). Note that a clear division is not possible because these methods are complex and combine several processing principles.

- Perceptual grouping of frequency partials. MFFE and sound separation are closely linked, as the human auditory system is very effective in separating and recognizing individual sound sources in mixture signals (see also Section 5.1). This cognitive function is called auditory scene analysis (ASA). The computational ASA (CASA) is usually viewed as a two-stage process, where an incoming signal is first decomposed into its elementary time–frequency components and these are then organized to their respective sound sources. Provided that this is successful, a conventional F_0 estimation of each of the separated component sounds, or in practice the F_0 estimation, often takes place as a part of the grouping process.
- Auditory model-based approach. Models of the human auditory periphery are also useful for MFFE, especially for preprocessing the signals. The most popular unitary pitch model described in (Meddis and Hewitt, 1991) is used in the algorithms of (Klapuri, 2004) or (Shandilya and Rao, 2003).

  An efficient calculation method for this auditory model is presented in (Klapuri and Astola, 2002). The basic processing steps are: a bandpass filter bank modelling the frequency selectivity of the inner ear, a half-wave rectifier modelling the neural transduction, the calculation of autocorrelation functions in each bandpass channel, and the calculation of the summary autocorrelation function of all channels.
- Blackboard architectures. Blackboard architectures emphasize the integration of knowledge. The name blackboard refers to the metaphor of a group of experts working around a physical blackboard to solve a problem, see (Klapuri, 2001). Each expert can see the solution evolving and makes additions to the blackboard when requested to do so.

  A blackboard architecture is composed of three components. The first component, the blackboard, is a hierarchical network of hypotheses. The input data is at the lowest level and analysis results on the higher levels. Hypotheses have relationships and dependencies on each other. Blackboard architecture is often also viewed as a data representation hierarchy, since hypotheses encode data at varying abstraction levels. The intelligence of the system is coded into knowledge sources (KSs). The second component of the system comprises processing algorithms that may manipulate the content of the blackboard. A third component, the scheduler, decides which knowledge source is in turn to take its actions. Since the state of analysis is completely encoded in the blackboard hypotheses, it is relatively easy to add new KSs to extend a system.

- Signal-model-based probabilistic inference. It is possible to describe the task of MFFE in terms of a signal model, and the fundamental frequency is the parameter of the model to be estimated.

  (Goto, 2000) proposed a method which models the short-time spectrum of a music signal. He uses a tone model consisting of a number of harmonics which are modelled as Gaussian distributions centred at multiples of the fundamental frequency. The expectation and maximization (EM) algorithm is used to find the predominant fundamental frequency in the sound mixtures.

- Data-adaptive techniques. In data-adaptive systems, there is no parametric model or other knowledge of the sources; see (Klapuri, 2004). Instead, the source signals are estimated from the data. It is not assumed that the sources (which refer here to individual notes) have harmonic spectra. For real-world signals, the performance of, for example, independent component analysis alone is poor. By placing certain restrictions on the sources, the data-adaptive techniques become applicable in realistic cases.

  Further details can be found in (Klapuri, 2004) or (Hainsworth, 2003).

In Figure 5.20 an overview of the system PreFEst (Goto, 2000) is shown. The audio signal is fed into a multi-rate filter bank containing five branches, and the signal is down-sampled stepwise from $\frac{F_s}{2}$ to $\frac{F_s}{16}$ in the last branch, where F_s is the sample rate. A short-time Fourier transform (STFT) is used with a constant

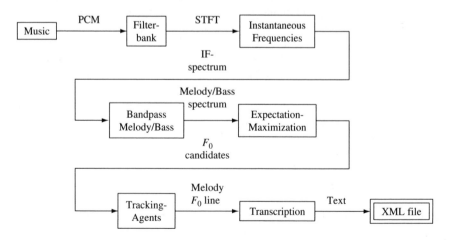

Figure 5.20 Overview of the system PreFEst by (Goto, 2000). This method can be seen as a technique with signal-model-based probabilistic inference

window length N in each branch to obtain a better time–frequency resolution for lower frequencies.

The following step is the calculation of the instantaneous frequencies of the STFT spectrum. Assume that $X(\omega, t)$ is the STFT of $x(t)$ using a window function $h(t)$. The instantaneous frequency $\lambda(\omega, t)$ is given by:

$$\lambda(\omega, t) = \frac{d\phi(\omega, t)}{dt} \tag{5.8}$$

with $X(\omega, t) = A(\omega, t) \exp^{(j\phi(\omega,t))}$. It is easily calculated using the time–frequency reassignment method, which can be interpreted as estimating the instantaneous frequency and group delay for each point (bin) on the time–frequency plane, see (Hainsworth, 2003). Quantization of frequency values following the equal temperated scale leads to a sparse spectrum with clear harmonic lines. The bandpass simply selects the range of frequencies that is examined for the melody and the bass lines.

The EM algorithm uses the simple tone model described above to maximize the weight for the predominant pitch in the examined signal. This is done iteratively leading to a maximum a posteriori estimate, see (Goto, 2000). An example of

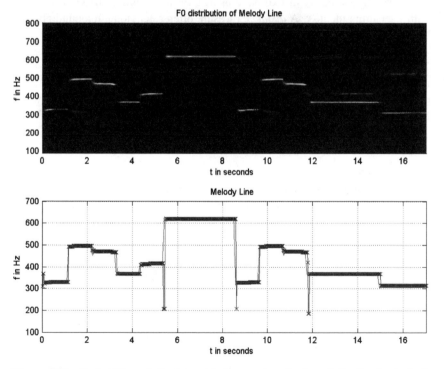

Figure 5.21 Probability of fundamental frequencies (top) and finally tracked F_0 progression (bottom): solid line = exact frequencies; crosses = estimated frequencies

the distribution of weights for F_0 is shown in Figure 5.21 (top). A set of F_0 candidates is passed to the tracking agents that try to find the most dominant and stable candidates. In Figure 5.21 (bottom) the finally extracted melody line is shown. These frequency values are transcribed to a symbolic melody description, e.g. the MPEG-7 *MelodyContour*.

5.4.3 Comparison of Melody Contours

To compare two melodies, different aspects of the melody representation can be used. Often, algorithms only take into account the contour of the melody, disregarding any rhythmical aspects. Another approach is to compare two melodies solely on the basis of their rhythmic similarity. Furthermore, melodies can be compared using contour and rhythm. (McNab *et al.*, 1996b) also discuss other combinations, like interval and rhythm.

This section discusses the usability of matching techniques for the comparison of MPEG-7 compliant with the *MelodyContour DS*. The goal is to determine the similarity or distance of two melodies' representations. A *similarity* measure represents the similarity of two patterns as a decimal number between 0 and 1, with 1 meaning identity. A *distance* measure often refers to an unbound positive decimal number with 0 meaning identity.

Many techniques have been proposed for music matching, see (Uitdenbogerd, 2002). Techniques include dynamic programming, n-grams, bit-parallel techniques, suffix trees, indexing individual notes for lookup, feature vectors, and calculations that are specific to melodies, such as the sum of the pitch differences between two sequences of notes. Several of these techniques use string-based representations of melodies.

N-gram Techniques
N-gram techniques involve counting the common (or different) n-grams of the query and melody to arrive at a score representing their similarity, see (Uitdenbogerd and Zobel, 2002). A melody contour described by M interval values is given by:

$$C = [m(1), m(2), \ldots, m(M)]. \tag{5.9}$$

To create an n-gram of length N we build vectors:

$$G(i) = [m(i), m(i+1), \ldots, m(i+N-1)], \tag{5.10}$$

containing N consecutive interval values, where $i = 1, \ldots M - N + 1$. The total amount of all n-grams is $M - N + 1$.

Q represents the vector with contour values of the query, and D is the piece to match against. Let Q_N and D_N be the sets of n-grams contained in Q and D, respectively.

- *Coordinate matching (CM)*: also known as count distinct measure, CM counts the n-grams $G(i)$ that occur in both Q and D:

$$R_{CM} = \sum_{G(i) \in Q_N \cap D_N} 1. \qquad (5.11)$$

- *Ukkonen*: the Ukkonen measure (UM) is a difference measure. It counts the number of n-grams in each string that do not occur in both strings:

$$R_{UM} = \sum_{G(i) \in S_N} |U(Q, G(i)) - U(D, G(i))|, \qquad (5.12)$$

where $U(Q, G(i))$ and $U(D, G(i))$ are the numbers of occurrences of the n-gram $G(i)$ in Q and D, respectively.
- *Sum of frequencies (SF)*: on the other hand SF counts how often the n-grams $G(i)$ common in Q and D occur in D:

$$R_{SF} = \sum_{G(i) \in Q_N \cap D_N} U(G(i), D) \qquad (5.13)$$

where $U(G(i), D)$ is the number of occurrences of n-gram $G(i)$ in D.

Dynamic Programming
The description of a melody as a sequence of symbols can been seen as a string. Therefore it is possible to apply string matching techniques to compare melodies. As stated in (Uitdenbogerd, 2002), one established way of comparing strings is to use edit distances. This family of string matching techniques has been widely applied in related applications including genomics and phonetic name matching.

- *Local Alignment*: the dynamic programming approach *local alignment* determines the best match of the two strings Q and D, see (Uitdenbogerd and Zobel, 1999, 2002). This technique can be varied by choosing different penalties for insertions, deletions and replacements.

   Let A represent the array, Q and D represent query and piece, and index i ranges from 0 to query length and index j from 0 to piece length:

$$A[i, j] = \max \begin{cases} A[i-1, j] + c_d & (i \geq 1) \\ A[i, j-1] + c_d & (j \geq 1) \\ A[i-1, j-1] + c_e & (Q(i) = D(j), \text{ and } i, j \geq 1) \\ A[i-1, j-1] + c_m & (Q(i) \neq D(j)) \\ 0 \end{cases} \qquad (5.14)$$

where c_d is the cost of an insertion or deletion, c_e is the value of an exact match, and c_m is the cost of mismatch.

- *Longest common subsequence*: for this technique, array elements $A[i, j]$ are incremented if the current cell has a match, otherwise they are set to the same value as the value in the upper left diagonal, see (Uitdenbogerd and Zobel, 2002). That is, inserts, deletes and mismatches do not change the score of the match, having a cost of zero.

String Matching with Mismatches

Since the vectors Q and D can be understood as strings, also string matching techniques can be used for distance measurement. Baeza-Yates describes in (Baeza-Yates, 1992) an efficient algorithm for string matching with mismatches suitable for QBH systems. String Q is sliding along string D, and each character $q(n)$ is compared with its corresponding character $d(m)$. R contains the highest similarity score after evaluating D. Matching symbols are counted, e.g if $q(n) = d(m)$ the similarity score is incremented. R contains the highest similarity score.

Direct Measure

Direct measure is an efficiently computable distance measure based on dynamic programming developed by (Eisenberg *et al.*, 2004). It compares only the melodies' rhythmic properties. MPEG-7 *Beat* vectors have two crucial limitations, which enable the efficient computation of this distance measure. All vectors' elements are positive integers and every element is equal to or bigger than its predecessor. The *direct measure* is robust against single note failures and can be computed by the following iterative process for two beat vectors U and V:

1. Compare the two vector elements $u(i)$ and $v(j)$ (starting with $i = j = 1$ for the first comparison).
2. If $u(i) = v(j)$, the comparison is considered a match. Increment the indices i and j and proceed with step 1.
3. If $u(i) \neq v(j)$, the comparison is considered a miss:
   (a) If $u(i) < v(j)$, increment only the index i and proceed with step 1.
   (b) If $u(i) > v(j)$, increment only the index j and proceed with step 1.

The comparison process should be continued until the last element of one of the vectors has been detected as a match, or the last element in both vectors is reached. The distance R is then computed as the following ratio with M being the number of misses and V being the number of comparisons:

$$R = \frac{M}{V}. \tag{5.15}$$

The maximum number of iterations for two vectors of length N and length M is equal to the sum of the lengths $(N + M)$. This is significantly more efficient than a computation with classic methods like the dot plot, which needs at least $N \cdot M$ operations.

TPBM I

The algorithm *TPBM I* (Time Pitch Beat Matching I) is described in (Chai and Vercoe, 2002) and (Kim et al., 2000) and directly related to the MPEG-7 *MelodyContour DS*. It uses melody and beat information plus time signature information as a triplet *time, pitch, beat*, e.g. $\langle t, p, b \rangle$. To compute the similarity score S of a melody segment $m = \langle t_m, p_m, b_m \rangle$ and a query $q = \langle t_q, p_q, b_q \rangle$, the following steps are necessary:

1. If the numerators of t_m and t_q are not equal, return 0.
2. Initialize measure number, $n = 1$.
3. Align p_m and p_q from measure n of m.
4. Calculate beat similarity score for each beat:
   (a) Get subsets of p_m and p_q that fall within the current beat as s_q and s_m.
   (b) Set $i = 1, j = 1, s = 0$.
   (c) While $i \leq |s_q|$ and $j \leq |s_m|$

       i. if $s_q[i] = s_m[j]$ then
           $s = s + 1, i = i + 1, j = j + 1$
       ii. else
           $k = j$
           if $s_q[i] \neq 0$ then $j = j + 1$
           if $s_m[k] \neq 0$ then $i = i + 1$

   (d) Return $S = \frac{s}{|S_q|}$.
5. Average the beat similarity score over total number of beats in the query. This results in the overall similarity score starting at measure n: S_n.
6. If n is not at the end of m, then $n = n + 1$ and repeat step 3.
7. Return $S = \max S_n$, the best overall similarity score starting at a particular measure.

An evaluation of distance measures for use with MPEG-7 *MelodyContour* can be found in (Batke et al., 2004a).

REFERENCES

Baeza-Yates R. (1992) "Fast and Practical Approximate String Matching", *Combinatorial Pattern Matching, Third Annual Symposium*, pp. 185–192, Barcelona, Spain.

Batke J. M., Eisenberg G., Weishaupt P. and Sikora T. (2004a) "Evaluation of Distance Measures for MPEG-7 Melody Contours", *International Workshop on Multimedia Signal Processing*, IEEE Signal Processing Society, Siena, Italy.

Batke J. M., Eisenberg G., Weishaupt P. and Sikora T. (2004b) "A Query by Humming System Using MPEG-7 Descriptors", *Proceedings of the 116th AES Convention*, AES, Berlin, Germany.

Boersma P. (1993) "Accurate Short-term Analysis of the Fundamental Frequency and the Harmonics-to-Noise Ratio of a Sampled Sound", *IFA Proceedings 17*, Institute of Phonetic Sciences of the University of Amsterdam, the Netherlands.

Chai W. and Vercoe B. (2002) "Melody Retrieval on the Web", *Proceedings of ACM/SPIE Conference on Multimedia Computing and Networking*, Boston, MA, USA.

Clarisse L. P., Martens J. P., Lesaffre M., Baets B. D., Meyer H. D. and Leman M. (2002) An Auditory Model Based Transcriber of Singing Sequences", *Proceedings of the ISMIR*, pp. 116–123, Ehent, Belgium.

Eisenberg G., Batke J. M. and Sikora T. (2004) "BeatBank – An MPEG-7 compliant query by tapping system", *Proceedings of the 116th AES Convention*, Berlin, Germany.

Goto M. (2000) "A Robust Predominant-f0 Estimation Method for Real-time Detection of Melody and Bass Lines in CD Recordings", *Proceedings of ICASSP*, pp. 757–760, Tokyo, Japan.

Goto M. (2001) "A Predominant-f0 Estimation Method for CD Recordings: Map Estimation Using EM Algorithm for Adaptive Tone Models", *Proceedings of ICASSP*, pp. V–3365–3368, Tokyo, Japan.

Hainsworth S. W. (2003) "Techniques for the Automated Analysis of Musical Audio", PhD Thesis, University of Cambridge, Cambridge, UK.

Haus G. and Pollastri E. (2001) "An Audio Front-End for Query-by-Humming Systems", *2nd Annual International Symposium on Music Information Retrieval*, ISMIR, Bloomington, IN, USA.

Hoos H. H., Renz K. and Görg M. (2001) "GUIDO/MIR—An experimental musical information retrieval system based on Guido music notation", *Proceedings of the Second Annual International Symposium on Music Information Retrieval*, Bloomington, IN, USA.

ISO (2001a) *Information Technology – Multimedia Content Description Interface – Part 4: Audio*, 15938-4:2001(E).

ISO (2001b) *Information Technology – Multimedia Content Description Interface – Part 5: Multimedia Description Schemes*, 15938-5:2001(E).

Kim Y. E., Chai W., Garcia R. and Vercoe B. (2000) "Analysis of a Contour-based Representation for Melody", *Proceedings of the International Symposium on Music Information Retrieval*, Boston, MA, USA.

Klapuri A. (2001) "Means of Integrating Audio Content Analysis Algorithms", *110th Audio Engineering Society Convention*, Amsterdam, the Netherlands.

Klapuri A. (2004) "Signal Processing Methods for the Automatic Transcription of Music", PhD Thesis, Tampere University of Technology, Tampere, Finland.

Klapuri A. P. and Astola J. T. (2002) "Efficient Calculation of a Physiologically-motivated Representation for Sound", *IEEE International Conference on Digital Signal Processing*, Santorini, Greece.

Manjunath B. S., Salembier P. and Sikora T. (eds) (2002) *Introduction to MPEG-7*, 1 Edition, John Wiley & Sons, Ltd, Chichester.

McNab R. J., Smith L. A. and Witten I. H. (1996a) "Signal Processing for Melody Transcription", *Proceedings of the 19th Australasian Computer Science Conference*, Waikato, New Zealand.

McNab R. J., Smith L. A., Witten I. H., Henderson C. L. and Cunningham S. J. (1996b) "Towards the Digital Music Library: Tune retrieval from acoustic input", *Proceedings of the first ACM International Conference on Digital Libraries*, pp. 11–18, Bethesda, MD, USA.

Meddis R. and Hewitt M. J. (1991) "Virtual Pitch and Phase Sensitivity of a Computer Model of the Auditory Periphery. I: Pitch identification", *Journal of the Acoustical Society of America*, vol. 89, no. 6, pp. 2866–2882.

Musicline (n.d.) "Die Ganze Musik im Internet", QBH system provided by phononet GmbH.

Musipedia (2004) "Musipedia, the open music encyclopedia", www.musipedia.org.

N57 (2003) *Information technology - Multimedia content description interface - Part 4: Audio, AMENDMENT 1: Audio extensions*, Audio Group Text of ISO/IEC 15938-4:2002/FDAM 1.

Prechelt L. and Typke R. (2001) "An Interface for Melody Input", *ACM Transactions on Computer-Human Interaction*, vol. 8, no. 2, pp. 133–149.

Scheirer E. D. (1998) "Tempo and Beat Analysis of Acoustic Musical Signals", *Journal of the Acoustical Society of America*, vol. 103, no. 1, pp. 588–601.

Shandilya S. and Rao P. (2003) "Pitch Detection of the Singing Voice in Musical Audio", *Proceedings of the 114th AES Convention*, Amsterdam, the Netherlands.

Uitdenbogerd A. L. (2002) "Music Information Retrieval Technology", PhD Thesis, Royal Melbourne Institute of Technology, Melbourne, Australia.

Uitdenbogerd A. L. and Zobel J. (1999) "Matching Techniques for Large Music Databases", *Proceedings of the ACM Multimedia Conference* (ed. D. Bulterman, K. Jeffay and H. J. Zhang), pp. 57–66, Orlando, Florida.

Uitdenbogerd A. L. and Zobel J. (2002) "Music Ranking Techniques Evaluated", *Proceedings of the Australasian Computer Science Conference* (ed. M. Oudshoorn), pp. 275–283, Melbourne, Australia.

Viitaniemi T., Klapuri A. and Eronen A. (2003) "A Probabilistic Model for the Transcription of Single-voice Melodies", *Finnish Signal Processing Symposium, FINSIG* Tampere University of Technology, Tampere, Finland.

Wikipedia (2001) "Wikipedia, the free encyclopedia", http://en.wikipedia.org.

6

Fingerprinting and Audio Signal Quality

6.1 INTRODUCTION

This chapter is dedicated to audio fingerprinting and audio signal quality description. In general, the MPEG-7 low-level descriptors in Chapter 2 can be seen as providing a fingerprint for describing audio content. We will focus in this chapter on fingerprinting tools specifically developed for the identification of a piece of audio and for describing its quality.

6.2 AUDIO SIGNATURE

6.2.1 Generalities on Audio Fingerprinting

This section gives a general introduction to the concept of fingerprinting. The technical aspects will be detailed in Sections 6.2.2–6.2.4 quoted out of (Cano *et al.*, 2002a) and (Herre *et al.*, 2002).

6.2.1.1 Motivations

The last decades have witnessed enormous growth in digitized audio (music) content production and storage. This has made available to today's users an overwhelming amount of audio material. However, this scenario created great new challenges for search and access to audio material, turning the process of finding or identifying the desired content efficiently into a key issue in this context.

MPEG-7 Audio and Beyond: Audio Content Indexing and Retrieval   H.-G. Kim, N. Moreau and T. Sikora
© 2005 John Wiley & Sons, Ltd

Audio fingerprinting or content-based audio identification (CBID) technologies[1] are possible and effective solutions to the aforementioned problems, providing the ability to link unlabelled audio to corresponding metadata (e.g. artist and song name), perform content-based integrity verification or watermarking support (Cano *et al.*, 2002c).

Audio *watermarking* is also another possible and much proposed solution. It is somewhat related to audio fingerprinting, but that topic is beyond the scope of this section. There are some references that explain the differences and similarities between watermarking and fingerprinting, and evaluate the applications where each technology is best suited for use (Cano *et al.*, 2002c; Gómez *et al.*, 2002; Gomes *et al.*, 2003).

The basic concept behind an audio fingerprinting system is the identification of a piece of audio content by means of a compact and unique signature extracted from it. This signature, also known as the *audio fingerprint*, can be seen as a summary or perceptual digest of the audio recording. During a training phase, those signatures are created from a set of known audio material and are then stored in a database. Unknown content, even if distorted or fragmented, should afterwards be identified by matching its signature against the ones contained in the database.

However, great difficulties arise when trying to identify audio-distorted content automatically (i.e. comparing a PCM music audio clip against the same clip compressed as MP3 audio).

Fingerprinting eliminates the direct comparison of the (typically large) digitized audio waveform as an efficient and effective approach to audio identification. Also hash methods, such as MD5 (Message Digest 5) or CRC (Cyclic Redundancy Checking), can be used to obtain a more compact representation of the audio binary file (which would allow a more efficient matching). It is difficult to achieve an acceptable robustness to compression or minimal distortions of any kind in the audio signals using hash methods, since the obtained hash values are very fragile to single bit changes.

Hash methods fail to perform the desired perceptual identification of the audio content. In fact, these approaches should not be considered as content-based identification, since they do not consider the content, just the bit information in the audio binary files (Cano *et al.*, 2002a).

When compared with the direct matching of multimedia content based on waveforms, fingerprint systems present important advantages in the identification of audio contents. Fingerprints have small memory and storage requirements and perform matching efficiently. On the other hand, since perceptual irrelevancies have already been removed from the fingerprints, fingerprinting systems should be able to achieve much more robust matching results.

---

[1] Audio fingerprinting is also known as robust matching, robust or perceptual hashing, passive watermarking, automatic music recognition, content-based digital signatures and content-based audio identification (Cano *et al.*, 2002c).

6.2.1.2 Requirements

An audio fingerprinting system should fulfil the following basic, application-dependent requirements (Cano *et al.*, 2002a, Haitsma and Kalker, 2002):

- *Robustness*: the system should be able to identify an audio item accurately, regardless of the level of compression, distortion or interference in the transmission channel. Additionally, it should be able to deal gracefully with other sources of degradation, such as pitch shifting, time extension/compression, equalization, background noise, A/D and D/A conversion, speech and audio coding artefacts (e.g. GSM, MP3), among others. In order to achieve high robustness, the audio fingerprint should be based on features strongly invariant with respect to signal degradations, so that severely degraded audio still leads to similar fingerprints. The false negative rate (i.e. very distinct audio fingerprints corresponding to perceptually similar audio clips) is normally used to express robustness.
- *Reliability*: highly related to the robustness, this parameter is inversely related to the rate at which the system identifies an audio clip incorrectly (false positive rate). A good fingerprinting system should make very few such mismatch errors, and when faced with a very low (or below a specified threshold) identification confidence it should preferably output an "unknown" identification result. Approaches to deal with false positives have been treated for instance in (Cano *et al.*, 2001).
- *Granularity*: depending on the application, it should be able to identify whole titles from excerpts a few seconds long (this property is also known as robustness to cropping), which requires methods for dealing with shifting. This problem addresses a lack of synchronization between the extracted fingerprint and those stored in the database.
- *Efficiency*: the system should be computationally efficient. Consequently, the size of the fingerprints, the complexity of the corresponding fingerprint extraction algorithms, as well as the speed of the searching and matching algorithms, are key factors in the global efficiency of a fingerprinting system.
- *Scalability*: the algorithms used in the distinct building blocks of a fingerprinting system should scale well with the growth of the fingerprint database, so that the robustness, reliability and efficiency parameters of the system remain as specified independently of the register of new fingerprints in the database.

There is an evident interdependency between the above listed requirements. In most cases, this is when improving one parameter implies losing performance in another. A more detailed enumeration of requirements can be found in (Kalker, 2001; Cano *et al.*, 2002c).

An audio fingerprint system generally consists of two main building blocks: one responsible for the extraction of the fingerprints and another one that performs the search and matching of fingerprints. The fingerprint extraction module

should try to obtain a set of relevant perceptual features out of an audio recording, and the resultant audio fingerprint should respect the following requirements
(Cano *et al.*, 2002c):

- *Discrimination power over huge numbers of other fingerprints*: a fingerprint
  is a perceptual digest of the recording, and so must retain the maximum of
  acoustically relevant information. This digest should allow discrimination over
  a large number of fingerprints. This may conflict with other requirements,
  such as efficiency and robustness.
- *Invariance to distortions*: this derives from the robustness requirement.
  Content-integrity applications, however, may relax this constraint for content
  preserving distortions in order to detect deliberate manipulations.
- *Compactness*: a small-sized representation is important for efficiency, since
  a large number (e.g. millions) of fingerprints need to be stored and compared. However, an excessively short representation might not be sufficient to
  discriminate among recordings, thus affecting robustness and reliability.
- *Computational simplicity*: for efficiency reasons, the fingerprint extraction
  algorithms should be computationally efficient and consequently not very time
  consuming.

The solutions proposed to fulfil the above requirements normally call for a
trade-off between dimensionality reduction and information loss, and such a
compromise is usually defined by the needs of the application in question.

6.2.1.3 General Structure of Audio Identification Systems

Independent of the specific approach to extract the content-based compact
signature, a common architecture can be devised to describe the function-
ality of fingerprinting when used for identification (RIAA/IFPI, 2001). This
general architecture is depicted in Figure 6.1. Two distinct phases can be
distinguished:

- Building the database: off-line a memory of the audio to be recognized is
  created. A series of sound recordings is presented to a fingerprint generator.
  This generator processes audio signals in order to generate fingerprints derived
  uniquely from the characteristics of each sound recording. The fingerprint (e.g.
  the compact and unique representation) that is derived from each recording
  is then stored in a database and can be linked with a tag or other metadata
  relevant to each recording.
- Content identification: in the identification mode, unlabelled audio (in either
  streaming or file format) is presented to the input of a fingerprint generator.
  The fingerprint generator function processes the audio signal to produce a

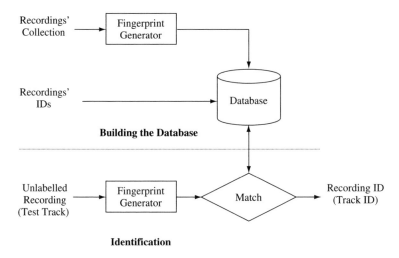

Figure 6.1 Content-based audio identification framework

fingerprint. This fingerprint is then used to query the database and is compared with the stored fingerprints. If a match is found, the resulting track identifier (Track ID) is retrieved from the database. A confidence level or proximity associated with each match may also be given.

The actual implementations of audio fingerprinting normally follow this scheme with differences on the acoustic features observed and the modelling of audio as well as in the matching and indexing algorithms.

6.2.2 Fingerprint Extraction

The overall extraction procedure is schematized in Figure 6.2. The fingerprint generator consists of a front-end and a fingerprint modelling block. These two modules are described in the following sections.

6.2.2.1 Front-End

The front-end converts an audio signal into a sequence of relevant features to feed the fingerprint model block. Several driving forces co-exist in the design of the front-end: dimensionality reduction, extraction of perceptually meaningful parameters (similar to those used by the human auditory system), design towards invariance or robustness (with respect to channel distortions, background noise, etc.), temporal correlation (systems that capture spectral dynamics).

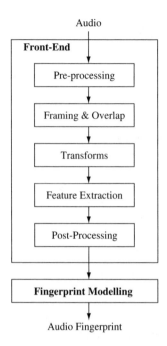

Figure 6.2 Fingerprint generator: frond-end and fingerprint modelling (Cano *et al.*, 2002a)

The front-end comprises five blocks: pre-processing, framing and overlap, transformation, feature extraction and post-processing (see Figure 6.2).

Pre-Processing
Most of the front-ends for audio fingerprinting start with a pre-processing step, where the audio is digitized (if necessary) and converted to a general digital audio format (e.g. 16-bit PCM, 5–44.1 kHz, mono). The signal may also be subjected to other types of processing, such as GSM encoding/decoding in a mobile phone system, pre-emphasis, amplitude normalization (bounding the dynamic range to $[-1, 1]$), among others. In the training phase (i.e. when adding a new fingerprint to the database), the fingerprint is usually extracted from an audio source with the best quality possible, trying to minimize interference, distortion or unnecessary processing of the original audio recording.

Framing and Overlap
The audio signal is then divided into frames (whose size should be chosen so that measurements can be assumed to be a stationary signal), windowed (in order to minimize discontinuities) and finally overlapped (this assures some robustness to shifting). The choice of the frame size, window type and overlap factor is again a trade-off between the rate of change in the spectrum and system complexity.

Typical values for frame size and overlap factor are in the ranges 10–500 ms and 50–80%, respectively.

Linear Transforms: Spectral Estimates

In order to achieve the desired reduction of redundancy in the audio signal, the audio frames are first submitted to a suitably chosen linear transformation. The most common transformation used in audio fingerprinting systems is the fast Fourier transform (FFT), but some other transforms have also been proposed: the discrete cosine transform (DCT), the Haar transform or the Walsh–Hadamard transform (Subramanya et al., 1997), and the modulated complex lapped transform (MCLT) (Mihcak and Venkatesan, 2001; Burges et al., 2002). Richly et al. did a comparison of the DFT and the Walsh–Hadamard transform that revealed that the DFT is generally less sensitive to shifting (Richly et al., 2000). The MCLT exhibits approximate shift invariance properties.

There are optimal transforms in the sense of information packing and decorrelation properties, like Karhunen–Loève (KL) or singular value decomposition (SVD) (Theodoris and Koutroumbas, 1998). These transforms, however, are signal dependent and computationally complex. For that reason, lower-complexity transforms using fixed basis vectors are more common. Most content-based audio identification methods therefore use standard transforms to facilitate efficient compression, noise removal and subsequent processing (Lourens, 1990; Kurth et al., 2002).

Feature Extraction

Once a time–frequency representation of the audio signal has been transformed, additional transformations are applied to the audio frames to generate the final acoustic vectors. The purpose is again to reduce the dimensionality, and at the same time to increase the invariance to distortions. A large number of algorithms have been proposed to generate the final feature vectors, and many of them extract several features by means of a critical-band analysis of the spectrum.

It is very common to include knowledge of the human auditory system to extract more perceptually meaningful parameters. Therefore, many systems extract several features performing a critical-band analysis of the spectrum. In (Papaodysseus et al., 2001; Cano et al., 2002a), mel-frequency cepstrum coefficients (MFCCs) are used. In (Allamanche et al., 2001), the choice is the spectral flatness measure (SFM), which is an estimation of the tone-like or noise-like quality for a band in the spectrum. Papaodysseus et al. proposed a solution based on "band representative vectors", which are an ordered list of indexes of bands with prominent tones (Papaodysseus et al., 2001). Kimura et al. use the energy of each frequency band (Kimura et al., 2001), and Haitsma and Kalker propose the use of the energies of 33 bark-scaled bands to obtain a "hash string", which is the sign of the energy band differences, in both the time and in frequency axes (Haitsma and Kalker, 2002).

Sukittanon and Atlas claim that spectral estimates and related features are only inadequate when audio channel distortion occurs (Sukittanon and Atlas, 2002). They proposed modulation frequency analysis to characterize the time varying behaviour of audio signals. In this case, features correspond to the geometric mean of the modulation frequency estimation of the energy of 19 bark-spaced band filters.

Approaches for music information retrieval include features that have proved valid for comparing sound: harmonicity, bandwidth, loudness, ZCR, etc. (Blum *et al.*, 1999).

(Burges *et al.*, 2002) point out that the features commonly used are heuristic, and as such may not be optimal. For that reason they use a modified Karhunen–Loève (KL) transform, namely oriented principal component analysis (OPCA), to find the optimal features in an unsupervised way. If KL (which is also known as principal component analysis, PCA) finds a set of orthogonal directions which maximize the signal variance, OPCA obtains a set of possible non-orthogonal directions which take some predefined distortions into account.

Post-Processing

Most of the above-mentioned features are absolute measurements. In order to characterize better the temporal variations in the signal, higher-order time derivatives are added to the feature vector. In (Batlle *et al.*, 2002; Cano *et al.*, 2002a), the feature vector is the concatenation of MFCCs, their derivative (Δ) and the acceleration ($\Delta\Delta$), as well as the Δ and $\Delta\Delta$ of the energy. In order to minimize the tendency of derivative features to amplify noise, (Batlle *et al.*, 2002) use cepstrum mean normalization (CMN) to reduce slowly varying channel distortions. They both use transforms (e.g. PCA) to compact the feature vector representation. Some other systems use only the derivative of the features, discarding their absolute values (Allamanche *et al.*, 2001; Kurth *et al.*, 2002). It is quite common to apply a very low-resolution quantization to the features: ternary (Richly *et al.*, 2000) or binary (Haitsma and Kalker, 2002; Kurth *et al.*, 2002). This allows the gaining of robustness against distortions (Haitsma and Kalker, 2002; Kurth *et al.*, 2002), normalizes (Richly *et al.*, 2000), eases hardware implementations and reduces memory requirements. Binary sequences are required to extract error correcting words. In (Mihcak and Venkatesan, 2001), the discretization is designed to increase randomness in order to minimize fingerprint collision probability.

6.2.2.2 Fingerprint Modelling

The fingerprint modelling block usually receives a sequence of feature vectors calculated on a frame-by-frame basis. This is a sequence of vectors where redundancies may be exploited in the frame time vicinity, inside a recording and across the whole database to reduce the fingerprint size further. The type of model chosen conditions the distance metric and also the design of indexing algorithms for fast retrieval.

A very concise form of fingerprint is achieved by summarizing the multi-dimensional vector sequences of a whole song (or a fragment of it) in a single vector.

In Etantrum,[1] the fingerprint was calculated from the means and variances of the 16 bank-filtered energies corresponding to 30 s of audio encoding with a signature of up to 512 bits, which along with information on the original audio format was sent to a server for identification (Cano *et al.*, 2002a). MusicBrainz's[2] TRM audio fingerprint is composed of the average zero crossing rate feature, the estimated beats per minute (BPM), an average representation of the spectrum and some more features of a piece of audio. This fingerprint model proved to be computationally efficient and compact, addressing the requirements of the application for which this system was designed: linking MP3 files to metadata (title, artist, etc.). This application gives priority to low complexity (on both the client and server side) to the detriment of robustness.

Fingerprints can also be simple sequences of features. In (Haitsma and Kalker, 2002) and (Papaodysseus *et al.*, 2001), the fingerprint, which consists of a sequence of band representative vectors, is binary encoded for memory efficiency. Some systems include high-level musically meaningful attributes, like rhythm (BPM) or prominent pitch (Blum *et al.*, 1999).

Following the reasoning on the possible sub-optimality of heuristic features, (Burges *et al.*, 2002) employs several layers of OPCA to decrease the local statistical redundancy of feature vectors with respect to time, reducing dimensionality and achieving better robustness to shifting and pitching.

(Allamanche *et al.*, 2001) propose the exploration of "global redundancies" within an audio piece, assuming that the audio features of a given audio item are similar among them. From this assumption, a compact representation can be generated by clustering the feature vectors, thus approximating the sequence of feature vectors by a much lower number of representative code vectors, a codebook. However, the temporal evolution of the extracted features is lost with such an approximation. In order to achieve higher recognition results and faster matching, short-time statistics are collected over regions of time, which allows taking into account certain temporal dependencies and shortening the length of each sequence.

(Cano *et al.*, 2002b) and (Batlle *et al.*, 2002) use a fingerprint model much inspired by speech research, and which further exploits global redundancy. They view a corpus of music as sentences constructed of concatenating sound classes of a finite alphabet (e.g. "perceptually equivalent" drum sounds occur in a great number of pop songs). This approximation yields a fingerprint which consists of sequences of indexes to a set of sound classes representative of a collection of audio items. The sound classes are estimated via unsupervised clustering and

---

[1] Available on-line at: http://www.freshmeat.net/project/songprint.

[2] MusicBrainz: http://www.musicbrainz.org.

modelled with hidden Markov models (HMMs). This fingerprint representation retains the information on the evolution of audio through time.

In (Mihcak and Venkatesan, 2001), discrete sequences are mapped to a dictionary of error correcting words. In (Kurth *et al.*, 2002), the error correcting codes form the basis of their indexing method.

6.2.3 Distance and Searching Methods

After an audio database has been indexed with the extracted fingerprints of individual recordings, it can be searched by the fingerprint identification module as depicted in Figure 6.1.

In order to compare fingerprints, it is necessary to define some sort of metric. Distance metrics are closely related to the type of model chosen. Correlation is a common option, but the Euclidean distance, or variations of it that deal with sequences of different lengths, are used for instance in (Blum *et al.*, 1999). In (Sukittanon and Atlas, 2002), the classification is nearest neighbour using a cross-entropy estimation. In systems where the vector feature sequences are quantized, a Manhattan distance (or Hamming distance when the quantization is binary) is common (Richly *et al.*, 2000; Haitsma and Kalker, 2002). Another error metric called the *exponential pseudo norm* (EPM), suggested by (Mihcak and Venkatesan, 2001), could be more appropriate to distinguish between close and distant values with an emphasis stronger than linear.

So far, the presented identification frameworks are based on a template matching paradigm (Theodoris and Koutroumbas, 1998): both the reference fingerprints (the ones stored in the database) and the test fingerprints (the ones extracted from the unknown audio) are in the same format and are thus compared according to some distance metric, e.g. Hamming distance, a correlation and so on.

However, in some systems only the reference items are actually fingerprints, compactly modelled as a codebook or a sequence of indexes to HMMs (Allamanche *et al.*, 2001; Batlle *et al.*, 2002), and in these cases the distances are computed directly between the feature sequence extracted from the unknown audio and the reference audio fingerprints stored in the repository. In (Allamanche *et al.*, 2001), the feature vector sequence is matched to the different codebooks using a distance metric. For each codebook, the errors are accumulated. The unknown items are then assigned to the class which yields the lowest accumulated error. In (Batlle *et al.*, 2002), the feature sequence is run against the fingerprints (a concatenation of indexes pointing at HMM sound classes) using the Viterbi algorithm and the most likely passage in the database is selected.

Besides the definition of a distance metric for a fingerprint comparison, a fundamental issue for the usability of such a system is how the comparison of the unknown audio will in fact be made efficiently against all the possibly millions of fingerprints, and this depends heavily on the fingerprint model being used. Vector spaces allow the use of efficient, existing spatial access methods (Baeza-Yates and Ribeiro-Neto 1999). The general goal is to build a data structure, an index, to reduce the number of distance evaluations when a query is presented. As stated by (Chávez *et al.*, 2001), most indexing algorithms for proximity searching build sets of equivalence classes, discard some classes and exhaustively search the rest. They use a simpler distance to eliminate many hypotheses quickly, and the use of indexing methods to overcome the brute-force exhaustive matching with a more expensive distance function is found in the content-based audio identification literature, e.g. in (Kenyon, 1999). Haitsma and Kalker proposed an efficient search algorithm: instead of following a brute-force approach where the distance to every position in the database would be calculated, the distance is calculated for a few candidate positions only (Haitsma and Kalker, 2002). These candidates contain, with very high probability, the best-matching position in the database. In (Cano *et al.*, 2002a), heuristics similar to those used in computational biology for the comparison of DNA are used to speed up a search in a system where the fingerprints are sequences of symbols. (Kurth *et al.*, 2002) presents an index that uses code words extracted from binary sequences representing the audio. These approaches, although very fast, make assumptions on the errors permitted in the words used to build the index. This could result in false dismissals; the simple coarse distance used for discarding unpromising hypotheses must lower bound the more expensive fine distance.

The final step in an audio fingerprinting system is to decide whether the query is present or not in the repository. The result of the comparison of the extracted fingerprint with the database of fingerprints is a score which results from the calculated distances. The decision for a correct identification must be based on a score that is beyond a certain threshold. However, this threshold is not trivial to define, and dependent on the fingerprint model, on the discriminative information of the query, on the similarity of the fingerprints in the database and on the database size. The larger the database, the higher the probability of returning a false positive, and consequently the lower the reliability of the system.

6.2.4 MPEG-7-Standardized *AudioSignature*

The MPEG-7 audio standard provides a generic framework for the descriptive annotation of audio data. The *AudioSignature* high-level tool is a condensed representation of an audio signal, designed to provide a unique content identifier for the purpose of robust automatic identification. It is a compact-sized audio signature which can be used as a fingerprint. This tool also provides an example of how to use the low-level MPEG-7 framework.

6.2.4.1 Description Scheme

The *AudioSignature* description essentially consists of a statistical summariza-tion of *AudioSpectrumFlatness* low-level descriptors (LLDs) over a period of time. These *AudioSpectrumFlatness* descriptors (see Chapter 2) are extracted on a frame-by-frame basis. The spectral flatness LLDs are stored in the unique attribute of the *AudioSignature* description scheme, which is called *Flatness*.

There are some restrictions regarding the instantiations of the *AudioSpectrum-Flatness* descriptors. In order to constitute a valid *AudioSignature* description, the following requirements have to be satisfied:

- The *AudioSpectrumFlatness* descriptions contained by the *Flatness* attribute must be stored as a *SeriesOfVectorBinary* description.
- Both the *Mean* and the *Variance* fields of the *SeriesOfVectorBinary* series containing the *Flatness* features have to be instantiated.
- The scaling ratio (i.e. the *ratio* attribute of the *SeriesOfVectorBinary*) must range between 2 and 128. The default value is 32.
- The *loEdge* attribute of the *AudioSpectrumFlatness* descriptor is fixed at 250 Hz.
- The *hiEdge* attribute of the *AudioSpectrumFlatness* descriptor must be at least 500 Hz. The default value is 4000 Hz.

6.2.4.2 Scalability

The *AudioSignature* description scheme instantiates the *AudioSpectrumFlatness* LLDs in such a way that an interoperable hierarchy of scalable audio signatures can be established with regard to the following parameters:

- Temporal scope of the audio signatures.
- Temporal resolution of the audio signatures.
- Spectral coverage/bandwidth of the audio signatures.

The temporal scope of the audio signatures represents a first degree of freedom and relates to the start position and the length of the audio item for which the feature extraction is carried out. The signal segment used for signature generation can be chosen freely and depends on the type of application envisaged.

The temporal resolution of the fingerprint is an important parameter which can be used to control the trade-off between fingerprint compactness and its descriptive power (i.e. its ability to discriminate between many different audio signals). This temporal scalability is obtained by using the mean and variance of the LLD values, as provided by the generic *SeriesOfVectorBinary* construct, with selectable degrees of decimation, and thus temporal resolution. Consequently, signatures may be rescaled (scaled down) in their temporal resolution according to the standard *SeriesOfVectorBinary* scaling procedures as desired, e.g. in order to achieve a compatible temporal resolution between two signatures.

A second dimension of *AudioSignature* scalability resides in its spectral coverage/bandwidth. The *AudioSpectrumFlatness* descriptor provides a vector of feature values, each value corresponding to a specific quarter-octave frequency band. The number of frequency bands above a fixed base frequency (250 Hz) can be selected as a further parameter of scalability. While signatures may provide different numbers of frequency bands, a meaningful comparison between them is always possible for the bands common to the compared signatures, since these relate to common fixed band definitions.

6.2.4.3   Use in Fingerprinting Applications

The main application for the *AudioSignature* description scheme is the automatic identification of an unknown piece of audio based on a database of registered audio items. An *AudioSignature* is extracted from the item to be identified and then matched to all previously registered *AudioSignature* descriptions in a database. The best-matching reference *AudioSignature* description is the most likely candidate to correspond to the unknown signal.

In a wider sense, the *AudioSignature* structure may be used to identify corresponding MPEG-7 descriptions for audio items which are delivered without any other descriptive data. To this end, the MPEG-7 descriptions available at some server have to include an *AudioSignature* description of each described item.

An example of an MPEG-7-based audio identification system is depicted in Figure 6.3 (Herre *et al.*, 2002). It consists mainly of the two basic extraction and identification modes of operation already introduced in Figure 6.1.

The first steps in the signal processing chain are the same for training and classification: the audio signal is converted to a standard format (e.g. monophonic PCM) at the pre-processing stage of the feature extractor. This stage is followed by the extraction of the *AudioSpectrumFlatness* LLD features.

A feature processor is then used to decrease the description size by means of statistical data summarization. In the MPEG-7 framework, this is done by applying the appropriate rescaling operation to the MPEG-7 *ScalableSeries* of

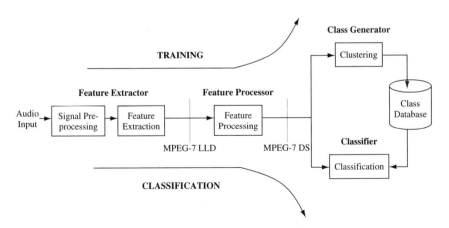

Figure 6.3   MPEG-7 standard audio identification system (Herre *et al.*, 2002)

vectors containing the *AudioSpectrumFlatness* features. The final result is an MPEG-7 *AudioSignature* description that can be interpreted as a fingerprint of the original piece of audio.

Based on this representation, matching between fingerprints can be done in numerous different ways. Since the choice of the matching approach or distance metric does not affect the interoperability of different applications using such a fingerprint, this choice is beyond the scope of the MPEG-7 standardization and left up to the individual application.

(Herre *et al.*, 2002) proposes a simple matching of MPEG-7 *AudioSignature* descriptions that is performed based on a vector quantization (VQ) and nearest-neighbour approach. During the training phase, the class generator in Figure 6.3 performs clustering (e.g. LBG vector quantization (Linde *et al.*, 1980)) using a set of training items. The resulting reference codebooks are then stored in the system's class database. During the classification phase, the signal at the output of the feature processor is compared by the classifier with the codebooks stored in the reference database. The item with the shortest distance (matching error) is presented at the system's output as a result. More sophisticated techniques can be used in the MPEG-7 *AudioSignature* framework to increase both matching robustness and speed.

As mentioned above, the scalability of the MPEG-7-based fingerprinting framework comes from the ability to vary some extraction parameters, such as temporal scope, temporal resolution and number of spectral bands. In this way, a flexible trade-off between the compactness of the fingerprint and its recognition robustness can be achieved.

From an application point of view, this is a powerful concept which helps satisfy the need for a wide range of applications by a single framework. More importantly, the fingerprint representation still maintains interoperability so that fingerprints extracted for one application can still be compared with a fingerprint database set up for a different purpose.

The specification for the *AudioSignature* extraction method guarantees worldwide compatibility between all standards-compliant applications. Numerous different applications, such as broadcast monitoring, Internet services or mobile audio identification services using cellular phones, are currently under development.

6.3 AUDIO SIGNAL QUALITY

The description of the "objective" or "subjective" quality of an audio signal is of great interest for many applications. In the following we describe the MPEG-7 tools developed for this purpose.

The MPEG-7 *AudioSignalQuality* descriptor contains several features reflecting the quality of a signal stored in an *AudioSegment* descriptor. The *AudioSignalQuality* features are often extracted without any perceptual or psycho-acoustical considerations and may not describe the subjective sound quality of audio signals.

The quality information enclosed in *AudioSignalQuality* descriptions could be used, for example, to select the files that should be downloaded among a list of audio documents retrieved on the Internet. More generally, this information helps to decide if a file is of sufficient quality to be used for a particular purpose. The *AudioSignalQuality* can also be used to guide the retrieval of audio documents in a database, based on the quality information.

6.3.1 *AudioSignalQuality* Description Scheme

The *AudioSignalQuality* description scheme is a set of descriptors that have been designed to handle and describe audio signal quality information. In particular the handling of single error events in audio streams is considered. An *AudioSignalQuality* description scheme comprises the following attributes:

- *Operator*: designates the person who is responsible for the audio quality information.
- *UsedTool*: designates the system that was used by the *Operator* to create the quality information. *UsedTool* is stored in a *CreationTool* descriptor.
- *BroadcastReady*: describes whether or not the sound material is ready for broadcasting. *BroadcastReady* is a Boolean parameter (false or true).
- *IsOriginalMono*: describes if a signal was originally mono if it presently has more than one channel. *IsOriginalMono* is a Boolean parameter (false or true).
- *BackgroundNoiseLevel*: contains the estimations of the noise levels in the different channels of a stereo signal.
- *CrossChannelCorrelation*: describes the correlations between the channels of a stereo signal.
- *RelativeDelay*: describes the relative delays between the channels of a stereo signal.
- *Balance*: describes the relative level between the channels of a stereo signal.
- *DcOffset*: describes the mean relative to the maximum of each channel of a stereo signal.
- *Bandwidth*: describes the upper limit of the signal's bandwidth for each channel.
- *TransmissionTechnology*: describes the technology with which the audio file was transmitted or recorded using a predefined set of categories.
- *ErrorEventList*: contains different *ErrorEvent* descriptors. An *ErrorEvent* describes the event time of a specified error type in the signal. The type of error is labelled according to a predefined set of categories.

These quality attributes are detailed in the following sections.

6.3.2 BroadcastReady

BroadcastReady indicates if the sound material is ready for broadcasting (value set to "true") or not (value set to "false"). Its value should generally result from the subjective evaluation of an operator, according to the context of the application. For example, the quality of a piece of audio may be quite bad, but it may be ready for broadcasting (e.g. a historical piece of audio, or a news report recorded in adverse conditions).

6.3.3 IsOriginalMono

IsOriginalMono describes whether or not a stereo signal (with N_{CH} channels) was originally recorded as a mono signal. The extraction of the *IsOriginalMono* descriptor is not normative. The standard recommends a method based on the calculation of normalized cross-correlations between the N_{CH} channels. If any of the derived coefficients is greater than a threshold reflecting correlation between the channels, *IsOriginalMono* is set to "true". Otherwise it is set to "false".

6.3.4 BackgroundNoiseLevel

The *BackgroundNoiseLevel* attribute indicates the noise level within an *AudioSegment*. A noise-level feature is computed separately in each channel of the signal. These values, expressed in dB, are in the range $[-\infty, 0]$. The extraction of the *BackgroundNoiseLevel* for an N_{CH}-channel signal is not standardized. A simple method consists of the following steps:

1. The absolute maximum amplitude $A_{dBmax}(i)$ is computed in dB, for each channel $i(1 \leq i \leq N_{CH})$, as:

$$A_{dBmax}(i) = 20 \log_{10} \left(\max_n |s_i(n)| \right) \quad (1 \leq i \leq N_{CH}), \qquad (6.1)$$

where $s_i(n)$ represents the digital signal in the ith channel.

2. The signal is divided into blocks (5 ms long, typically), in which the mean power is estimated as:

$$P_i(j) = \frac{1}{L_B} \sum_{n=(j-1)L_B}^{j.L_B-1} s_i^2(n) \quad (1 \leq j \leq \text{number of blocks}),$$

$$(1 \leq i \leq N_{CH}) \qquad (6.2)$$

where j is the block index, L_B is the length of a block (in number of samples), and $P_i(j)$ is the mean power of the jth block in the ith channel signal $s_i(n)$.

3. Then, the minimum block power of each channel is computed in dB:

$$P_{dBmin}(i) = 10\log_{10}\left(\min_j |P_i(j)|\right) \quad (1 \le i \le N_{CH}).$$ (6.3)

4. Finally, the *BackgroundNoiseLevel* feature of the *i*th channel is defined by the difference:

$$BNL(i) = P_{dBmin}(i) - A_{dBmax}(i) \quad (1 \le i \le N_{CH}).$$ (6.4)

The noise level features should be normalized in each channel by the maximum amplitude of the signal, in order to make the descriptor independent of the recording level. Finally, the extraction process yields values, which are stored in a vector, as a summary of the noise level in one *AudioSegment*.

6.3.5 *CrossChannelCorrelation*

The *CrossChannelCorrelation* attribute describes the correlation between the channels of a signal stored in an *AudioSegment*. It is a measurement of the relationship between the first channel and the $N_{CH} - 1$ other channels of a multi-channel signal, independently of their levels. The extraction of the *CrossChannelCorrelation* features from an N_{CH}-channel signal is not standardized. A possible method consists of the following steps:

1. Each channel is normalized to its maximum value.
2. The cross-correlations $\Gamma_{s1,si}$ between the first channel and the $N_{CH} - 1$ other channels $(2 \le i \le N_{CH})$ are estimated.
3. Each correlation $\Gamma_{s1,si}$ is normalized by the geometric mean of the first channel's autocorrelation $\Gamma_{s1,s1}$ and the *i*th channel's autocorrelation $\Gamma_{si,si}$.
4. Finally, the $(i - 1)$th *CrossChannelCorrelation* feature is defined as the middle coefficient of the *i*th channel's normalized cross correlation:

$$Cor(i-1) = \frac{\Gamma_{s_1,s_i}(0)}{\sqrt{\Gamma_{s_1,s_1}(0)\Gamma_{s_i,s_i}(0)}} \quad (2 \le i \le N_{CH}).$$ (6.5)

This procedure yields a vector of $N_{CH} - 1$ *CrossChannelCorrelation* features $Cor(i)(1 \le i \le N_{CH} - 1)$, used to describe the audio segment. Each *CrossChannelCorrelation* feature *Cor* ranges between -1 and $+1$:

- $Cor = +1$: the channels are completely correlated.
- $Cor = 0$: the channels are uncorrelated.
- $Cor = -1$: the channels are out of phase.

In the case of two sine signals ($N_{CH} = 2$), the *CrossChannelCorrelation* is defined by a unique feature $Cor = \cos(\varphi)$, where φ is the phase shift between the two channels.

6.3.6 RelativeDelay

The *RelativeDelay* attribute describes the relative delays between two or more channels of a stereo signal. The delay values are expressed in milliseconds. They are restricted to the range $[-0.5\,\text{ms}, +0.5\,\text{ms}]$, in order to prevent ambiguity with pitch or other correlations in the signal. The extraction of the *RelativeDelay* features from an N_{CH}-channel signal is not standardized. A possible method consists of the following steps:

1. An *unscaled* cross-correlation function $UCC_{s1,si}$ between the first channel and each of the $N_{CH} - 1$ other channels is estimated as:

$$UCC_{s_1,s_i}(m) = \begin{cases} \displaystyle\sum_{n=0}^{L_S - m - 1} s_1(n)s_i(n+m) & (m \geq 0) \\ UCC_{s_1,s_i}(-m) & (m < 0) \end{cases} \quad (2 \leq i \leq N_{CH}), \quad (6.6)$$

where L_S is the length of the input signal in number of samples. The $UCC_{s1,si}$ cross-correlation functions have $2L_S - 1$ coefficients.

2. The extraction system searches the position $m_{max}(i)$ of the maximum of $UCC_{s1,si}$ in a search region corresponding to $\pm 0.5\,\text{ms}$ (defined according to the sampling frequency).

3. The $(i-1)$th *RelativeDelay* feature is then estimated for the ith channel by taking the difference between the position of the maximum $m = m_{max}(i)$ and the position of the middle coefficient $m = 0$. This time interval is converted to ms:

$$RD(i-1) = \frac{m_{max}(i)}{F_s} \quad (2 \leq i \leq N_{CH}), \quad (6.7)$$

where F_s is the sample rate of the input signal.

This procedure yields a vector of $N_{CH} - 1$ *RelativeDelay* features $RD(i)(1 \leq i \leq N_{CH} - 1)$ for the whole audio segment. For a mono signal, a single *RelativeDelay* value is set to 0.

6.3.7 Balance

The *Balance* attribute describes the relative level between two or more channels of an *AudioSegment*. The *Balance* features are expressed in dB within a

$[-100\,\mathrm{dB}, 100\,\mathrm{dB}]$ range. The extraction of the *Balance* features from an N_{CH}-channel signal is not standardized. A possible method consists of the following steps:

1. The mean power is calculated in each channel as:

$$P_i = \frac{1}{L_S} \sum_{n=0}^{L_S-1} s_i^2(n) \quad (1 \le i \le N_{CH}), \tag{6.8}$$

where L_S is the length of the input signal.
2. The $(i-1)$th *Balance* feature is defined by the ratio (in dB) between the first channel's power and the ith channel's power:

$$Bal(i-1) = 10 \log_{10} \left(\frac{P_1}{P_i} \right) \quad (2 \le i \le N_{CH}). \tag{6.9}$$

The extraction procedure yields a vector of $N_{CH} - 1$ *Balance* features $Bal(i)(1 \le i \le N_{CH} - 1)$ for the whole audio segment. For a mono signal, a single *Balance* value is set to 0.

6.3.8 DcOffset

The *DcOffset* attribute describes the mean relative to the maximum of each channel of an *AudioSegment*. As audio signals should have a zero mean, a DC offset may indicate a bad analogue–digital conversion. The *DcOffset* features take their values in the $[-1, 1]$ range. The extraction of the *DcOffset* features from an N_{CH}-channel signal is not standardized. A possible method consists of the following steps:

1. The mean amplitude is first calculated within each channel:

$$\overline{s_i} = \frac{1}{L_S} \sum_{n=0}^{L_S-1} s_i(n) \quad (1 \le i \le N_{CH}), \tag{6.10}$$

where L_S is the length of the input signal.
2. The *DcOffset* features are obtained by normalizing these values by the maximum of the absolute magnitude value in each channel:

$$DC(i) = \frac{\overline{s_i}}{\max_n |s_i(n)|} \quad (1 \le i \le N_{CH}). \tag{6.11}$$

The extraction procedure yields a vector of N_{CH} *DcOffset* features $DC(i)$ $(1 \le i \le N_{CH})$ for the whole audio segment.

6.3.9 Bandwidth

Bandwidth describes the upper limit of the signal's bandwidth for each channel. The *Bandwidth* features are expressed in Hz, and take their values within the range $[0\,\text{Hz}, F_s/2]$, where F_s is the sample rate of the input signal. These features give an estimation of the original signal bandwidth in each channel. This gives an indication of the technical quality of the original recording.

To extract the *Bandwidth* description from an N_{CH}-channel signal, the following method is proposed. First, the local power spectra of the signal are calculated from successive overlapping frames (e.g. 30 ms frames starting every 10 ms) within each channel. A maximum filter is then used over the local spectra to get a maximum power spectrum $MPS_i(k)$ for each channel. A logarithmic maximum power spectrum (LMPS) is defined in each channel as:

$$LMPS_i(k) = 10\log_{10}(MPS_i(k)) \quad (1 \le i \le N_{CH}). \tag{6.12}$$

A boundary is used to find the edge of the bandwidth of the LMPS of each channel. The maximum value LMP_{max} and minimum value LMP_{min} of each LMPS are calculated. The boundary LMP_{bound} for the upper limit of the bandwidth is set to 70% of $(LMP_{max} - LMP_{min})$ below LMP_{max}. The upper edge of the bandwidth is the frequency BW above which the power spectrum falls below LMP_{bound}. The extraction procedure yields a vector of N_{CH} *Bandwidth* features $BW(i)$ $(1 \le i \le N_{CH})$ for the whole audio segment.

6.3.10 TransmissionTechnology

The *TransmissionTechnology* attribute describes the technology in which the audio file was transmitted or recorded. The description uses a predefined set of categories describing different possible transmission and recording technologies.

The extraction of *TransmissionTechnology* has to be made manually by a human operator. The sound can be labelled with 10 categories defined by the standard. The operator has to be familiar with the different transmission or recording technologies in order to choose a proper category. Some categories may pack different types of signals together, which share similar acoustic qualities. For instance, the *Category 6*, as defined by the standard, stands for two distinct types of bad-quality recordings: speech over telephones with a [50 Hz–8 kHz] bandwidth and vinyl before 1960.

6.3.11 ErrorEvent and ErrorEventList

The *ErrorEventList* description contains a list of *ErrorEvent* descriptors. An *ErrorEvent* descriptor is used to describe a type of error occurring in the input audio signal. It consists of the following attributes:

- *ErrorClass*: describes the error type using a predefined set of categories. The standard defines 12 error categories: *Click* (a high-frequency burst of short duration), *ClickSegment* (a segment containing many clicks), *DropOut* (absence of high frequencies for a short period), *Pop* (a low-frequency burst), *DigitalClip* (distortion occurring when a digital signal is clipped), *AnalogClip* (distortion occurring when an analogue signal is clipped), *SampleHold* (click at start and end, short muting of signal), *BlockRepeating* (repetition of a short block), *Jitter* (single sample click), *MissingBlock* (click at the transition caused by missing blocks), *DigitalZero* (click at the transition caused by zero-valued samples) and *Other* (any other error).
- *ChannelNo*: specifies the channel in which the error occurs.
- *TimeStamp*: specifies the temporal location of the error.
- *Relevance*: is the degree of relevance of the error. The possible integer values range from 0 (relevance not specified) to 7 (high relevance). An error with low relevance (e.g. *Relevance* $= 1$) is hardly audible. An error with high relevance (e.g. *Relevance* $= 7$) is very disturbing.
- *DetectionProcess*: describes the process of detection: *Manual* or *Automatic*.
- *Status*: describes the current status of the error. This label is set automatically or by a listener. Five labels are possible: *Undefined* (default), *checked* (the error has been checked), *needs restoration* (the error needs to be restored), *restored* (the error has been restored) and *deleted* (the detected error was a false alarm).
- *Comment*: contains any comment about the detected error.

The *ErrorEvent* is used to describe typical errors that occur in audio data, in particular those resulting from an analogue–digital conversion. The *ErrorClass* category may be set manually by a human listener, or automatically extracted from the input signal, for instance through a click detection algorithm. A given audio segment can be indexed with different *ErrorEvent* descriptors due to the *ErrorEventList* attribute.

REFERENCES

Allamanche E., Herre J., Helmuth O., Fröba B., Kasten T. and Cremer M. (2001) "Content-based Identification of Audio Material Using MPEG-7 Low Level Description", *International Symposium on Music Information Retrieval*, Bloomington, NI, USA, October.

Baeza-Yates R. and Ribeiro-Neto B. (1999) *Modern Information Retrieval*, Addison-Wesley, Reading, MA.

Batlle E., Masip J. and Guaus E. (2002) "Automatic Song Identification in Noisy Broadcast Audio", *International Conference on Signal and Image Processing (SIP 2002)*, Kauai, HI, USA, August.

Blum T., Keislar D., Wheaton J. and Wold E. (1999) "Method and Article of Manufacture for Content-Based Analysis, Storage, Retrieval and Segmentation of Audio Information", US Patent 5918.223.

Burges C., Platt J. and Jana S. (2002) "Extracting Noise-Robust Features from Audio Data", *ICASSP 2002*, Orlando, FL, USA, May.

Cano P., Kaltenbrunner M., Mayor O. and Batlle E. (2001) "Statistical Significance in Song-Spotting in Audio", *International Symposium on Music Information Retrieval (MUSIC IR 2001)*, Bloomington, IN, USA, October.

Cano P., Batlle E., Kalker T. and Haitsma J. (2002a) "A Review of Algorithms for Audio Fingerprinting", *International Workshop on Multimedia Signal Processing (MMSP 2002)*, St Thomas, Virgin Islands, December.

Cano P., Batlle E., Mayer H. and Neuschmied H. (2002b) "Robust Sound Modeling for Song Detection in Broadcast Audio", *AES 112th International Convention*, Munich, Germany, May.

Cano P., Gómez E., Batlle E., Gomes L. and Bonnet M. (2002c) "Audio Fingerprinting: Concepts and Applications", *International Conference on Fuzzy Systems Knowledge Discovery (FSKD'02)*, Singapore, November.

Chávez E., Navarro G., Baeza-Yates R. A. and Marroquín J. L. (2001) "Searching in Metric Spaces", *ACM Computing Surveys*, vol. 23, no. 3, pp. 273–321.

Gomes L., Cano P., Gómez E., Bonnet M. and Batlle E. (2003) "Audio Watermarking and Fingerprinting: For Which Applications?", *Journal of New Music Research*, vol. 32, no. 1, pp. 65–81.

Gómez E., Cano P., Gomes L., Batlle E. and Bonnet M. (2002) "Mixed Watermarking-Fingerprinting Approach for Integrity Verification of Audio Recordings", *International Telecommunications Symposium (ITS 2002)*, Natal, Brazil, September.

Haitsma J. and Kalker T. (2002) "A Highly Robust Audio Fingerprinting System", *3rd International Conference on Music Information Retrieval (ISMIR2002)*, Paris, France, October.

Herre J., Hellmuth O. and Cremer M. (2002) "Scalable Robust Audio Fingerprinting Using MPEG-7 Content Description", *IEEE Workshop on Multimedia Signal Processing (MMSP 2002)*, Virgin Islands, December.

Kalker T. (2001) "Applications and Challenges for Audio Fingerprinting", *111th AES Convention*, New York, USA, December.

Kenyon S. (1999) "Signal Recognition System and Method", US Patent 5.210.820.

Kimura A., Kashino K., Kurozumi T. and Murase H. (2001) "Very Quick Audio Searching: Introducing Global Pruning to the Time-Series Active Search", *ICASSP'01*, vol. 3, pp. 1429–1432, Salt Lake City, UT, USA, May.

Kurth F., Ribbrock A. and Clausen M. (2002) "Identification of Highly Distorted Audio Material for Querying Large Scale Databases", *112th AES International Convention*, Munich, Germany, May.

Linde Y., Buzo A. and Gray R. M. (1980) "An Algorithm for Vector Quantizer Design", *IEEE Transactions on Communications*, vol. 28, no. 1, pp. 84–95.

Lourens J. G. (1990) "Detecting and Logging Advertisements Using its Sound", *IEEE Transactions on Broadcasting*, vol. 36, no. 3, pp. 231–233.

Mihcak M. K. and Venkatesan R. (2001) "A Perceptual Audio Hashing Algorithm: A Tool for Robust Audio Identification and Information Hiding", *4th Workshop on Information Hiding*, Pittsburgh, PA, USA, April.

Papaodysseus C., Roussopoulos G., Fragoulis D. and Alexiou C. (2001) "A New Approach to the Automatic Recognition of Musical Recordings", *Journal of the AES*, vol. 49, no. 1/2, pp. 23–35.

RIAA/IFPI (2001) "Request for Information on Audio Fingerprinting Technologies", available at http://www.ifpi.org/site-content/press/20010615.html.

Richly G., Varga L., Kovács F. and Hosszú G. (2000) "Short-term Sound Stream Characterization for Reliable, Real-Time Occurrence Monitoring of Given Sound-Prints", *10th IEEE Mediterranean Electrotechnical Conference (MELECON 2000)*, pp. 29–31, Cyprus, May.

Subramanya S., Simba R., Narahari B. and Youssef A. (1997) "Transform-Based Indexing of Audio Data for Multimedia Databases", *IEEE International Conference on Multimedia Computing and Systems (ICMCS '97)*, pp. 211–218, Ottawa, Canada, June.

Sukittanon S. and Atlas L. (2002) "Modulation Frequency Features for Audio Fingerprinting", *ICASSP 2002*, Orlando, FL, USA, May.

Theodoris S. and Koutroumbas K. (1998) *Pattern Recognition*, Academic Press, San Diego, CA.

7
Application

7.1 INTRODUCTION

Audio content contains very important clues for the retrieval of home videos, because different sounds can indicate different important events. In most cases it is easier to detect events using audio features than using video features. For example, when interesting events occur, people are likely to talk or laugh or cry out. So these events can be easily detected by audio content, while it is very difficult or even impossible using visual content. For these reasons, effective video retrieval techniques using audio features have been investigated by many researchers in the literature (Srinivasan *et al.*, 1999; Bakker and Lew, 2002; Wang *et al.*, 2000; Xiong *et al.*, 2003).

The purpose of this chapter is to outline example applications using the concepts developed in the previous chapters.

To retrieve audiovisual information in semantically meaningful units, a system must be able to scan multimedia data automatically like TV or radio broadcasts for the presence of specific topics. Whenever topics of users' interests are detected, the system could alert a related user through a web client. Figure 7.1 illustrates on a functional level how multimedia documents may be processed by a multimedia mining system (MMS).

A multimedia mining system consists of two main components: a multimedia mining indexer and a multimedia mining server. The input signal, received for example through a satellite dish, is passed on to a video capture device or audio capture device, which in turn transmits it to the multimedia mining indexer. If the input data contains video, joint video and audio processing techniques may be used to segment the data into scenes, i.e. ones that contain a news reader or a single news report, and to detect story boundaries. The audio track is processed using audio analysis tools.

The multimedia mining indexer produces indexed files (e.g. XML text files) as output. This output, as well as the original input files, are stored in a

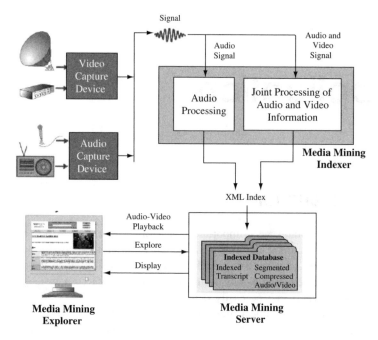

Figure 7.1 Multimedia mining system

multimedia-enabled database for archiving and retrieval. The multimedia mining server application then makes the audio, video, index and metadata files available to the user. All output and functionalities may be presented to the user through a web client.

Based on data contained in the mining server it could be possible to understand whether a TV programme is a news report, a commercial, or a sports programme without actually watching the TV or understanding the words being spoken. Often, analysis of audio alone can provide excellent understanding of scene content. More sophisticated visual processing can be saved. In this chapter we focus on indexing audiovisual information based on audio feature analysis.

The indexing process starts with audio content analysis, with the goal to achieve audio segmentation and classification. A hierarchical audio classification system, which consists of three stages, is shown in Figure 7.2.

Audio recordings from movies or TV programmes are first segmented and classified into basic types such as speech, music, environmental sounds and silence. Audio features including non-MPEG-7 low-level descriptors (LLDs) or MPEG-7 LLDs are extracted. The first stage provides coarse-level audio classification and segmentation. In the second stage, each basic type is further processed and classified.

Even without a priori information about the number of speakers and the identities of speakers the speech stream can be segmented by different approaches, such

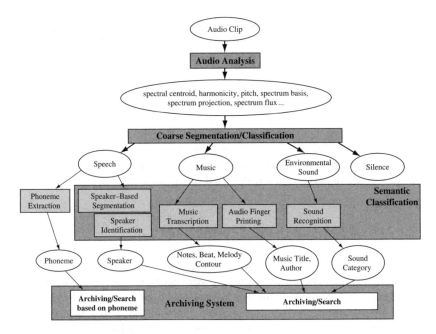

Figure 7.2 A hierarchical system for audio classification

as metric-based, model-based or hybrid segmentation. In speaker-based segmentation the speech stream is cut into segments, such that each segment corresponds to a homogeneous stretch of audio, ideally a single speaker. Speaker identification groups the individual speaker segments produced by speaker change detection into putative sets from one speaker. For speakers known to the system, speaker identification (classification) associates the speaker's identity to the set. A set of several hundred speakers may be known to the system. For unknown speakers, their gender may be identified and an arbitrary index assigned.

Speech recognition takes the speech segment outputs and produces a text transcription of the spoken content (words) tagged with time-stamps. A phone-based approach processes the speech data with a lightweight speech recognizer to produce either a phone transcription or some kind of phonetic lattice. This data may then be directly indexed or used for word spotting.

For the indexing of sounds, different models are constructed for a fixed set of acoustic classes, such as applause, bells, footstep, laughter, bird's cry, and so on. The trained sound models are then used to segment the incoming environmental sound stream through the sound recognition classifier.

Music data can be divided into two groups based on the representational form: that is, music transcription, and the audio fingerprinting system.

As outlined in Chapter 5, transcription of music implies the extraction of specific features from a musical acoustic signal resulting in a symbolic representation that comprises notes, their pitches, timings and dynamics. It may also include the identification of the beat, meter and the instruments being played. The resulting notation can be traditional music notation or any symbolic representation which gives sufficient information for performing the piece using musical instruments.

Chapter 6 discussed the basic concept behind an audio fingerprinting system, the identification of audio content by means of a compact and unique signature extracted from it. This signature can be seen as a summary or perceptual digest of the audio recording. During a training phase, the signatures are created from a set of known audio material and are then stored in a database. Afterwards unknown content may be identified by matching its signature against the ones contained in the database, even if distorted or fragmented.

7.2 AUTOMATIC AUDIO SEGMENTATION

Segmenting audio data into speaker-labelled segments is the process of determining where speakers are engaged in a conversation (start and end of their turn). This finds application in numerous speech processing tasks, such as speaker-adapted speech recognition, speaker detection and speaker identification. Example applications include speaker segmentation in TV broadcast discussions or radio broadcast discussion panels.

In (Gish and Schmidt, 1994; Siegler *et al.*, 1997; Delacourt and Welekens, 2000), distance-based segmentation approaches are investigated. Segments belonging to the same speaker are clustered using a distance measure that measures the similarity of two neighbouring windows placed in evenly spaced segments of time intervals. The advantage of this method is that it does not require any a priori information. However, since the clustering is based on distances between individual segments, accuracy suffers when segments are too short to describe sufficiently the characteristics of a speaker.

In (Wilcox *et al.*, 1994; Woodland *et al.*, 1998; Gauvain *et al.*, 1998; Sommez *et al.*, 1999), a model-based approach is investigated. For every speaker in the audio recording, a model is trained and then an HMM segmentation is performed to find the best time-aligned speaker sequence. This method places the segmentation within a global maximum likelihood framework. However, most model-based approaches require a priori information to initialize the speaker models.

Similarity measurement between two adjacent windows is based on a comparison of their parametric statistical models. The decision of a speaker change is performed using a model-selection-based method (Chen and Gopalakrishnan, 1998; Delacourt and Welekens, 2000), called the Bayesian information criterion (BIC). This method is robust and does not require thresholding. In (Kemp *et al.*, 2000; Yu *et al.*, 2003; Kim and Sikora, 2004a), it is shown that a hybrid algorithm, which combines metric-based and model-based techniques, works significantly better than all other approaches. Therefore, in the following we describe a hybrid segmentation approach in more detail.

7.2.1 Feature Extraction

The performance of the segmentation depends on the feature representation of audio signals. Discriminative and robust features are required, especially when the speech signal is corrupted by channel distortion or additive noise. Various features have been proposed in the literature:

- Mel-frequency cepstrum coefficients (MFCCs): one of the most popular sets of features used to parameterize speech is MFCCs. As outlined in Chapter 2, these are based on the human auditive system model of critical frequency bands. Linearly spaced filters at low frequencies and logarithmically at high frequencies have been used to capture the phonetically important characteristics of speech.
- Linear prediction coefficients (LPCs) (Rabiner and Schafer, 1978): the LPC-based approach performs spectral analysis with an all-pole modelling constraint. It is fast and provides extremely accurate estimates of speech parameters.
- Linear spectral pairs (LSPs) (Kabal and Ramachandran, 1986): LSPs are derived from LPCs. Previous research has shown that LSPs may exhibit explicit differences in different audio classes. LSPs are more robust in noisy environments.
- Cepstral mean normalization (CMN) (Furui, 1981): the CMS method is used in speaker recognition to compensate for the effect of environmental conditions and transmission channels.
- Perceptual linear prediction (PLP) (Hermansky, 1990): this technique uses three concepts from the psychophysics of hearing to derive an estimate of the auditory spectrum: (1) the critical-band spectral resolution, (2) the equal-loudness curve and (3) the intensity–loudness power law. The auditory spectrum is then approximated by an autoregressive all-pole model. A fifth-order all-pole model is effective in suppressing speaker-dependent details of the auditory spectrum. In comparison with conventional linear predictive (LP) analysis, PLP analysis is more consistent with human hearing.
- RASTA-PLP (Hermansky and Morgan, 1994): the word RASTA stands for *RelAtive SpecTrAl technique*. This technique is an improvement on the traditional PLP method and incorporates a special filtering of the different frequency channels of a PLP analyser. The filtering is employed to make speech analysis less sensitive to the slowly changing or steady-state factors in speech. The RASTA method replaces the conventional critical-band short-term spectrum in PLP and introduces a less sensitive spectral estimation.
- Principal component analysis (PCA): PCA transforms a number of correlated variables into a number of uncorrelated variables called principal components. The first principal component accounts for as much of the variability in the

data as possible, and each succeeding component accounts for as much of the remaining variability as possible.

- MPEG-7 audio spectrum projection (ASP): the MPEG-7 ASP feature extraction was described in detail in chapter.

7.2.2 Segmentation

In model-based segmentation, a set of models for different acoustic speaker classes from a training corpus is defined and trained prior to segmentation. The incoming speech stream is classified using the models. The segmentation system finds the best time-aligned speaker sequence by maximum likelihood selection over a sliding window. Segmentation can be made at the locations where there is a change in the acoustic class. Boundaries between the classes are used as segment boundaries. However, most model-based approaches require a priori information to initialize the speaker models. The process of HMM model-based segmentation is shown in Figure 7.3.

In the literature several algorithms have been described for model-based segmentation. Most of the methods are based on VQ, the GMM or the HMM. In

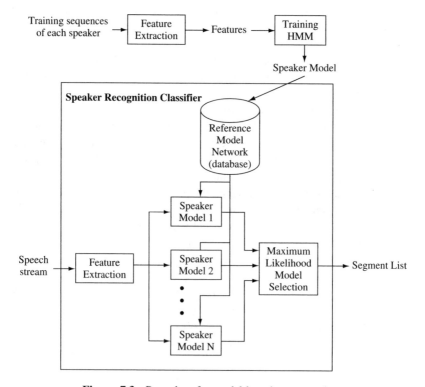

Figure 7.3 Procedure for model-based segmentation

the work of (Sugiyama *et al.*, 1993), a simple application scenario is studied, in which the number of speakers to be clustered was assumed to be known. VQ and the HMM are used in the implementation. The algorithm proposed by (Wilcox *et al.*, 1994) is also based on HMM segmentation, in which an agglomerative clustering method is used when the speakers are known or unknown. (Siu *et al.*, 1992) proposed a system to separate controller speech and pilot speech with a GMM. Speaker discrimination from telephone speech signals was studied in (Cohen and Lapidus, 1996) using HMM segmentation. However, in this system, the number of speakers was limited to two. A defect of these models is that iterative algorithms need to be employed. This makes these algorithms very time consuming.

7.2.3 Metric-Based Segmentation

The metric-based segmentation task is divided into two main parts: speaker change detection and segment clustering. The overall procedure of metric-based segmentation is depicted in Figure 7.4.

First, the speech signal is split into smaller segments that are assumed to contain only one speaker. Prior to the speaker change detection step, acoustic feature vectors are extracted. Speaker change detection measures a dissimilarity value between feature vectors in two consecutive windows. Consecutive distance values are often low-pass filtered. Local maxima exceeding a heuristic threshold indicate segment boundaries.

Various speaker change detection algorithms differ in the kind of distance function they employ, the size of the windows, the time increments for the shifting of the two windows, and the way the resulting similarity values are evaluated and thresholded. The feature vectors in each of the two adjacent windows are assumed to follow some probability density (usually Gaussian) and the distance is represented by the dissimilarity of these two densities. Various similarity measures have already been proposed in the literature for this purpose.

Consider two adjacent portions of sequences of acoustic vectors $X_1 = \{x_1, \ldots, x_i\}$ and $X_2 = \{x_{i+1}, \ldots, x_{N_X}\}$, where N_X is the number of acoustic vectors in the complete sequence of subset X_1 and subset X_2:

- Kullback–Leibler (KL) distance. For Gaussian variables X_1 and X_2, KL can be written as:

$$d_{KL}(X_1, X_2) = \frac{1}{2}(\mu_{X_2} - \mu_{X_1})^T \left(\Sigma_{X_1}^{-1} + \Sigma_{X_2}^{-1}\right)(\mu_{X_2} - \mu_{X_1})$$

$$+ \frac{1}{2}tr\left(\left(\Sigma_{X_1}^{1/2}\Sigma_{X_2}^{-1/2}\right)\left(\Sigma_{X_1}^{1/2}\Sigma_{X_2}^{-1/2}\right)^T\right)$$

$$+ \frac{1}{2}tr\left(\left(\Sigma_{X_1}^{-1/2}\Sigma_{X_2}^{1/2}\right)\left(\Sigma_{X_1}^{-1/2}\Sigma_{X_2}^{1/2}\right)^T\right) - p \qquad (7.1)$$

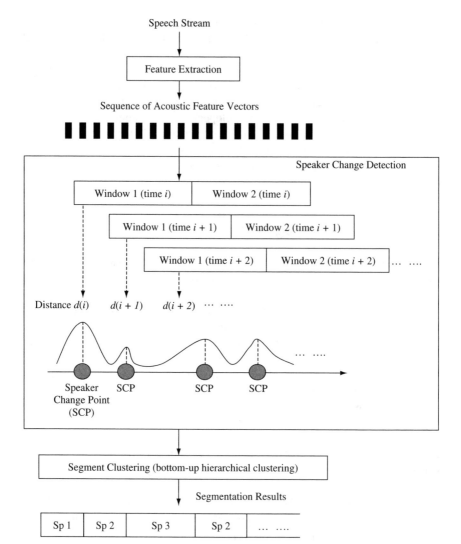

Figure 7.4   Procedure for metric-based segmentation

where *tr* denotes the trace of a matrix, μ_{X_1}, μ_{X_2} are respectively the mean values of the subsets X_1 and $X_2, \sum_{X_1}, \sum_{X_2}$ are respectively the covariance matrices of X_1 and X_2, and p is the dimension of the feature vectors.

- Mahalanobis distance:

$$d_{MAH}(X_1, X_2) = \frac{1}{2}(\mu_{X_2} - \mu_{X_1})^T (\Sigma_{X_1} \Sigma_{X_2})^{-1} (\mu_{X_2} - \mu_{X_1}) \qquad (7.2)$$

- Bhattacharyya distance:

$$d_{BHA}(X_1, X_2) = \frac{1}{4}(\mu_{X_2} - \mu_{X_1})^T (\Sigma_{X_1} + \Sigma_{X_2})^{-1}(\mu_{X_2} - \mu_{X_1})$$
$$+ \frac{1}{2} \log \frac{|\Sigma_{X_1} + \Sigma_{X_2}|}{2\sqrt{|\Sigma_{X_1} \Sigma_{X_2}|}}. \tag{7.3}$$

- Generalized likelihood ratio (GLR). The GLR is used by (Gish and Schmidt, 1994) and (Gish et al., 1991) for speaker identification. Let us consider testing the hypothesis for a speaker change at time i:

H_0: both X_1 and X_2 are generated by the same speaker. Then the reunion of both portions is modelled by a multi-dimensional Gaussian process:

$$X = X_1 \cup X_2 \sim N(\mu_x, \Sigma_x). \tag{7.4}$$

H_1: X_1 and X_2 are pronounced by a different speaker. Then each portion is modelled by a multi-Gaussian process:

$$X_1 \sim N(\mu_{x_1}, \Sigma_{x_1}) \text{ and } X_2 \sim N(\mu_{x_2}, \Sigma_{x_2}). \tag{7.5}$$

The GLR between the hypothesis H_0 and H_1 is defined by:

$$R = \frac{L(X, N(\mu_X, \Sigma_X))}{L(X_1, N(\mu_{X_1}, \Sigma_{X_1}))L(X_2, N(\mu_{X_2}, \Sigma_{X_2}))} \tag{7.6}$$

where $L(X, N(\mu_X, \Sigma_X))$ represents the likelihood of the sequence of acoustic vectors X given the multi-dimensional Gaussian process $N(\mu_X, \Sigma_X)$.

A distance is computed from the logarithm of this ratio:

$$d_{GLR} = -\log R. \tag{7.7}$$

A high value of R (i.e. a low value of d_{GLR}) indicates that the one multi-Gaussian modelling (hypothesis H_0) fits the data well. A low value of R (i.e. a high value of d_{GLR}) indicates that the hypothesis H_1 should be preferred so that a speaker change is detected at time i.

- Divergence shape distance (DSD). The DSD (Cambell, 1997; Lu and Zhang, 2001; Lu et al., 2002; Wu et al., 2003) is used to measure the dissimilarity between two neighbouring sub-segments at each time slot. It is defined as the distance between their reliable speaker-related sets:

$$d_{DSD} = \frac{1}{2} tr\left[(\Sigma_{X_1} - \Sigma_{X_2})(\Sigma_{X_1}^{-1} - \Sigma_{X_2}^{-1})\right]. \tag{7.8}$$

A potential speaker change is found between the ith and the $(i+1)$th sub-segments, if the following conditions are satisfied:

$$d_{DSD}(i, i+1) > d_{DSD}(i+1, i+2)$$

$$d_{DSD}(i, i+1) > d_{DSD}(i-1, i) \tag{7.9}$$

$$d_{DSD}(i, i+1) > Th_i$$

where $d_{DSD}(i, i+1)$ is the distance between the ith and the $(i+1)$th sub-segments, and Th_i is a threshold.

The first two conditions guarantee that a local peak exists, and the last condition can prevent very low peaks from being detected. The threshold setting is affected by many factors, such as insufficiently estimated data and various environmental conditions. For example, the distance between speech sub-segments will increase if the speech is in a noisy environment. Accordingly, the threshold should increase in such a noisy environment. The dynamic threshold Th_i is computed as:

$$Th_i = \alpha \frac{1}{N} \sum_{n=0}^{N} d_{DSD}(i-n-1, i-n) \tag{7.10}$$

where N is the number of previous distances used for predicting the threshold, and α is a coefficient as amplifier.

Thus, the threshold is automatically set according to the previous N successive distances. The threshold determined in this way works well in various conditions, but false detections still exist.

The next step merges speech segments containing the same speaker. Segments belonging to the same speaker are clustered using a distance measure between segments detected by the speaker change step, such that each cluster contains speech from only one speaker. Also speech from the same speaker is classified in the same cluster. For this, bottom-up hierarchical clustering (Siu *et al.*, 1992; Everitt, 1993) of the distance matrix between speech segments is often used. The algorithm picks the closest pair of clusters according to the distance metric, and merges them. This step is repeated until there is only one cluster. There are several agglomerative schemes, as illustrated in Figure 7.5:

- Single linkage: the distance between two clusters is defined as the distance between their two closest members.
- Complete linkage: the distance between two clusters is defined as the distance between their two farthest members.
- Average linkage between groups: the distance between two clusters is defined as the average of the distances between all pairs of members, one segment taken in each cluster.

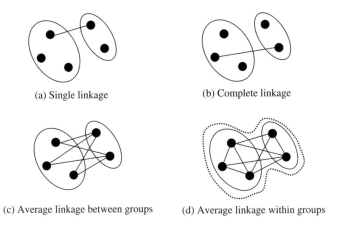

(a) Single linkage   (b) Complete linkage

(c) Average linkage between groups   (d) Average linkage within groups

Figure 7.5   Various distances between groups used in neighbourhood clustering schemes

- Average linkage within groups: the distance between two clusters is defined
  as the average of the distances between all pairs in the cluster, which would
  result from combining the two clusters.

The output from the scheme is generally represented by a dendrogram, a tree of
clusters, in which each node corresponds to a cluster. The cutting (or pruning)
of the dendrogram produces a partition composed of all the segments. Several
techniques exist in the literature (Solomonoff *et al.*, 1998; Reynolds *et al.*, 1998)
for selecting a partition. These techniques consist of cutting the dendrogram at
a given height or of pruning the dendrogram by selecting clusters at different
heights. Figure 7.6 shows a dendrogram to illustrate the consecutive grouping
of clusters.

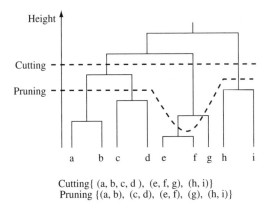

Cutting{ (a, b, c, d), (e, f, g), (h, i)}
Pruning {(a, b), (c, d), (e, f), (g), (h, i)}

Figure 7.6   Example of dendrogram: cluster selection methods

The metric-based method is very useful and very flexible, since no or little information about the speech signal is needed a priori to decide the segmentation points. It is simple and applied without a large training data set. Therefore, metric-based methods have the advantage of low computation cost and are thus suitable for real-time applications. The main drawbacks are: (1) It is difficult to decide an appropriate threshold. (2) Each acoustic change point is detected only by its neighbouring acoustic information. (3) To deal with homogeneous segments of various lengths, the length of the windows is usually short (typically 2 seconds). Feature vectors may not be discriminative enough to obtain robust distance statistics.

7.2.4 Model-Selection-Based Segmentation

The challenge of model identification is to choose one from among a set of candidate models to describe a given data set. Candidates of a series of models often have different numbers of parameters. It is evident that when the number of parameters in the model is increased, the likelihood of the training data is also increased. However, when the number of parameters is too large, this might cause the problem of overtraining. Further, model-based segmentation does not generalize to acoustic conditions not presented in the model.

Several criteria for model selection have been introduced in the literature, ranging from non-parametric methods such as cross-validation to parametric methods such as the BIC. The BIC permits the selection of a model from a set of models for the same data: this model will match the data while keeping complexity low. Also, the BIC can be viewed as a general change detection algorithm since it does not just take into account prior knowledge of speakers. Instead of making a local decision based on the distance between two adjacent sliding windows of fixed size, (Chen and Gopalakrishnan, 1998) applied the BIC to detect the change point within a window.

The maximum likelihood ratio between H_0 (no speaker turn) and H_1 (speaker turn at time i) applied to the GLR is then defined by:

$$R_{BIC}(i) = \frac{N_X}{2} \log |\Sigma_X| - \frac{N_{X_1}}{2} \log |\Sigma_{X_1}| - \frac{N_{X_2}}{2} \log |\Sigma_{X_2}| \qquad (7.11)$$

where $\Sigma_X, \Sigma_{X_1}, \Sigma_{X_2}$ are the covariance matrices of the complete sequence, the subset $X_1 = \{x_1, \ldots, x_i\}$ and the subset $X_2 = \{x_{i+1}, \ldots, x_{N_X}\}$ respectively. N_X, N_{X_1}, N_{X_2} are the number of acoustic vectors in the complete sequence, sub-set X_1 and sub-set X_2.

The speaker turn point is estimated via the maximum likelihood ratio criterion as:

$$\hat{t} = \arg \max_i R_{BIC}(i). \qquad (7.12)$$

The variations of the BIC value between the two models is then given by:

$$\Delta BIC(i) = -R_{BIC}(i) + \lambda D \qquad (7.13)$$

with the penalty

$$D = \frac{1}{2}\left(d + \frac{1}{2}d(d+1)\right)\log N_X, \qquad (7.14)$$

where d is the dimension of the acoustic feature vectors.

If the ΔBIC value is negative, this indicates a speaker change. If there is no change point detected, the window will grow in size to have more robust distance statistics.

Because of this growing window, Chen and Gopalakrishnan's BIC scheme suffers from high computation costs, especially for audio streams that have many long homogeneous segments. The ΔBIC computation relies on a similar approach as the one used in the GLR computation, but there is a penalty for the complexity of the models. ΔBIC is actually thresholding the GLR with $D(1 \leq D \leq 4)$. The advantage of using ΔBIC for the distance measure is that the appropriate threshold can be easily designed by adjusting the penalty factor, λ.

Two improved BIC-based approaches were proposed to speed up the detection process (Tritschler and Gopinath, 1999; Zhou and John, 2000). A variable window scheme and some heuristics were applied to the BIC framework while the T^2 statistic was integrated into the BIC. (Cheng and Wang, 2003) propose a sequential metric-based approach which has the advantage of low computation cost for the metric-based methods. It yields comparable performance to the model-selection-based methods. The Delacourt segmentation technique (Delacourt and Welekens, 2000) takes advantage of these two types of segmentation techniques. First, a distance-based segmentation combined with a thresholding process is applied to detect the most likely speaker change points. Then the BIC is used during a second pass to validate or discard the previously detected change points.

7.2.5 Hybrid Segmentation

Hybrid segmentation is a combination of metric-based and model-based approaches. A distance-based segmentation algorithm is used to create an initial set of speaker models. Starting with these, model-based segmentation performs more refined segmentation.

Figure 7.7 depicts the algorithm flow chart of a system introduced by (Kim and Sikora, 2004a). The hybrid segmentation can be divided into seven modules: silence removal, feature extraction, speaker change detection, segment-level clustering, speaker model training, model-level clustering and model-based resegmentation using the retrained speaker models. First, silence segments in the input audio recording are detected by a simple energy-based algorithm. The detected

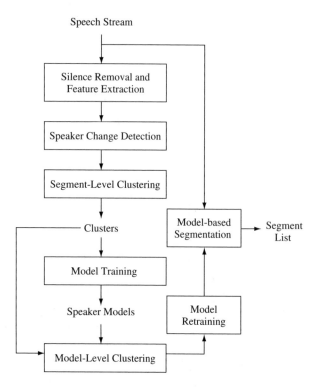

Figure 7.7   Block diagram of the hybrid speaker-based segmentation system

silence part is used to train a silence model. The speech part is transformed into a feature vector sequence and fed into the speaker change detection step, which splits the conversational speech stream into smaller segments.

The speech segments found by speaker change detection are classified using segment-level clustering, such that each cluster is assumed to contain the speech of only one speaker. After training a model for every cluster, model–cluster merging is performed by L-best likelihood scores from all cluster speaker models, thus yielding a target cluster number equal to the actual number of speakers. After merging the two clusters, the new cluster models are retrained. The retrained speaker models are used to resegment the speech stream. Finally, the model-based resegmentation step is achieved using a Viterbi algorithm to determine the maximum likelihood score.

The detailed procedure is described in the following:

- Speaker change detection: speech signals are first parameterized in terms of acoustic feature vectors. The distance between two neighbouring segments is sequentially calculated for speaker change detection using the GLR, BIC or DSD.

- Segment-level clustering: since this set of cluster models is to be used as the starting point of the subsequent model-level clustering, the aim is high cluster purity (every cluster should consist of segments from only one speaker). Because of this, initial segment clustering is terminated at a target cluster number larger than the actual speaker number.

  The segment-level clustering is a simple, greedy, bottom-up algorithm. Initially, every segment is regarded as a cluster. The GLR or BIC can be applied to the segment-level clustering. The GLR is most accurate when the segments have uniform length. In the approach of (Kim and Sikora, 2004a), clustering of segments of the same speaker is done using the BIC as the distance between two clusters. Given a set of speech segments $Seg_1 \ldots Seg_k$ found by speaker change detection, one step of the algorithm consists of merging two of them. In order to decide if it is advisable to merge Seg_i and Seg_j, the difference between the BIC values of two clusters is computed. The more negative the ΔBIC is, the closer the two clusters are.

  At the beginning, each segment is considered to be a single segment cluster and distances between this and the other clusters are computed. The two closest clusters are then merged if the corresponding ΔBIC is negative. In this case, the distances between the new cluster and the other ones are computed, and the new pair of closest clusters is selected at the new iteration. Otherwise, the algorithm is terminated.

- Model building and model-level clustering: after segment-level clustering the cluster number may be larger than the actual speaker number. Starting with speaker models trained from these clusters, model-based segmentation cannot achieve higher accuracy. We perform model-level clustering using speaker model scores (likelihood).

  In order to train a statistical speaker model for each cluster, GMMs or HMMs can be used, which consist of several states. (Kim and Sikora, 2004b) employed an ergodic HMM topology, where each state can be reached from any other state and can be revisited after leaving. Given the feature vectors of one cluster, an HMM with seven states for the cluster is trained using a maximum likelihood estimation procedure (the Baum–Welch algorithm). All cluster GMMs or HMMs are combined into a larger network which is used to merge the two clusters.

  The feature vectors of each cluster are fed to the GMM or HMM network containing all reference cluster speaker models in parallel. The reference speaker model scores (likelihoods) are calculated over the whole set of feature vectors of each cluster. All these likelihoods are passed to the *Likelihood Selection block*, where the similarity between all combinations of two reference scores is measured by the likelihood distance:

$$d_i(i, l) = P(C_i|\lambda_i) - P(C_l|\lambda_l) \qquad (7.15)$$

where C_l denotes the observations belonging to cluster l, $P(C_l|\lambda_l)$ the cluster model score and λ_l the speaker model.

If $d_i(i, l) \leq \Delta$, Δ being a threshold, the index j is stored as the candidate in the L-best likelihood table T_i. This table also provides ranking of the cluster models similar to C_i. In order to decide if the candidate models j in the table T_i belong to the same speaker, we check the L-best likelihood table T_j, where the distances between the j cluster model and an other reference model i is computed:

$$d_j(j, i) = P(C_j|\lambda_j) - P(C_i|\lambda_i). \qquad (7.16)$$

If $d_j(j, i) \leq \Delta$, it is assumed that GMM or HMM λ_i and GMM or HMM λ_j represent the same speaker and thus cluster C_i and cluster C_j can be merged. Otherwise, λ_i and λ_j represent different speakers. The algorithm checks all entries in table T_i and similar clusters are merged. In this way we ensure that model-level clustering achieves higher accuracy than direct segment-level clustering. After merging the clusters, the cluster models are retrained.

- Model-based resegmentation: for this, the speech stream is divided into 1.5 second sub-segments, which overlap by 33%. It is assumed that there is no speaker change within each sub-segment. Therefore, speaker segmentation can be performed at the sub-segment level. Given a sub-segment as input, the MFCC features are extracted and fed to all reference speaker models in parallel. In the case of the GMM, model-based segmentation is performed using GMM cluster models. Using the HMM, the Viterbi algorithm finds the maximum likelihood sequence of states through the HMMs and returns the most likely classification label for the sub-segment.

  The sub-segment labels need to be smoothed out. A low-pass filter can be applied to enable more robust segmentation by correcting errors. The filter stores A adjacent sub-segments of the same label to decide on the beginning of a segment. Errors can be tolerated within a segment, but once B adjacent classifications of any other models are found, the segment is ended. For our data, the optimum values were $A = 3$ and $B = 3$.

7.2.6 Hybrid Segmentation Using MPEG-7 ASP

Hybrid segmentation using MPEG-7 ASP features may be implemented as shown in Figure 7.8 (Kim and Sikora, 2004a). In the following, this MPEG-7-compliant system together with system parameters used in the experimental setup described by (Kim and Sikora, 2004a) is described in more detail to illustrate the concept.

7.2.6.1 MPEG-7-Compliant System

The speech streams are digitized at 22.05 kHz using 16 bits per sample and divided into successive windows, each 3 seconds long. An overlap of 2.5 seconds is used. Detected silence segments are first removed. For each non-silence

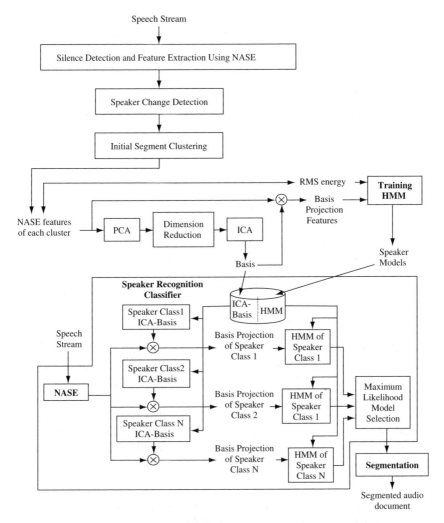

Figure 7.8 Block diagram of segmentation using a speaker recognition classifier

segment, the segment is divided into overlapping frames of duration 30 ms with 15 ms overlapping for consecutive frames. Each frame is windowed using a Hamming window function. To extract audio spectrum envelope (ASE) features, the observed audio signal is analysed using a 512-point FFT. The power spectral coefficients are grouped in logarithmic subbands spaced in non-overlapping 7 octave bands spanning between a low boundary (62.5 Hz) and high boundary (8 kHz). The resulting 30-dimensional ASE is next converted to the decibel scale. Each decibel-scale spectral vector is further normalized with the RMS energy envelope, thus yielding a normalized log-power version of the ASE (NASE).

The speaker change detection step is performed using a NASE DSD between two successive windows. This splits the speech stream into smaller segments that are assumed to contain only one speaker. These segments created by the speaker change detection are selected to form initial clusters of similar segments with the hierarchical agglomerative method. The initial clusters are then used to train an initial set of speaker models.

Given the NASE features of every cluster, the spectral basis is extracted with one of three basis decomposition algorithms: PCA for dimension reduction, FastICA for information maximization or NMF. For NMF there are two choices: (1) In NMF method 1 the NMF basis is extracted from the NASE matrix and the ASP projected onto the NMF basis is applied directly to the HMM sound classifier. (2) In NMF method 2 the audio signal is transformed to the spectrogram. NMF component parts are extracted from the segmented spectrogram image patches. Basis vectors computed by NMF are selected according to their discrimination capability. Sound features are computed from these reduced vectors and fed into the HMM classifier. This process is well described in (Cho *et al.*, 2003).

The resulting spectral basis vectors are multiplied with the NASE matrix, thus yielding the ASP features. The resulting ASP features and RMS-norm gain values are used for training a seven-state ergodic HMM for each cluster.

The speech stream is then resegmented based on the resulting speaker HMMs. The input speech track is cut into 1.5 second sub-segments, which overlap by 33%. Thus, the hop size is 1 second. Overlapping increases the input data to be classified by 50%, but yields more robust sound/speaker segmentation results due to the filtering technique described with the model-based resegmentation. Given a sub-segment 1.5 seconds long as input, the NASE features are extracted and projected against basis functions of each speaker class. Then, the Viterbi algorithm is applied to align each projection with its corresponding speaker class HMM. Resegmentation is achieved using the Viterbi algorithm to determine the maximum likelihood state sequence through the speaker recognition classifier.

7.2.6.2 Selection of Suitable ICA Basis Parameters for the Segmentation Using MPEG-7 ASP Features

In this section we describe how suitable parameters for the MPEG-7 system in Figure 7.8 can be derived in an experimental framework.

Two audio tracks from TV panel discussions and broadcast news were used for our purpose. The TV broadcast news (N) was received from a TV satellite and stored as MPEG-compressed files. The set contained five test files; every file was about 5 minutes long and contained the speech of between three and eight speakers. The video part of the signal was not used for our experiments. We further used two audio tracks from TV talk show programmes: "Talk Show 1 (TS1)" was approximately 15 minutes long and contained only four speakers; "Talk Show 2 (TS2)" was 60 minutes long and contained much more challenging content with seven main speakers (five male and two female). The studio audience often responded to comments with applause. The speakers themselves were mostly German politicians arguing about tax reforms, so they interrupted each other frequently.

For each audio class, the spectral basis was extracted by computing the PCA to reduce the dimensions and the FastICA to maximize information.

To select suitable ICA basis parameters, we measured the classification rate of the sub-segments 3 seconds long from "Talk Show 2". Two minutes from each speaker's opening talk were used to train the speaker models and the last 40 minutes of the programme were used for testing. In this case, we assumed that the ergodic topology with seven states would suffice to measure the quality of the extracted data. The parameter with the most drastic impact turned out to be the horizontal dimension E of the PCA matrix. If E was too small, the PCA matrix reduced the data too much, and the HMMs did not receive enough information. However, if E was too large, then the extra information extracted was not very important and was better ignored. The total recognition rate of the sub-segments vs. E from the ICA method for "Talk Show 2" is depicted in Figure 7.9.

As can be seen in the figure, the best value for E was 24, yielding a recognition rate of 84.3%. The NASE was then projected onto the first 24 PCA/ICA basis vectors of every class. The final output consisted of 24 basis projection features plus RMS energy.

For the classification with these features, we tested the recognition rate for the different HMM topologies. Table 7.1 depicts the classification results for different HMM topologies given the features with $E = 24$. The number of states includes two non-emitting states, so seven states implies that only five non-emitting states were used.

The HMM classifier yields the best performance when the number of states is 7 and topology is ergodic. The corresponding classification accuracy is 85.3%; three iterations were used to train the HMMs.

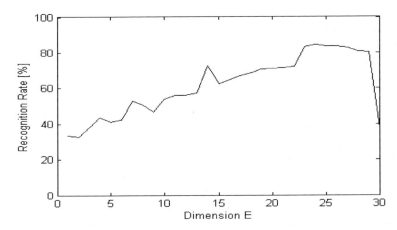

Figure 7.9 Comparison of recognition rates for different values of E of ICA

Table 7.1 Sub-segment recognition rate for three different HMMs

	Number of states				
HMM topology	4	5	6	7	8
Left–right HMM	76.3%	75.5%	79.5%	81.1%	80.2%
Forward and backward HMM	64.9%	79.3%	74.3%	77.1%	76.3%
Ergodic HMM	61.7%	78.8%	81.5%	85.3%	82.9%

7.2.7 Segmentation Results

For measuring the performance of various techniques for speaker segmentation, the recognition rate and F-measure were used. The F-measure F is a combination of the recall (RCL) rate of correct boundaries and the precision (PRC) rate of the detected boundaries. When RCL and PRC errors are weighted as being equally detractive to the quality of segmentation, F is defined as:

$$F = \frac{2 \cdot PRC \cdot RCL}{PRC + RCL}. \tag{7.17}$$

The recall is defined by $RCL = ncf/tn$, while precision $PRC = ncf/nhb$, where ncf is the number of correctly found boundaries, tn is the total number of boundaries, and nhb is the number of hypothesized boundaries (meaning the total number of boundaries found by the segmentation module). F is bounded between 0 and 100, where $F = 100$ is a perfect segmentation result and $F = 0$ implies segmentation to be completely wrong.

7.2.7.1 Results for Model-Based Segmentation

We compare the MFCC-based technique vs. MPEG-7 ASP. An HMM was trained for each acoustic class model with between 1 and 2 minutes of audio for every sound/speaker. These models were used by the segmentation module. The segmentation module consists of recognition classifiers, each containing an HMM (and a set of basis functions in the case of MPEG-7 ASP features). There is a classifier for each speaker and for other audio sources that may occur, such as applause. The audio stream can be parsed in terms of these models. Segmentation can be made at the locations where there is a change in the acoustic class.

The results of model-based segmentation are summarized in Table 7.2. The segmentation performance for "Talk Show 1" was quite good because there were only four speakers, and they rarely interrupted each other. The algorithms run fast enough so they can be implemented for real-time applications. The F-measure for "Talk Show 2" was not as good, but still impressive in view of the numerous interruptions.

Table 7.2 Results for model-based segmentation

Data	FD	FE	Reco. rate (%)	RCL (%)	PRC (%)	F (%)
TS1	13	ASP	83.2	84.6	78.5	81.5
		MFCC	87.7	92.3	92.3	92.3
	23	ASP	89.4	92.3	92.3	92.3
		MFCC	95.8	100	92.8	96.2
TS2	13	ASP	61.6	51.5	28.8	36.9
		MFCC	89.2	63.6	61.7	62.6
	23	ASP	84.3	66.6	61.1	63.7
		MFCC	91.6	71.2	73.8	73.4

TS1: Talk Show 1; TS2: Talk Show 2; FD: feature dimension; FE: feature extraction methods; Reco. rate: recognition rate.

The training data also differed somewhat from the test data because the speakers (politicians) did not raise their voices until later in the show. That is, we used their calm introductions as training data, while the test data sounded quite different. The segmentation results show that the MFCC features yield far better performance compared with the MPEG-7 features with dimensions 13 and 23.

Figure 7.10 depicts a demonstration user interface for the model-based segmentation. The audio stream is automatically segmented into four speakers. The system indicates for each speaker the speaker segments in the stream. In the demonstration system the user can access the audio segments of each speaker directly to skip forwards and backwards quickly through the stream.

7.2.7.2 Hybrid- vs. Metric-Based Segmentation

Table 7.3 shows the results of a metric-based segment clustering module for the TV broadcast news data and the two panel discussion materials.

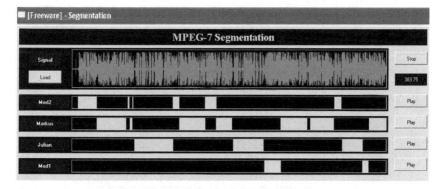

Figure 7.10 Demonstration of the model-based segmentation using MPEG-7 audio features (TU-Berlin)

Table 7.3 Metric-based segmentation results based on several feature extraction methods

Data	FD	FE	Reco. Rate (%)	F (%)
N	30	NASE	78.5	75.3
	13	MFCC	82.3	79.9
	24	MFCC	89.7	88.1
TS1	30	NASE	79.5	79.5
	13	MFCC	85.4	87.5
	24	MFCC	93.3	94.6
TS2	30	NASE	66.3	49.9
	13	MFCC	81.6	65.5
	24	MFCC	87.5	73.7

N: TV broadcast news; TS1: Talk Show 1; TS2: Talk Show 2; FD: feature dimension; FE: feature extraction methods; Reco. rate: recognition rate.

The recognition accuracy, recall, precision and F-measure of the MFCC features in the case of both 13 und 24 feature dimensions are far superior to the NASE features with 30 dimensions for TV broadcast news and "Talk Show 1". For "Talk Show 2" the MFCC features show a remarkable improvement over the NASE features.

Table 7.4 depicts the results for hybrid segmentation. The hybrid approach significantly outperforms direct metric-based segmentation, given the suitable initialization of speaker models. MFCC features yield higher recognition accuracy and F-measure than MPEG-7 ASP features in the case of both 13 and 24 feature dimensions for all test materials including broadcast news, "Talk Show 1" and "Talk Show 2".

Table 7.4 Hybrid segmentation results based on several feature extraction methods

Data	FD	FE	Reco. rate (%)	F(%)
N	13	ASP	83.2	88.9
		MFCC	87.1	92.1
	24	ASP	88.8	93.3
		MFCC	94.3	95.7
TS1	13	ASP	86.2	88.5
		MFCC	90.5	93.5
	24	ASP	91.5	94.7
		MFCC	96.8	98.1
TS2	13	ASP	72.1	56.1
		MFCC	87.2	69.7
	24	ASP	88.9	75.2
		MFCC	93.2	82.7

N: TV broadcast news; TS1: Talk Show 1; TS2: Talk Show 2; FD: feature dimension; FE: feature extraction methods; Reco. rate: recognition rate.

Figure 7.11 depicts further results for a video sequence. The audio clip recorded from "Talk Show" (TS1) contains only four speakers. Figure 7.11(a) shows that the number of speakers detected by metric-based segmentation was 6. The correct number of speakers was detected by model-level clustering using hybrid segmentation in Figure 7.11(b).

(a) Metric-based segmentation

(b) Hybrid segmentation

Figure 7.11 Demonstration of metric-based and hybrid segmentation applied to TV panel discussions (TU-Berlin)

Figure 7.12 Demonstration of metric-based segmentation applied to TV broadcast news (TU-Berlin)

Figure 7.12 illustrates a result for metric-based segmentation applied to TV broadcast news. The technique identifies several speakers. Only one speaker was contained in the scene. Hybrid segmentation resulted in correct segmentation.

7.3   SOUND INDEXING AND BROWSING OF HOME VIDEO USING SPOKEN ANNOTATIONS

In this section we describe a simple system for the retrieval of home video abstracts using MPEG-7 standard ASP features. Our purpose here is to illustrate some of the innovative concepts supported by MPEG-7, namely the combination of spoken content description and sound classification. The focus on the "home video" is due to the fact that it becomes more feasible for users to annotate video with spoken content. For measuring the performance we compare the classification results of the MPEG-7 standardized features vs. MFCCs.

7.3.1   A Simple Experimental System

For the retrieval of home video abstracts the system consists of a two-level hierarchy method using speech recognition and sound classification. Figure 7.13 depicts the block diagram of the system.

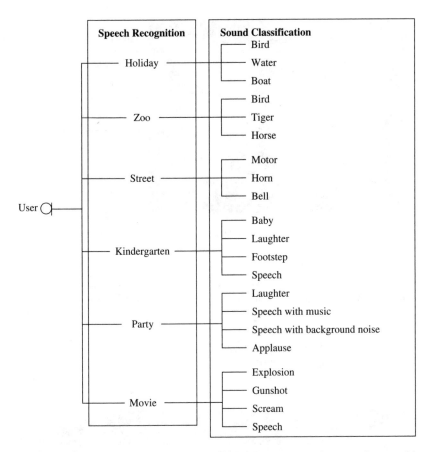

Figure 7.13 Block diagram of a two-level hierarchy method using speech recognition and sound classification

At the first/top level, a spoken annotation is recorded by the user for each home video abstract of the database. A speech recognizer extracts a spoken content descriptor from each spoken annotation. In our example, each abstracted home video is annotated with one word of the six-keyword lexicon: holiday, zoo, kindergarten, movie, party and street. Each keyword of the description vocabulary is modelled by concatenating the phone models. By uttering keywords, the user can automatically retrieve the corresponding home video abstracts.

At the second/bottom level, each home video of the database includes its own sound. For example, audio segments of home videos according to keyword category "holiday" is classified into bird, water, boat.

The sounds of home videos are modelled according to category labels and presented in a set of model parameters. Sound retrieval is achieved based on sound classification. Given a selected query sound, the extracted sound features

Figure 7.14 A home video abstract is described as a key frame annotated with spoken content and sound descriptors

are used to run the sound classifier, which compares the pre-indexed sounds in the sound database with the audio query and outputs the classification results.

Figures 7.14–7.17 show the graphical interfaces of the system. Each home video abstract includes two MPEG-7 descriptors: the spoken content descriptor and sound descriptor as shown in Figure 7.14.

Figure 7.15 illustrates the global view of all home video abstracts. If the user is looking for home video abstracts of holiday videos, he or she starts with the

Figure 7.15 Examples of key frames of videos contained in the database (TU-Berlin)

Figure 7.16 The results of a query using the speech input word "holiday". Speech recognition is used to identify the appropriate class of videos (TU-Berlin)

Figure 7.17 The query is refined using the query sound "water". Sound recognition is used to identify videos in the class "holiday" that contain sounds similar to the query sound (TU-Berlin)

global view and refines the search by processing query keywords to the system. Figure 7.16 illustrates the result of a query using speech as the query input. The system recognizes that the user selected the category "holiday" using speech input. The search can be refined by querying for the sound of "water" using a sound sample. The system then matches the "water" sound sample against the sounds contained in the audio streams of videos in the "holiday" category. Figure 7.17 depicts the results of an audio query belonging to the "water" class.

7.3.2 Retrieval Results

We collected 180 home video abstracts from a controlled audio environment with very low background interference. Each of them was hand-labelled into one of 18 audio classes. Their durations differed from around 7 seconds to more than 12 seconds long. The recorded audio signals were in PCM format sampled at 22.05 kHz with 16 bits/sample.

For the feature extraction we used two approaches, MPEG-7 ASP features and MFCC. The ASP features based on PCA/ICA were derived from speech frames of length 30 ms with a frame rate of 15 ms. The spectrum was split logarithmically into 7 octaves with the low and high boundaries at 62.5 Hz and 8 kHz respectively. For each audio class, the spectral basis was extracted by computing the PCA to reduce the dimensions and FastICA to maximize information.

In the case of MFCC the power spectrum bins were grouped and smoothed according to the perceptually motivated mel-frequency scaling. Then the spectrum was segmented into 40 critical bands by means of a filter bank that consisted of overlapping triangular filters. The first 13 filters for low frequencies had triangular frequency responses whose centre frequencies were linearly spaced by a difference of 133.33 Hz. The last 27 filters for high frequencies had triangular frequency responses whose centre frequencies were logarithmically spaced by a factor of 1.071 170 3. A discrete cosine transform applied to the logarithm of the 40 filter banks provided the vectors of decorrelated MFCC.

As feature parameters for speech recognition, 13th-order MFCCs plus delta and acceleration calculations were used. In order to compare the performance of MPEG-7 standardized features vs. the MFCC approach for sound classification we used MFCCs only without delta and acceleration calculations.

For speech recognition at the first level, the recognition rate was always excellent, because only six keywords were used.

The results of the sound classification are shown in Table 7.5. These results show that the sound classification system achieves a high recognition rate, because only three or four sound classes in each of the eight categories were tested.

Table 7.5 Sound classification accuracy (%)

FD	Feature extraction	Holiday	Zoo	Street	Kindergarten	Movie	Party	Average
7	PCA-ASP	92.5	95.5	92.1	91.3	96.5	75.1	90.05
	ICA-ASP	91.3	96.2	90.7	90.5	96.9	82.3	91.32
	MFCC	97.08	97.6	95.3	96.3	97.6	94	96.31
13	PCA-ASP	96.3	97.6	95.7	95.8	98	82.4	94.3
	ICA-ASP	97.9	94.3	96.6	96.6	98.7	93.9	96.33
	MFCC	100	99	96.6	99	100	90.1	97.45
23	PCA-ASP	100	98.8	98.5	98.5	100	88.2	97.33
	ICA-ASP	99	99.4	97.8	99	100	94	98.2
	MFCC	100	100	99	100	100	93.4	98.73
	Average	97.12	97.6	95.81	96.28	98.63	88.15	95.56

FD: feature dimension.

On average, MPEG-7 ASP based on ICA yields better performance than ASP based on PCA. However, the recognition rates using MPEG-7 ASP results appear to be significantly lower than the recognition rate of MFCC. Overall MFCC achieves the best recognition rate.

7.4 HIGHLIGHTS EXTRACTION FOR SPORT PROGRAMMES USING AUDIO EVENT DETECTION

Research on the automatic detection and recognition of events in sport video data has attracted much attention in recent years. Soccer video analysis and events/highlights extraction are probably the most popular topics in this research area. Based on goal detection it is possible to provide viewers with a summary of a game.

Audio content plays an important role in detecting highlights for various types of sports, because often events can be detected easily by audio content.

There has been much work on integrating visual and audio information to generate highlights automatically for sports programmes. (Chen *et al.*, 2003) described a shot-based multi-modal, multimedia, data mining framework for the detection of soccer shots at goal. Multiple cues from different modalities including audio and visual features are fully exploited and used to capture the semantic structure of soccer goal events. (Wang *et al.*, 2004) introduced a method to detect and recognize soccer highlights using HMMs. HMM classifiers can automatically find temporal changes of events.

In this section we describe a system for detecting highlights using audio features only. Visual information processing is often computationally expensive and thus not feasible for low-complex, low-cost devices, such as set-top boxes.

Detection using audio content may consist of three steps: (1) feature extraction to extract audio features from the audio signals of a video sequence; (2) event candidate detection to detect the main events (i.e. using an HMM); and (3) goal event segment selection to determine finally the video intervals to be included in the summary. The architecture of such a system is shown in Figure 7.18 on the basis that an HMM is used for classification.

In the following we describe an event detection approach and illustrate its performance. For feature extraction we compare MPEG-7 ASP vs. MFCC (Kim and Sikora, 2004b).

Our event candidate detection focuses on a model of highlights. In the soccer videos, the sound track mainly includes the foreground commentary and the background crowd noise. Based on observation and prior knowledge, we assume that: (1) exciting segments are highly correlated with announcers' excited speech; and (2) the audience ambient noise can also be very useful, because the audience reacts loudly to exciting situations.

To detect the goal events we use one acoustic class model for the announcers' excited speech, the audience's applause and cheering for a goal or shot. An ergodic HMM with seven states is trained with approximately 3 minutes of audio using the well-known Baum–Welch algorithm. The Viterbi algorithm determines the most likely sequence of states through the HMM and returns the most likely classification/detection event label for the event segment (sub-segments).

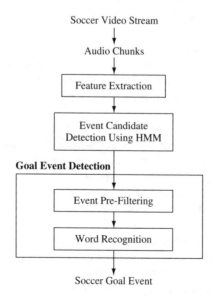

Figure 7.18   Architecture for detection of goal events in soccer videos

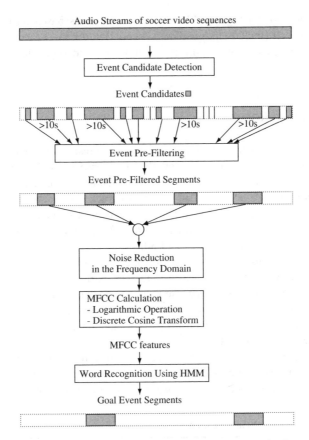

Figure 7.19   Structure of the goal event segment selection

7.4.1 Goal Event Segment Selection

When goals are scored in a soccer game, commentators as well as audiences get excited for a longer period of time. Thus, the classification results for successive sub-segments can be combined to arrive at a final, robust segmentation. This is then achieved using a pre-filtering step as illustrated in Figure 7.19.

To detect a goal event it is possible to employ a sub-system for excited speech classification. The speech classification is composed of two steps, as shown in Figure 7.19:

1. Speech endpoint detection: in TV soccer programmes, the presence of noise can be as strong as the speech signal itself. To distinguish speech from other audio signals (noise) a noise reduction method based on smoothing of the spectral noise floor (SNF) may be employed (Kim and Sikora, 2004c).

2. Word recognition using HMMs: the classification is based on two models, excited speech (including "goal" and "score") and non-excited speech. This model-based classification performs a more refined segmentation to detect the goal event.

7.4.2 System Results

Our first aim was to identify the type of sport present in a video clip. We employed the above system for basketball, soccer, boxing, golf and tennis.

Table 7.6 illustrates that it is possible in general to recognize which one of the five sport genres is present in the audio track. With feature dimensions 23–30 a recognition rate of more than 90% can be achieved. MFCC features yield better performance compared with MPEG-7 features based on several basis decompositions with dimension 23 and 30.

Table 7.7 compares the methods with respect to computational complexity.

Compared with the MPEG-7 ASP the feature extraction process of MFCC is simple and significantly faster because there are no bases used. MPEG-7 ASP is more time and memory consuming. For NMF, the divergence update algorithm was iterated 200 times. The spectrum basis projection using NMF is very slow compared with PCA or FastICA.

Table 7.8 provides a comparison of various noise reduction techniques (Kim and Sikora, 2004c). The above SNF algorithm is compared with the results of MM (multiplicatively modified log-spectral amplitude speech estimator) (Malah

Table 7.6 Sport genre classification results for four feature extraction methods.

Feature extraction	Classification accuracy			
	Feature dimension			
	7	13	23	30
ASP onto PCA	87.94%	89.36%	84.39%	83.68%
ASP onto ICA	85.81%	88.65%	85.81%	63.82%
ASP onto NMF	63.82%	70.92%	80.85%	68.79%
MFCC	82.97%	88.65%	93.61%	93.61%

Table 7.7 Processing time

Feature dimension	Feature extraction method			
	ASP onto PCA	ASP onto FastICA	ASP onto NMF	MFCC
23	75.6 s	77.7 s	1 h	18.5 s

Table 7.8 Segmental SNR improvement for different one-channel noise estimation methods

Method	Input SNR (dB)					
	White noise		Car noise		Factory noise	
	10	5	10	5	10	5
	SNR improvement (dB)					
MM	7.3	8.4	8.2	9.7	6.2	7.7
OM	7.9	9.9	9	10.6	6.9	8.3
SNF	8.8	11.2	9.7	11.4	7.6	10.6

MM: multiplicatively modified log-spectral amplitude speech estimator; OM: optimally modified LSA speech estimator and minima-controlled recursive averaging noise estimation.

et al., 1999) and OM (optimally modified LSA speech estimator and minima-controlled recursive averaging noise estimation) (Cohen and Berdugo, 2001). It can be expected that improved signal-to-noise ratio (SNR) will result in improved word recognition rates.

For evaluation the Aurora 2 database together with a hidden Markov toolkit (HTK) were used. Two training modes were selected: training on clean data and multi-condition training on noisy data. The feature vectors from the speech database with a sampling rate of 8 kHz consisted of 39 parameters: 13 MFCCs plus delta and acceleration calculations. The MFCCs were modelled by a simple left-to-right, 16-state, three-mixture whole-word HMM. For the noisy speech results, we averaged the word accuracies between 0 dB and 20 dB SNR.

Tables 7.9 and 7.10 confirm that different noise reduction techniques yield different word recognition accuracies. SNF provides better performance than MM front-end and OM front-end. The SNF method is very simple because it needs lower turning parameters compared with OM.

We employed MFCCs for the purpose of goal event detection in soccer videos. The result was satisfactory and encouraging: seven out of eight goals

Table 7.9 Word recognition accuracies for training with clean data

Feature extraction	Set A	Set B	Set C	Overall
Without noise reduction	61.37%	56.20%	66.58%	61.38%
MM	79.28%	78.82%	81.13%	79.74%
OM	80.34%	79.03%	81.23%	80.20%
SNF	84.32%	82.37%	82.54%	83.07%

Sets A, B and C: matched noise condition, mismatched noise condition, and mismatched noise and channel condition.

Table 7.10 Word recognition accuracies for training with multi-condition training data

Feature extraction	Set A	Set B	Set C	Overall
Without NR	87.81%	86.27%	83.77%	85.95%
MM	89.68%	88.43%	86.81%	88.30%
OM	90.93%	89.48%	88.91%	89.77%
SNF	91.37%	91.75%	92.13%	91.75%

NR: noise reduction; Set A, B and C: matched noise condition, mismatched noise condition, and mismatched noise and channel condition.

contained in four soccer games were correctly identified, while one goal event was misclassified.

Figure 7.20 depicts the user interface of our goal event system. The detected goals are marked in the audio signal shown at the top. The user can skip directly to these events.

It is possible to extend the above framework to more powerful indexing and browsing systems for soccer video based on audio content. The soccer game has high background noise from the excited audience. Separated acoustic class models, such as male speech, female speech, music for detecting the advertisements, and announcers' excited speech with the audience's applause and cheering, can be trained with between 5 and 7 minutes of audio. These models may be used for event detection using the ergodic HMM segmentation

Figure 7.20 Demonstration of goal event detection in soccer videos (TU-Berlin)

Figure 7.21   Demonstration of indexing and browsing system for soccer videos using audio contents (TU-Berlin)

module. To test for the detection of main events, a soccer game of 50 minutes' duration was selected. The graphical user interface is shown in Figure 7.21.

A soccer game is selected by the user. When the user presses the "Play" button at top right of the window, the system displays the soccer game. The signal at the top is the recorded audio signal. The second "Play" button on the right detects the video from the position where the speech of the woman moderator begins, while the third "Play" button detects the positions of two reporters, the fourth "Play" button is for the detection of a goal or shooting event section and the fifth "Play" button is for the detection of the advertisements.

7.5   A SPOKEN DOCUMENT RETRIEVAL SYSTEM FOR DIGITAL PHOTO ALBUMS

The graphical interface of a photo retrieval system based on spoken annotations is depicted in Figure 7.22. This is an illustration of a possible application for the MPEG-7 *SpokenContent* tool described in Chapter 4.

Each photo in the database is annotated by a short spoken description. During the indexing phase, the spoken content description of each annotation is extracted by an automatic speech recognition (ASR) system and stored. During the retrieval phase, a user inputs a spoken query word (or alternatively a query text). The spoken content description extracted from that query is matched against each spoken content description stored in the database. The system will return photos whose annotations best match the query word.

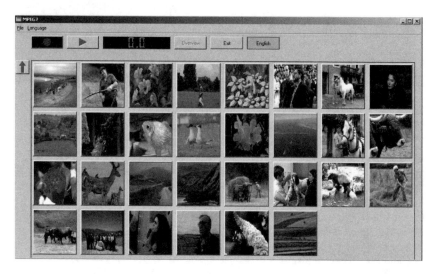

Figure 7.22   MPEG-7 SDR demonstration (TU-Berlin)

This retrieval system can be based on the MPEG-7 *SpokenContent* high-level tool. The ASR system first extracts an MPEG-7 *SpokenContent* description from each noise-reduced spoken document. This description consists of an MPEG-7-compliant lattice enclosing different recognition hypotheses output by the ASR system (see Chapter 4). For such an application, the retained approach is to use phones as indexing units: speech segments are indexed with phone lattices through a phone recognizer. This recognizer employs a set of phone HMMs and a bigram language model. The use of phones restrains the size of the indexing lexicon to a few units and allows any unknown indexing term to be processed. However, phone recognition systems have high error rates. The retrieval system exploits the phone confusion information enclosed in the MPEG-7 *SpokenContent* description to compensate for the inaccuracy of the recognizer (Moreau *et al.*, 2004). Text queries can also be used in the MPEG-7 context. A text-to-phone translator converts a text query into an MPEG-7-compliant phone lattice for this purpose.

REFERENCES

Bakker E. M. and Lew M. S. (2002) "Semantic Video Retrieval Using Audio Analysis", *Proceedings CIVR 2002*, pp. 271–277, London, UK, July.

Cambell J. R. (1997) "Speaker Recognition: A Tutorial", *Proceedings of the IEEE*, vol. 85, no. 9, pp. 1437–1462.

Chen S. and Gopalakrishnan P. (1998) "Speaker Environment and Channel Change Detection and Clustering via the Bayesian Information Criterion", *DARPA Broadcast News Transcription and Understanding Workshop 1998*, Lansdowne, VA, USA, February.

Chen S.-C., Shyu M.-L., Zhang C., Luo L. and Chen M. (2003) "Detection of Soccer Goal Shots Using Joint Multimedia Features and Classification Rules", *Proceedings of the Fourth International Workshop on Multimedia Data Mining (MDM/KDD2003)*, pp. 36–44, Washington, DC, USA, August.

Cheng S.-S and Wang H.-M. (2003) "A Sequential Metric-Based Audio Segmentation Method via the Bayesian Information Criterion", *Proceedings EUROSPEECH 2003*, Geneva, Switzerland, September.

Cho Y.-C., Choi S. and Bang S.-Y. (2003) "Non-Negative Component Parts of Sound for Classification", *IEEE International Symposium on Signal Processing and Information Technology*, Darmstadt, Germany, December.

Cohen A. and Lapidus V. (1996) "Unsupervised Speaker Segmentation in Telephone Conversations", *Proceedings, Nineteenth Convention of Electrical and Electronics Engineers*, Israel, pp. 102–105.

Cohen I. and Berdugo, B. (2001) "Speech Enhancement for Non-Stationary Environments", *Signal Processing*, vol. 81, pp. 2403–2418.

Delacourt P. and Welekens C. J. (2000) "DISTBIC: A Speaker-Based Segmentation for Audio Data Indexing", *Speech Communication*, vol. 32, pp. 111–126.

Everitt B. S. (1993) *Cluster Analysis*, 3rd Edition, Oxford University Press, New York.

Furui S. (1981) "Cepstral Analysis Technique for Automatic Speaker Verification", *IEEE Transactions on Acoustics, Speech, and Signal Processing*, vol. ASSP-29, pp. 254–272.

Gauvain J. L., Lamel L. and Adda G. (1998) "Partitioning and Transcription of Broadcast News Data", *Proceedings of ICSLP 1998*, Sydney, Australia, November.

Gish H. and Schmidt N. (1994) "Text-Independent Speaker Identification", *IEEE Signal Processing Magazine*, pp. 18–21.

Gish H., Siu M.-H. and Rohlicek R. (1991) "Segregation of Speaker for Speech Recognition and Speaker Identification", Proceedings of ICASSP, pp. 873–876, Toronto, Canada, May.

Hermansky H. (1990) "Perceptual Linear Predictive (PLP) Analysis of Speech", *Journal of the Acoustical Society of America*, vol. 87, no. 4, pp. 1738–1752.

Hermansky H. and Morgan N. (1994) "RASTA Processing of Speech", *IEEE Transactions on Speech and Audio Processing*, vol. 2, no. 4, pp. 578–589.

Kabal P. and Ramachandran R. (1986) "The Computation of Line Spectral Frequencies Using Chebyshev Polynomials", *IEEE Transactions on Acoustics, Speech, and Signal Processing*, vol. ASSP-34, no. 6, pp. 1419–1426.

Kemp T., Schmidt M., Westphal M. and Waibel A. (2000) "Strategies for Automatic Segmentation of Audio Data", *Proceedings ICASSP 2000*, Istanbul, Turkey, June.

Kim H.-G. and Sikora T. (2004a) "Automatic Segmentation of Speakers in Broadcast Audio Material", *IS&T/SPIE's Electronic Imaging 2004*, San Jose, CA, USA, January.

Kim H.-G. and Sikora T. (2004b) "Comparison of MPEG-7 Audio Spectrum Projection Features and MFCC Applied to Speaker Recognition, Sound Classification and Audio Segmentation", *Proceedings ICASSP 2004*, Montreal, Canada, May.

Kim H.-G. and Sikora T. (2004c) "Speech Enhancement based on Smoothing of Spectral Noise Floor", *Proceedings INTERSPEECH 2004 - ICSLP*, Jeju Island, South Korea, October.

Liu Z., Wang Y. and Chen T. (1998) "Audio Feature Extraction and Analysis for Scene Segmentation and Classification", *Journal of VLSI Signal Processing Systems for Signal, Image, and Video Technology*, vol. 20, no. 1/2, pp. 61–80.

Lu L. and Zhang H.-J. (2001) "Speaker Change Detection and Tracking in Real-time News Broadcasting Analysis", *Proceedings 9th ACM International Conference on Multimedia, 2001*, pp. 203–211, Ottawa, Canada, October.

Lu L., Jiang H. and Zhang H.-J. (2002) "A Robust Audio Classification and Segmentation Method", *Proceedings 10th ACM International Conference on Multimedia, 2002*, Juan les Pins, France, December.

Malah D., Cox R. and Accardi A. (1999) "Tracking Speech-presence Uncertainty to Improve Speech Enhancement in Non-stationary Noise Environments", *Proceedings ICASSP 1999*, vol. 2, pp. 789–792, Phoenix, AZ, USA, March.

Moreau N., Kim H.-G. and Sikora T. (2004) "Phonetic Confusion Based Document Expansion for Spoken Document Retrieval", *ICSLP Interspeech 2004*, Jeju Island, Korea, October.

Rabiner L. R. and Schafer R. W. (1978) *Digital Processing of Speech Signals*, Prentice Hall (Signal Processing Series), Englewood Cliffs, NJ.

Reynolds D. A., Singer E., Carlson B. A., McLaughlin J. J., O'Leary G.C. and Zissman M. A. (1998) "Blind Clustering of Speech Utterances Based on Speaker and Language Characteristics", *Proceedings ICASSP 1998*, Seattle, WA, USA, May.

Siegler M. A., Jain U., Raj B. and Stern R. M. (1997) "Automatic Segmentation, Classification and Clustering of Broadcast News Audio", *Proceedings of Speech Recognition Workshop*, Chantilly, VA, USA, February.

Siu M.-H., Yu G. and Gish H. (1992) "An Unsupervised, Sequential Learning Algorithm for the Segmentation of Speech Waveforms with Multiple Speakers", *Proceedings ICASSP 1992*, vol.2, pp. 189–192, San Francisco, USA, March.

Solomonoff A., Mielke A., Schmidt M. and Gish H. (1998) "Speaker Tracking and Detection with Multiple Speakers", *Proceedings ICASSP 1998*, vol. 2, pp. 757–760, Seattle, WA, USA, May.

Sommez K., Heck L. and Weintraub M. (1999) "Speaker Tracking and Detection with Multiple Speakers", *Proceedings EUROSPEECH 1999*, Budapest, Hungary, September.

Srinivasan S., Petkovic D. and Ponceleon D. (1999) "Towards Robust Features for Classifying Audio in the CueVideo System", *Proceedings 7th ACM International Conference on Multimedia*, pp. 393–400, Ottawa, Canada, October.

Sugiyama M., Murakami J. and Watanabe H. (1993) "Speech Segmentation and Clustering Based on Speaker Features", *Proceedings ICASSP 1993*, vol. 2, pp. 395–398, Minneapolis, USA, April.

Tritschler A. and Gopinath R. (1999) "Improved Speaker Segmentation and Segments Clustering Using the Bayesian Information Criterion", *Proceedings EUROSPEECH 1999*, Budapest, Hungary, September.

Wang J., Xu C., Chng E. S. and Tian Q. (2004) "Sports Highlight Detection from Keyword Sequences Using HMM", *Proceedings ICME 2004*, Taipei, China, June.

Wang Y., Liu Z. and Huang J. (2000) "Multimedia Content Analysis Using Audio and Visual Information", *IEEE Signal Processing Magazine* (invited paper), vol. 17, no. 6, pp. 12–36.

Wilcox L., Chen F., Kimber D. and Balasubramanian V. (1994) "Segmentation of Speech Using Speaker Identification", *Proceedings ICASSP 1994*, Adelaide, Australia, April.

Woodland P. C., Hain T., Johnson S., Niesler T., Tuerk A. and Young S. (1998) "Experiments in Broadcast News Transcription", *Proceedings ICASSP 1998*, Seattle, WA, USA, May.

Wu T., Lu L., Chen K. and Zhang H.-J. (2003) "UBM-Based Real-Time Speaker Segmentation for Broadcasting News", *ICME 2003*, vol.2, pp. 721–724, Hong Kong, April.

Xiong Z., Radhakrishnan R., Divakaran A. and Huang T. S. (2003) "Audio Events Detection Based Highlights Extraction from Baseball, Golf and Soccer Games in a Unified Framework", *Proceedings ICASSP 2003*, vol. 5, pp. 632–635, Hong Kong, April.

Yu P., Seide F., Ma C. and Chang E. (2003) "An Improved Model-Based Speaker Segmentation System", *Proceedings EUROSPEECH 2003*, Geneva, Switzerland, September.

Zhou B. W. and John H. L. (2000) "Unsupervised Audio Stream Segmentation and Clustering via the Bayesian Information Criterion", *Proceedings ICSLP 2000*, Beijing, China, October.

Index